BEYOND STOCKS

John F. Merrill

Tanglewood Publishing
Houston, Texas

Publisher's Cataloging-in-Publication

Merrill, John F.
    Beyond stocks / John F. Merrill.
    p. cm.
    Includes index.
    Preassigned LCCN: 97-60331
    ISBN 0-9657131-5-6

    1. Mutual funds. 2. Portfolio management. 3. Investments.
    I. Title.

HG4530.M47 1997   332.63'27
                                       QBI97-40324

ISBN 0-9657131-5-6

Acknowledgments

This book would not have been possible without a lot of encouragement and hard work by many people. My clients, associates and friends were all instrumental in different ways.

My associate, John Goott, was especially supportive of this effort early on and stayed steadfastly behind it all the way through. My right-hand for over 15 years, Debra Courson, provided the necessary backup to keep everything running smoothly at the office and therefore allow me the time to write. The most instrumental person has been Gwyn Welsh. She has dedicated herself to this project for more than a year, providing countless hours of research, computer data evaluations and day-to-day organization of the manuscript.

My two boys, Brian and Brady, were not only supportive, they also made life around the home conducive to this working sabbatical. My mother, Galva Merrill and my sister, Connie Snowden, were extremely encouraging, while providing good common sense.

Numerous friends and clients became personally involved in reviewing one or more chapters for content and clarity. Especially helpful were Bert Rosenbaum, Michael Yackira, Jonathan Kagan, Tom Pazera, Victor Lamanuzzi, Baker Mitchell, Chuck Bracht, Don Ward, Bruce Golubock, Fred Mitchell, John Creed, Ann Clinton, David Lampe, Bill Phillips, Milton Gray, Melinda Van Paasschen, Margaret Meaden, Ed Williamson, Eileen Black, Sharon Dodson and Mark Grenader.

I also owe a great deal of the credit for the final book to Lisa Sostack, my editor, and Bridgett Akin for graphic design. Each labored over the book and provided much needed guidance at crucial times.

John F. Merrill

Table of Contents

Introduction

Information, Knowledge and Noise

Over the past decade, there has been a major shift in responsibility for your retirement from Big Business and Big Government to YOU. This change in responsibility and consequent interest in investments by the public has not been lost on the media.

The attention given to the stock market, bonds, currencies, mutual funds, interest rates and all things financial has exploded in the past 5-10 years. Much of this is good. Certainly, there is a wealth of information, research and commentary available to every investor today that may have only been circulated around Wall Street 15 years ago.

On the other hand, information is not the same as knowledge. It is important to distinguish between the two. Hundreds of pieces of new information may not impart one new bit of knowledge. Knowledge is *understanding* the information and knowing what to discard and what few pieces add value to what is currently understood. New information without a proper context can be less than useful. It is just noise.

We receive the lion's share of our financial information from the media—print and broadcast. Therefore, it is important to understand both the motives and goals behind all this financial reporting.

First and foremost, the financial media is no different than other media. Job number one is to maintain and increase readers and viewers. This forces their focus on *today* to hook their audience on daily information (or weekly or monthly, depending on publishing or broadcasting dates). It is a huge challenge—to make each day's market activity seem meaningful.

Just reporting the daily numbers is not enough; they are too dry and too boring. In and of themselves, numbers won't hook the audience.

Therefore, much of the financial media move beyond the numbers to those aspects of human nature that will bring the audience back day-after-day, week-after-week.

Fear and Greed

One of the easiest ways to rope in an audience is by appealing to emotions. The market didn't rise—it *soared*! The market didn't decline—it *plunged*!

However, words alone would also get somewhat stale over time. To have the captivating effect desired, they must be tied to one of the two primal emotions of investors—fear or greed.

Greed is the harder of the two emotions to capture or stimulate by the traditional media. This particular emotion has been more broadly tapped by the investment newsletters. The idea is to let you in on something, to get the big bucks that only their subscribers get, to be privy to insights Wall Street would never want you to know, to take advantage of their closely guarded *black box* secret to financial success.

Hogwash. Study after study has proved that simple buy-and-hold strategies have greatly outperformed the investment newsletter industry over long periods of time (even more so after taxes and transaction costs).

Fear is the bigger emotional hook. This is the emotion that has proved to be far easier to tap for all of the financial media. Studies have shown that investors are twice as emotional about a 20% loss as they are about a 20% gain in their investments.

Therefore, much of the financial media has taken on a negative or pessimistic tone. "Technical trends are scary." "Fundamentals are overvalued." "The cycle is turning negative." "Public enthusiasm is speculative." "Downside risk is growing." "How much farther can these positive earnings continue?" Etc., etc., etc....

The Game

If emotions are the hook, then the market forecast is the game. The market forecast game is built around a dialog of bull and bear markets. Once set up, it seems axiomatic that the listener/reader would want to be **in** bull markets (greed) and **out** of bear markets (fear). Therefore, you need to keep up with their financial forecasts.

Actually, these are not the media's forecasts, but the forecasts of a parade of "experts." Most of the media prefers not to prepare its own analyses; that would not appear impartial. Worse, journalists and program hosts might be responsible for follow-up and evaluation of prior forecasts. So, the media brings in outside experts to provide market forecasts.

Most of these experts come from Wall Street brokerage firms. This works out well for both. The media needs experts in order to give credibility to the views expressed, so it is in the media's own interest to build up the reputations of its experts—even to *guru* status—so that their audiences feel privileged to get these insights and predictions. They rarely dwell on the expert's lousy market calls, choosing to sing the praises of his great ones instead. (Remember, a coin flip is right 50% of the time.) *Strict and thorough accountability would ruin the game—so it is ignored.*

An example will at least illustrate the point.

One high profile Wall Street expert is the Chief Portfolio Strategist of a major Wall Street firm. He is often quoted in the press and interviewed on business news shows. He has been consistently *bearish* since 1991!

In April 1991, for instance, this expert said that if the Dow Jones Industrial Average went above 3000, "it would be one of the great *sell* signals of all time."[1] Four thousand (4000) points higher, he is still bearish, still asked for his expert opinion and not too embarrassed to give it.

The next time you watch a business news show, notice that each expert must cooperate and play the game. "Are you a bull or a bear?" "Where will the market be in six months?" "What's your market forecast?"

In return, the expert and his firm get free advertising and the credibility of being referred to as an expert by a supposedly disinterested person. The expert's status is confirmed, his firm's prestige is enhanced, and perhaps the expert will get to tout some stocks for which his/her firm is interested in finding new buying power.

On a broader basis, all of Wall Street benefits from this game. Keep in mind that the real engine of Wall Street is *transactions*— buys and sells. The ongoing bull and bear game plays on greed and fear, which generates tickets (buys and sells). Wall Street is well aware that while long-term, buy-and-hold investors are not very profitable, *traders* are.

Therefore, the market forecast game is perfectly symbiotic. The media and Wall Street both win. It is the investor-turned-market-timer, trader or speculator who loses.

Wall Street will always be able to provide legions of very bright, articulate, well-educated, sincere experts who show complete confidence in their own forecasts, despite market history and their own past mistakes. At any point in time, some will be bullish and others will be bearish and both will be equally convincing.

Perhaps one day the Securities and Exchange Commission (SEC) will catch on to this game and enforce proper disclosure as it does with paid advertising. It would be nice to hear the following:

> *"The views expressed are the views of our guest and not that of this network. They may be unfounded, biased, self-serving and completely at odds with your long-term investment success. No due diligence on all past recommendations has been attempted."*

Or see this:

> *"Warning!! The following market analysis will likely be hazardous to your long-term investment strategy if acted upon. It is designed to motivate you to be a short-term trader (most of whom eventually fail) instead of a long-term investor (most of whom succeed)."*

You don't need daily, weekly or monthly market forecasts. They are a poor substitute for a long-term strategy, a well-designed portfolio and the patience and discipline to strictly apply them while avoiding the noise and excitement served up by the media.

This book will serve your long-term interests and be your ready antidote to the media's emotional noise.

Who Should Read This Book?

Beyond Stocks is written for long-term investors. It will have little value for market timers, active traders or speculators.

Based upon extensive new historical research, Beyond Stocks offers unique insights into the risks and rewards of all the major asset classes and, more importantly, complete portfolios of the most reliable and efficient of those asset classes. The objective is to provide you with all the tools and rationale for the structure of *your* best portfolio, the one most likely to meet your specific targeted rate of return with the least risk.

It is not an investment primer. Beyond Stocks is intended for investors who have already acquired an everyday knowledge of general investment terms and who are currently invested in mutual funds or similar pooled investment accounts such as company-sponsored 401(k) programs.

This book does not address the many related and important concepts that together provide a total financial plan. However, financial planning issues are addressed which have a direct bearing on investment decisions. For example, this book shows how to calculate the maximum amount of income a retirement portfolio can provide under various market conditions and different inflation scenarios.

Although not written specifically for investment professionals, **financial planners, money managers and security brokers** will benefit greatly from the original research, dramatic portfolio illustrations and client-friendly analogies throughout the book.

Mutual Fund Focus

Mutual funds have been available to investors since the mid-1920s. In recent years, both individual and institutional investors have increasingly turned to mutual funds as their investment medium of choice.

This is partly the result of the many innovations in the buying, selling and holding of mutual funds. Mutual fund marketplaces first pioneered by Charles Schwab & Company, Inc. offer one custodial account for all funds, fee-less and paperless trading, money market fund sweep privileges and electronic portfolio services, such as pricing, performance and tax accounting, all of which now allow mutual funds to be fully managed by individuals and institutions alike.

In addition, the breadth of mutual fund offerings has expanded geometrically. There are sector funds, international funds, country funds, micro-cap funds, single-state municipal bond funds and so on. This allows mutual funds to fulfill almost any role in a portfolio.

The end result: **managed portfolios of mutual funds**. It has been rightly said that mutual funds are the stocks and bonds of today's portfolios. Today's investors have moved *beyond stocks*.

For all these reasons, this book will use a mutual fund focus wherever relevant. It is believed that more readers will identify with the points and illustrations this way. However, most of the principles, concepts and illustrations are equally valid for portfolios of individual stocks and bonds.

Major Points Highlighted Throughout Text

The following symbols are placed in the margin next to major points in the text:

          Key Point

          Valuable New Research

Section I

Your
Wealth and Retirement
Portfolio

Overview
of Section I

Most investment professionals remain awed throughout their careers by the power of compounding returns. Maybe this is why Benjamin Franklin referred to it as the "eighth wonder of the world."

One aspect of compounding that never ceases to amaze is the magnified difference in wealth created by minuscule changes in rates of return over time. In this section, the impact of increasing rates of return will be taken one step further—to the bottom line. How does a change in the long-term rate of return of a portfolio increase or decrease the income the portfolio can provide during retirement?

This section also contains critical definitions of financial terms used throughout this book. Although these definitions are straightforward and easy to comprehend, they are sometimes at odds with conventional use.

In addition, this section introduces the term used throughout this book to signify an investor's long-term investments—the **Wealth and Retirement Portfolio**. The importance of viewing all long-term investments as a single unit with singular performance is a critical step in developing a comprehensive approach to investing.

1

Evaluating the Big Picture—Returns and Financial Risk

Many investors spend the majority of their time juggling their various investments in an attempt to gain a short-term advantage. Other investors are completely wrapped up in the attempt to avoid short-term market setbacks. All too often this preoccupation with individual investments or short-term risks ends up sidetracking investors from the big picture, their long-term retirement objectives. The best time spent on investments is that time taken to structure their entire portfolio. The sum is more important than the parts, and the long-term more important than today in reaching financial goals.

"A ship in port is safe, but that's not what ships are built for."
— Grace Murray Hooper, <u>A Kick in the Seat of the Pants</u>, 1986

The Sum is More Important than the Parts

In January of 1994, I had an appointment with a man I will call Mr. Smith. Mr. Smith, 55, had worked at Exxon for many years. A little more than two years before our meeting, Mr. Smith had elected early retirement. He received close to $500,000, which he rolled over into an IRA. He had been investing the money himself but was interested in our money management services. He was currently acting as a consultant and did not plan to retire for about 10 years, at which time he would live off his portfolio.

After a few minutes of getting to know each other, he asked me how we had performed in 1993. I told him that our firm had a good year, and the average account was up over 20%.

He was silent for a moment, then he came back with, "I beat you guys. I made 26%!" Well, I was impressed, so I asked him what he had invested in. He responded with the names of two Fidelity funds. He was right, I knew they had done well.

"That's it?" I asked, a little incredulously. "You invested your half million dollar portfolio in two Fidelity funds?"

"Oh, heaven forbid!" he quickly responded. "I had about $15,000 in each."

"Okay," I queried. "Where did you invest the bulk of your portfolio to earn such a good return?"

"No, you don't understand," he said. "Those are my investments. The rest I keep in CDs so it won't be at risk….so it will be safe."

"King's X," I threw out. "The $500,000 is your investment portfolio. The 26% return on the small part of it you call your investments is of little importance. What is important is the total return of the entire portfolio. The size of your retirement income in 10 years is completely dependent on the return you achieve from the **total portfolio.**"

We spent a few minutes reviewing his rollover IRA papers and determined that his total return for 1993 on his investment portfolio was just a little over 6%! That was 1993's contribution to the financial quality of his retirement.

The Hodge-Podge Portfolio

Most investors acquire their individual investments over time in a somewhat seat-of-the-pants fashion. A certificate of deposit (CD) here, a mutual fund there, this municipal bond, that stock and so on.

Many such decisions are based upon what is **convenient** (local bank), what options are **available** (401(k)), what's **promoted** (broker-dealer) or what's **advertised** (mutual funds). Each institution disseminates financial data—but only about the securities held at that institution.

Most investors are more or less like Mr. Smith. They don't look at their entire portfolio. Moreover, they don't <u>plan</u> their entire portfolio. As a result, they tend to follow and fret over the individual moves and short-term performance of each investment. This can easily cause excessive trading and bad decisions, or at the other end of the spectrum, a stagnant portfolio and no decisions at all.

The Big Picture

Do you know what your *entire* portfolio's return was last year...for the past five years...for the past ten years? Even most sophisticated investors do not have an accurate measurement of their total performance. And many investors who think they know how their portfolio is performing are seriously overestimating their overall results. A recent study showed that investors, on average, thought their portfolios were providing investment returns several percentage points greater than they actually were.

Do you know what your portfolio is currently worth? Do you have a computer program or ledger that contains a composite of all of your investments on one page? Do you update and evaluate it at least annually—as a portfolio, not a collection of individual investments? If you are like most individuals, you do not.

Your Wealth and Retirement Portfolio

The portfolio referred to here—and throughout the book—is your Wealth and Retirement Portfolio. This is your long-term portfolio, your wealth builder. This is the portfolio that may replace a substantial part of your income during retirement.

Your Wealth and Retirement Portfolio is made up of your "liquid investments," investments that are easily converted to cash, such as stocks, bonds, mutual funds, insurance cash values, certificates of deposit and mortgage notes.

It does not matter whether you own these investments directly or indirectly for portfolio management purposes. Directly owned investments are in your name or that of your spouse. Indirect ownership includes IRAs, company retirement and savings plans, trust accounts (of which you are a direct beneficiary) or any other portfolio assets that are earmarked for your future enjoyment and will be available for your retirement.

Your Wealth and Retirement Portfolio should *not* be broken into two periods—before retirement and after retirement. Economist Richard Thaler, a professor at the University of Chicago, pointed out in the September/October 1996 issue of <u>Fee Advisor</u> magazine, "People act like something magical happens on the day they retire, and it shrinks their (investment) time horizon to zero." Your investment time horizon should reach at least 30 years after retirement and perhaps well into the next generation of your heirs.

Defining Critical Terms

Before going any further, it is important that you have a quick reference to the precise meaning of certain critical terms as used throughout this book.

Definitions

Risk	Possibility of, or intensity of, a decline in market value
Loss	A decline in value that is not recovered
At Risk	The possibility of falling short of an investment objective
Volatility	Large random swings in market value
Fluctuation	Up and down movements in market values that are historically normal for a particular asset or set of assets
Decline	Downturn in market value from a prior level
Recovery	The period after a decline in which the market regains its former high value
Advance	Upturn in market value from a prior level
Return	Total Return - Includes all items of gain or loss, plus dividends and interest
Riskless Rate of Return	The return from 30-day U.S. Treasury bills
Reward	A measurement of the return above the riskless rate
Correlation	The degree with which the advances and declines of two separate investments parallel each other. Highly correlated assets tend to track each other's movements.
Efficiency Rating	The reward an asset class or portfolio provides for a given level of risk
Short-Term	A period of less than 5 years
Intermediate-Term	A period of between 5 and 15 years
Long-Term	A period exceeding 15 years (easily encompassing most wealth building or retirement portfolios)
Portfolio Design	Establishing a pre-determined mix of asset classes which is maintained indefinitely
Wealth	Purchasing power
SBBI	Stocks, Bonds, Bills & Inflation Yearbook, Ibbotson Associates, Chicago

CHART 1-1

Just How Important are Rates of Return?

Let's return to my conversation with Mr. Smith, the retiree from Exxon. He wanted an idea of what level of retirement income he could expect from his portfolio. Using Chart A1-1 in the Appendix, we can estimate the income that his retirement portfolio will provide. A portion of this chart is shown below in Chart 1-2.

How Much Retirement Income Will Your Current Tax-Sheltered Account Provide?

(Inflation-Adjusted, Retirement Income as a Percentage of Your Current Tax-Sheltered Retirement Account)

Years to Retirement	Annual Rates of Return							
	5%	6%	7%	8%	9%	10%	11%	12%
10	5.2%	6.6%	8.1%	10.1%	12.4%	14.9%	18.0%	21.8%

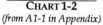

CHART 1-2
(from A1-1 in Appendix)

Note: In order to estimate future income from a portfolio, it is necessary to make certain assumptions:
- Inflation is assumed to be 3.0% per year (both before and after retirement).
- Retirement income will be adjusted annually by the increase in inflation.
- Retirement income will be paid out for 30 years before the investment principal is depleted.

As Mr. Smith is 10 years away from retirement, the only other variable needed to estimate his retirement income is the rate of return he can expect to achieve on his portfolio. For simplicity, this table assumes that the long-term rate of return from a portfolio is constant both before and after retirement.

As pointed out earlier, Mr. Smith's current portfolio experienced a rate of return of close to 6% the year prior to our discussion. If 6% were his average annual return for 40 years into the future (10 years until retirement plus 30 years after retirement), the chart reflects a retirement income that would be calculated as **6.6%** of his current retirement portfolio. Applied to his $500,000 portfolio, this chart indicates that he would be able to take an annual income worth $33,000—in today's dollars—for 30 years ($500,000 x **6.6%** = $33,000) after he retires fully in 10 years.

The point of this chart is to isolate one variable—the portfolio rate of return—and determine its impact on Mr. Smith's retirement income. As we reviewed this chart together, **Mr. Smith was very surprised by the increase in his retirement income that just a one percent change in his portfolio rate of return would make.** For example, if Mr. Smith's portfolio were to provide an average return of 7%, his retirement income would increase to $40,500 per year in current dollars. An 8% portfolio return provides him $50,500 per year. *This is 50% more retirement income for a 2% increase in his portfolio rate of return.* A 9% return provides $62,000 per year, a 10% return provides $74,500 per year—more than *double* the retirement income of a 6% return!

The rewards of better investing are real and significant. Of course, Mr. Smith already knew he could make higher returns than he had been making, but he had not understood the magnitude of change in his retirement income that comes from such small changes in his portfolio rate of return.

But what about the risk involved in investing for higher returns?

Which Financial Risk?

As presently constituted, Mr. Smith's portfolio is very low risk. With a large investment in CDs, 94% of his portfolio is insulated from market declines. However, there is a different kind of risk to which this portfolio is more exposed. His portfolio appears to be *at risk* of not achieving the return necessary to support his preferred lifestyle in retirement. Mr. Smith had suggested to me that his retirement needs would be about $50,000 per year (in today's buying power) at his retirement. For this objective, his current portfolio is highly *at risk* of falling far short of his needs.

Mr. Smith and I discussed changes to his current portfolio that would bring these two risks more into balance. If he could accept more short-term risk (intensity of portfolio declines), he could practically eliminate being at risk of not meeting his long-term retirement income needs.

Mr. Smith was becoming motivated to seek a higher portfolio rate of return. Yet he well understood his sensitivity to risk. Both his fears and needs are disclosed by his concluding comments.

> "I want my portfolio to be very predictable for the long term."

> "I want the least amount of risk possible that will still achieve my retirement income goal."

> "I want to know the worst that can happen. How would another big bear market like 1973-'74 affect my portfolio and its ability to maintain my income throughout retirement?"

Notice that the goals are specific to Mr. Smith's personal needs. Success is measured in terms of reaching a stated long-term return while minimizing risks along the way. This is so much more important than the elusive and fuzzy goals that most investors espouse, such as "maximizing my returns" or "beating the market." Either of these illusive goals may incur substantially more risk than an investor is willing to live with for a goal that is not meaningful to his or her own financial circumstances.

The two central points of this chapter are:

- Put it all together - assemble all of your long-term investments into one Wealth and Retirement Portfolio.

- Run your own race - measure the performance of your Wealth and Retirement Portfolio (as one value) against your own established objective.

With these two goals in place, this book provides a step-by-step blueprint for building the best portfolio design (stable combination of asset classes) for your Wealth and Retirement Portfolio. The end result is the presentation of the most efficient portfolio design for each type of investor—from the very conservative to the aggressive.

You Only Have One Investment *Portfolio* with Many Different Slices

Bottom Line: It is the performance of the portfolio as a whole that really matters.

Section II

Financial Asset Classes

Overview of Section II

Are Investment Returns Predictable?

No. Investment returns cannot be forecast with precision either in the short run or long term. However, the range of returns that are highly probable becomes smaller and smaller as the time horizon increases. The chart below illustrates this point.

The Longer Your Investment Horizon...
The Narrower the Range of Expected Returns

Range of average annual returns over increasing holding periods

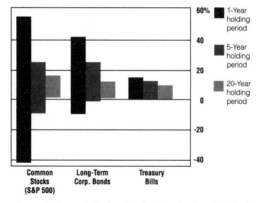

Source: © Computed using data from Stocks, Bonds, Bills & Inflation 1996 Yearbook™ with data updated January 1997, Ibbotson Associates, Chicago (annually updates work by Roger G. Ibbotson and Rex Sinquefield). Used with permission. All rights reserved.

One clear message of this chart is that investment returns become more predictable with time. A fundamental premise of this book is that investors with time horizons of 20 years or more should take full advantage of this tendency toward predictability in structuring their portfolios.

Asset Classes

Types of investments with similar characteristics are grouped together as asset classes. As a group, these securities will tend to react in the same way to economic or investment forces. It is critically important to understand the fundamentals of each of the alternative asset classes available to your portfolio, particularly the efficiency rating of each asset class, which is a measure of the degree of risk taken in order to deliver its return. Your portfolio's mix of asset classes will be far more important in determining its performance than will be your selection of individual securities or mutual funds.[2]

In the broadest sense, there are three families of asset classes: common stocks, bonds and cash equivalents. Each asset class family has provided the American investor with distinctly different long-term rewards and shorter term fluctuations.

The three asset class families comprise 13 separate asset classes that will be the focus of this section.

Asset Class Family	Asset Class
Stocks	Domestic Large Cap Stocks
	Domestic Mid/Small Cap Stocks
	Domestic Micro Cap Stocks
	International Stocks (Developed Country)
	International Stocks (Emerging Markets)
	Securitized Real Estate (REITs)
Bonds	U.S. Treasury Bonds - Intermediate Maturity
	U.S. Treasury Bonds - Long Maturity
	Domestic High-Quality Corporate Bonds
	Domestic High-Yield (Junk) Bonds
	International Bonds
Cash	U.S. Treasury Bills – 30-Day Maturity (equivalent to Money Market Accounts)
	Gold

Each asset class has unique characteristics and should be evaluated on its own merits. This section of the book will provide a discussion and evaluation of each of these liquid or tradable asset classes with the particular view of long-term inclusion in your Wealth and Retirement Portfolio.

2

The Impressive Record of Domestic Stocks

Domestic stocks, while volatile in the short-term, have been the most rewarding asset class for U.S. shareholders over the long term. Events like the 1987 crash lead to the belief that the market is irrational, but since 1926, long-term investors have enjoyed remarkably consistent long-term returns from the stocks of large and small companies. U.S. equities are a critical component of the well-designed Wealth and Retirement Portfolio.

"The market itself really represents nothing more than a pendulum that swings back and forth through the median line of rationality. It spends very little time at the point of rationality and most of the time on one side or the other."

— Robert Kirby, Research Paper at the Institute of Chartered Financial Analysts (1976)

Long-Term Rationality

A basic characteristic of the stock market is that it is both rational and irrational at the very same time. The difference is simply the time period under the microscope.

Measured over long periods of time, the market value of common stocks exhibits very rational and rewarding behavior. Essentially, market values track corporate earnings (profits). For example, the earnings of the stocks that make up the S&P 500 Index are up 4,258% for the six decades ending 1995. The market value of shares of those companies are up 4,486% for those same sixty years. Good tracking, indeed.

Short-Term Irrationality

Comparing the performance of the stock market relative to the underlying earnings of its companies over much shorter time periods, however, may show little connection between the two. This is what makes the stock market so frustrating. Earnings often go up while stock prices go down and vice versa.

The short-term fluctuations of any company's stock price is in large part a result of market participants (investors) not knowing what the company's earnings will be looking ahead. Keep in mind that, while investors know today's earnings, they are investing based upon what they estimate will be the future earnings of the individual companies in which they choose to invest.

This estimating of corporate earnings is further complicated by interest rates. In theory, the value of a company's stock today is the discounted present value of all future earnings that could be paid out as dividends to the current owner. The discount rate is arbitrary, yet many, if not most market participants believe the best discount rate is the current interest rate for 30-year U.S. Treasury bonds. Therefore, stock prices also reflect changes in interest rates and anticipated changes in interest rates…more guesswork.

With all of its uncertainties, frustrations and erratic behavior, market participation draws on investors' emotions. At times, the ever-changing market psychology (the collective enthusiasm or pessimism of participants) goes to extremes. The outlook for future earnings (or interest rates) will reach heights or depths that become very detached from the more probable, mundane reality, meaning stock prices in the shorter term don't necessarily reflect the reality of their underlying earnings potential.

1987 Blow-off and Crash

An extreme example of the entire process was provided in one fairly recent calendar year—1987. January to August of 1987 experienced an outbreak of market "fever"—one of those occasional periods of over-exuberant market psychology. Market prices as measured by the S&P 500 Index bolted upward by over 23% in just that eight-month period. Meanwhile, corporate earnings were flat to down, and interest rates were rising rapidly (usually a depressant to stock market prices because higher rates cause a heftier discounting of future earnings).

The infamous crash of 1987 occurred in the three months of September through November when stock prices lost over 30% from their August highs.

Unfortunately, this is *not* a singular aberration. Such bull market exuberance followed by bear market depression has occurred many times over the market's long history. What was new, and very unnerving, was the one-day 500+ point decline in the Dow Jones Industrial Average. This represented a record 22% loss in market value in a single day!

The crash of 1987 has received a lot more attention than the exuberant upside blow-off that preceded it. In reality, the crash of 1987 was a correction of market psychology as much as it was a correction of market prices. Such corrections have a way of bringing market expectations back to earth.

It is interesting to view the full calendar year of 1987 as one piece of market history. For that 12 months, the S&P 500 index was up 5.2%. Reviewing changing stock prices for the year-as-whole, one might assume that the year was a yawner (not a goner) and that it had exhibited perfectly rational long-term behavior.

Long-Term Rewards

Despite episodes like 1987, domestic stocks have been a very rewarding asset class for U.S. shareholders over the long term. Stocks, Bonds, Bills & Inflation (SBBI), published annually by Ibbotson Associates, Chicago, Illinois, has become the financial industry's bible of historical information on domestic asset classes. According to SBBI, from the beginning of 1926 through the end of 1996, the average annual compounded return from the S&P 500 (and its predecessor index) has been 10.7%. Over that same period, inflation has averaged just 3.1% annually. Thus, U.S. stockholders have earned the remarkable real return of 7.6% per year since 1926. This is meaningful wealth creation...more than doubling the real value of a diversified portfolio of stocks every 10 years.

Better still, this appears to be the normal, long-term, real return for stocks. Jeremy Siegel, a professor at the University of Pennsylvania's Wharton School, completed an extensive study of the U.S. stock market back into the last century in his book Stocks for the Long Run (1994). His major finding: stocks have delivered a consistent 6½% to 7½% over inflation in virtually any long period of time.

The attraction of common stocks is the significant and consistent long-term returns over inflation they have historically provided.

In addition, stocks have *always* outperformed cash and bonds after 20 years.

> *When the New York Stock Exchange celebrated its 200th birthday in May 1992, it could brag that a person who bought all the shares of all the companies listed on the exchange on **any** day in its history would have beaten bonds and T-bills over any period exceeding 20 years. Quite an accomplishment.*[3]

This attribute of domestic common stocks makes them an ideal candidate for your Wealth and Retirement Portfolio. However, investing in stocks is by no means a free ride.

Drawback to Stocks

The drawback to common stocks is their susceptibility to large and frequent declines in market value.

These wide swings in market values make stocks by themselves an inappropriate vehicle for most short-term funding goals. Money that will be needed in five years or less is taking on substantial risk of losing principal that cannot be recovered when invested solely in common stocks.

But most portfolios should include some portion of stocks. What portion should be invested in stocks is discussed in Section III – Designing Reliable and Efficient Portfolios.

Market Capitalization

Domestic, publicly-traded stocks are separated into asset classes by the size of companies (market capitalizations). The market capitalization (market cap) of a particular stock is simply its total market value—the number of shares outstanding times the market price of each share.

At year-end 1996, the largest U.S. company was General Electric with a market cap of close to $165 billion. The smallest publicly-traded company is well below $5 million.

The approximately 6,300 domestic, publicly-traded operating companies[*] on the New York Stock Exchange (NYSE), American Stock Exchange (AMEX) and the over-the-counter (OTC or NASDAQ) markets, are grouped by their market caps into three domestic stock asset classes: large cap, mid/small cap and micro cap.

Unfortunately, these terms are *not* uniformly applied to the same size firms by all Wall Street observers. This book will utilize the

---

[*] All publicly-traded companies include all common stocks of corporations domiciled in the U.S. in the database of the Center for Research in Security Prices at the University of Chicago (CRSP). Excluded are American Depository Receipts (ADRs) of foreign-based corporations, Real Estate Investment Trusts (REITs), and Closed-End Investment Companies.

convention set forth by the Center for Research in Security Pricing at the University of Chicago (CRSP) and more or less followed by Ibbotson's SBBI. CRSP's methodology divides all stocks listed on the NYSE into ten deciles. Deciles one and two, the largest 20% of all NYSE firms, are defined as large cap, and all listed securities on the AMEX or NASDAQ *of the same size* are included in this category. Deciles nine and ten, the smallest 20% of all NYSE firms, are defined as micro cap and all listed securities of the same size on the AMEX or NASDAQ are included. All of the stocks that fall in between, NYSE deciles three through eight and equivalent size firms on the AMEX and NASDAQ, are mid/small cap firms.

These definitions of market capitalization are somewhat different than those used by Morningstar Mutual Funds and some other mutual fund observers. The primary reason for adopting CRSP definitions is the extensive research this allows back to 1926 (with CRSP or SBBI data) and the wide use of Ibbotson charts and data. (The small companies in Ibbotson's SBBI are the micro cap universe.)

Asset Class	Range of Market Capitalizations	Approximate Number of Companies	Approximate Percentage of Total Stock Market Value
Large Cap (S&P 500)	Over $2 billion	500	72%
Mid/Small Cap	$170 million - $2 billion	2,300	25%
Micro Cap	Under $170 million	3,500	3%

CHART 2-1

As you can see on the accompanying Chart 2-1, Large Caps represent about 72% of the entire market value of all 6,300 stocks in the CRSP database even though they are represented by just 500 stocks. On the other end of the spectrum, Micro Cap stocks represent only about 3% of total market value, yet this group has more than 3,500 stocks.

If you want to own a domestic stock portfolio that matches the whole U.S. stock market—a market weight portfolio—you would not own an equal amount of each of the 6,300 stocks. Instead, your market weight portfolio would look close to this:

Market Capitalization	Your Ownership Percentage
Large Cap Stocks	72%
Mid Cap & Small Cap Stocks	25%
Micro Cap Stocks	3%

Size Effect

There is a straightforward reason why domestic stocks often are segregated in this way. The long-term returns from large cap stocks have been lower in aggregate than those from mid/small cap stocks, which in turn, have produced smaller returns than the returns from micro cap stocks (see Chart 2-2). This size effect has held true over time.

Given that micro cap stocks historically outperform larger cap issues, it would seem to make sense to concentrate on these companies. But investing in stocks of smaller companies is by no means an easy task. There are two substantial drawbacks:

- The smaller the market capitalization, the larger the fluctuation in market prices. (The volatility in micro cap stocks is about 50% greater on average than that of large cap stocks.)

- Over periods of time even longer than a decade, the returns from smaller company stocks can severely lag the returns of their larger brethren (see Chart 2-3). The size effect will be explored in more detail in Chapter 4.

In addition, the returns reflected for Micro Cap stocks in Chart 2-2 may be hard to duplicate. James O'Shaughnessy, author of What Works on Wall Street, points out the severe lack of *liquidity* or ease of purchase and sale of micro cap issues. The implication is that micro cap stock returns reflected in historical data may not actually be possible in the real world. The supply of micro cap stocks is limited and their true cost may be understated. Transaction costs (spreads between the bid and ask price and commissions) may be quite a bit higher than those of larger cap issues.

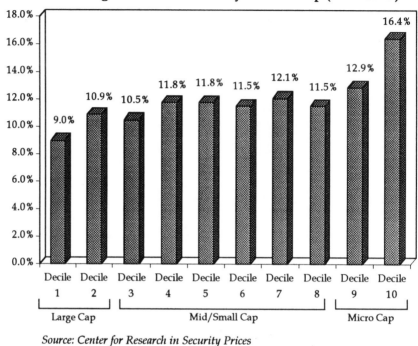

Average Annual Returns by Market Cap (1925-1995)

Source: Center for Research in Security Prices

CHART 2-2

This is undoubtedly a major factor behind Ibbotson Associates' decision at the end of 1981 to switch from using the complete micro cap data (as collected and published by CRSP) in its historical analysis to using the real world results of a dedicated micro cap mutual fund—DFA 9-10 Fund from Dimensional Fund Advisors, which typically invests in more than 2,500 micro cap stocks.

As part of the research analysis conducted for this book, the performance of the DFA 9-10 Fund (as reported in SBBI as Small Companies) was compared to the complete results of all micro cap stocks (as recorded by CRSP). It was anticipated that the performance of the DFA 9-10 Fund (which reflects all transaction costs and bid/ask spreads) would be substantially below that of the full micro cap index (calculated without the impact of transaction costs and spreads.)

U.S. Stock Performance – History of the Size Effect

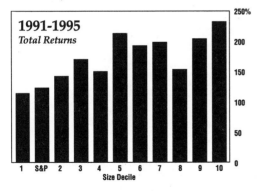

THE SIZE EFFECT CAN PERSIST IN EITHER DIRECTION FOR LONG PERIODS OF TIME.

This chart illustrates the total returns of Large Cap stocks (Deciles 1 & 2), Mid/Small Cap stocks (Deciles 3 to 8), and Micro Cap stocks (Deciles 9 & 10) from 1965 to 1995. This data was organized to illustrate the extreme variance in returns within "the market" over periods of time as long as 9 years.

Sources: Center for Research in Security Prices (CRSP)

CHART 2-3

The actual results were the exact opposite of what was expected. The DFA 9-10 fund outperformed the entire micro cap asset class — and by a wide margin. The micro cap universe of stocks as recorded by CRSP produced an annualized return of 12.4% between 1982-1996 while the DFA 9-10 Fund, which experienced the illiquidity pricing and costs of the real world, produced an annualized return of 14.4%.[*]

☞ The performance of the DFA 9-10 fund demonstrates that micro cap results are, in fact, achievable by the average mutual fund investor. (O'Shaughnessy's observation is true for large institutional investors who would undoubtedly experience great difficulty in moving large dollar amounts into micro cap stocks.)

Advantage USA: Big Picture

Thus far, we have only addressed domestic stocks. And for good reason. The old expression "you can't see the forest for the trees" is very apropos for the American investor today. There are many advantages to investing at home that are simply taken for granted, such as:

- Currency invisibility – no direct consideration of currency movements or costs

- Ease of purchase and sale (liquidity), particularly for large, mid and small cap issues

- Most transparent and accurate accounting standards for company reporting in the world

- Best regulatory supervision (Securities and Exchange Commission) to prevent market manipulation and unfair insider trading practices

---

[*] Part of the explanation lies in the fact that the DFA 9-10 fund is not run like large cap index funds. A large cap index fund constantly monitors its target asset class and buys or sells stocks within the fund in order to closely replicate the asset class. The poor liquidity of micro cap stocks makes this precision impossible. Therefore, the managers of the DFA 9-10 fund mainly buy those micro caps that become available for purchase — typically when they are out of favor. This gives the fund a contrarian bent, but still indicates that the returns of this asset class are possible in the real world.

- Wide availability and easy access to markets

- *English* is the de facto business language of the world—but everything is in English here—nothing is lost in the translation and

- Relatively low transaction costs, no transaction taxes.

While these inherent advantages may diminish in the future, they are very real and significant in the 1990s and will remain so for many years to come.

Advantage USA: Culture

Beyond certain indisputable advantages of U.S. investment markets, there are also cultural advantages that bode especially well for American investment:

- **Incubation of new ideas** – America's fertile intellectual fields are the envy of the world, particularly the depth of our graduate and post-graduate programs.

- **Entrepreneurship** – The U.S. is unique in small business creation, as well as small business funding through venture capital, initial public offerings, small business loans, etc. Entrepreneurs from around the globe consider the U.S. the best place to launch an innovative new business. No other country in the world comes close to developing great growth companies like the U.S according to Ralph Wanger, Manager of the Acorn Fund.

- **Technological leadership** – The U.S. has a major or dominant position in almost every industry of the future including: computers, software, telecommunications, biotechnology "and the largest proportion of companies with world-class productivity advantages."[4] This technological edge may be expanding. The Wall Street Journal (September 26, 1996) reported that the Internet "is overwhelmingly U.S. centric, inundated with English language sites and U.S. generated content." This is the information technology platform of the future.

- **Relatively pro-business government** – Although far from perfect, the degree of government regulation of business in America is far less intrusive than our major trading partners. This is particularly important in areas of hiring and firing, subsidies and taxation.

☞ **Taxation is very important, as any corporation's earnings are subject to the tax policy (whims) of its domestic government.** Keep firmly in mind, the number one shareholder of every corporation is the government where it is domiciled. The government has first claim to all profits—even the assets—of the corporation through tax policies and the ultimate tax — confiscation.

- And finally, as Shelby Davis, portfolio manager of Davis New York Venture Fund and Selected American Shares, posed to an audience at Morningstar's June 1996 investment conference, "What other country in the world has people lined up to be let in?"

Advantage USA: Shareholder Value Imperative

Last, but not least, investing in U.S. companies has a major, under-appreciated advantage over companies virtually anywhere in the world—a management imperative to deliver increasing value to shareholders. Perhaps more than any other single factor, this imperative is why the U.S. stock market has outperformed its international brethren in the 1990s and is uniquely positioned to continue to outperform in the future. The tangible evidence of this benefit to stockholders in U.S. companies lies in:

- **Share buy-backs** to increase earnings-per-share

- **Downsizing** to create more efficient use of capital and labor

- **Return-on-equity** results that are close to double that of Europe and eight times that of Japan (summer 1996)

- **Management accession** policies that develop and grow management talent without regard to family ties

- **Third-party shareholders** that want (demand?) returns on their investment. (In Japan or Europe, business partners and/or banks own majority stakes in business and, therefore, have other ways of being compensated than through increasing share value. In many emerging markets, family ties are often more important than the corporate officer/shareholder relationship. Here again, other compensation methods can supersede adding value for shareholders.)

- **Aggressive management** that aids U.S. competitiveness; the threat of hostile takeovers (almost non-existent in Japan and Europe) allows for poor performers to be removed.

Conclusion

All three of the domestic stock asset classes—large cap, mid/small cap and micro cap stocks—offer long-term investors these advantages:

- Risks and rewards that have been meticulously recorded over seven decades

- Significant real returns over prevailing inflation over virtually any long-term period

- Big picture advantages in areas of access to the markets and reliability of securities regulation

- Cultural advantages that support entrepreneurship, new technology and pro-business regulation and

- A shareholder imperative by corporate managements to deliver increasing value.

While domestic stocks may be volatile and fluctuate irrationally in the short-term, U.S. equities have proved to be the best performing asset classes for the long term. They are a critical component of the well-designed Wealth and Retirement Portfolio.

3

Attractions and Drawbacks of Domestic Cash and Bonds

Cash and its equivalents, such as Certificates of Deposit (CDs) and Treasury bills, offer both a safe haven for principal and interest rates that adjust quickly to inflation. Cash has produced consistently low real returns, however, over the past seven decades. Bonds typically pay higher yields than cash and have produced higher total returns over the long term. Yet bonds must endure significant fluctuations in their principal value due to changing levels of interest rates and changes in the credit quality of a bond's issuer.

For long-term portfolios, the significant attraction of these two asset classes is their consistent and uncorrelated returns with those of stocks.

*"...Diversification is the nearest an investor or
business manager can ever come to a free lunch."*
— Peter Bernstein, <u>Against the Gods</u>, 1996

Cash Asset Class

Money market accounts are a necessary component of virtually every portfolio. This is the account that transaction proceeds flow through for purchases, sales, contributions and withdrawals. Cash is an ideal vehicle for parking funds that will be needed soon or for which the timing of the use is uncertain.

While the daily moves in the stock market are often "fast and *curious*," the daily moves in cash equivalent securities ("cash") are monotonously "*low* but sure." One of the main attractions of cash is that you will not read the newspaper and see that the investment you made yesterday is down in value today.

Cash equivalent securities come in many popular forms: money market accounts, certificates of deposit (CDs), commercial paper (short-term notes issued by corporations) and U.S. Treasury bills (T-bills) guaranteed by the U.S. Government.

The return from cash is so nearly certain (little or no fluctuation in the value of principal—up or down) that investors have accepted a very small return over the prevailing inflation rate in exchange for this safety. The excess return over the current inflation rate is called the **inflation premium** for cash equivalents or bonds.

Attractions

The three attractions of cash are thus:

- As a depository account for collecting and disbursing funds

- Little or no fluctuation in principal value and

- An income stream that adjusts quickly to changes in inflation.

On the other hand, these short-term positives are overwhelmed by the long-term negatives of cash equivalents when viewed as a major component of your Wealth and Retirement Portfolio.

Drawbacks

The two big drawbacks of cash for long-term portfolios are:

- Lack of stable or dependable income level and
- Little real return (over inflation).

An extreme personal example of the first drawback happened in 1981. A fairly young, new retiree (late 50s) came into my office to discuss his financial plans. He had just received a pension distribution of approximately $300,000, which was all *invested* in a money market account at the then current rate of 16%. He told me he retired because he could make it on the $48,000 per year that his money market account would pay him. (He assumed the 16% rate was permanent!)

This man fell prey to what might be called the "current trend myopia," which posits that whatever has been happening in the financial markets for a couple of years or more will go on forever. Regrettably, he stuck with his plan, and when interest rates fell from this lofty but temporary perch, he had to find another job.

The second drawback, the dismal *real* return over inflation provided by cash over time, is analyzed in the next chapter.

Bond Asset Classes

A bond is very similar to the cash equivalent securities discussed above, but with a longer period until maturity. Bonds are segregated in three different ways:

- Domestic or foreign
- Taxable or tax free and
- High grade or high yield (junk).

SBBI has provided detailed information back to the beginning of 1926 for three domestic, high-quality bond asset classes:

- **Long-Term Government Bonds**   U.S. Treasury bonds 20-year constant maturity

- **Intermediate-Term Government Bonds**   U.S. Treasury bonds 5-year constant maturity

- **Long-Term Corporate Bonds**   High-grade bonds of domestic issuers with long-term maturities

Intermediate-term Government bonds offer much less volatility in returns than long-term Government bonds, yet have outperformed the long-term Treasury bonds for the full 1926-1996 period (5.2% versus 5.1%), according to SBBI. Receiving lower returns at a higher level of risk is not the desired attribute of a long-term position in a profitable portfolio. Therefore, long-term U.S. Treasury bonds are discarded as a potential asset class to include in the model portfolios developed in Section III.

Long-term corporate bonds are even more volatile than long-term U.S. Treasury bonds but have at least produced a higher long-term rate of return (5.6%) than intermediate-term U.S. Treasury bonds. But corporate bonds must be evaluated more closely than Treasury bonds because of their **credit risk**, the risk that not all interest payments or all principal (at maturity) will be paid as due. In addition, the credit quality of the corporate bond issuer can change significantly over a bond's long life and have a direct effect on the price of the bond in the open market.

Attractions

The attractions of bonds as a stand-alone asset class are:

- Stable, locked-in rate of income until maturity and

- Typically higher *inflation premium* (interest rate) than that of cash equivalents.

These attributes of bonds make them an ideal choice for a significant portion of short-term and intermediate-term funding requirements (like college educations) and to match specific financial obligations of a longer-term nature (like known pension liabilities for retiring employees).

For most long-term portfolios, the central attraction of bonds is the attributes they bring to a planned portfolio:

- Relatively high and stable income as compared to stocks and

- Relatively low correlation of returns with domestic stocks.

☞ These are very powerful features of bonds that have been overlooked in recent years due to the typical, oversimplified heads-up comparison between stocks and bonds on a stand-alone basis. The significant and important role of bonds within portfolios will be evaluated in detail in Section III.

Drawbacks

The two drawbacks of bonds as a free-standing asset class are:

- No interest rate adjustments on bonds during long periods of rising rates, and

- Over long periods of time, the inflation premium of bonds has not compared favorably with the real returns of common stocks.

The first drawback was realized in spades by the bond buyers of the 1940s, 1950s and 1960s. They were never adequately compensated for the rising levels of both inflation and interest rates. An extreme example was the buyer of a 30-year U.S. Treasury bond in the early 1950s. This investor was stuck with an interest rate of about 1.0% for *three decades* in which inflation rose as high as 14% and interest rates to over 20%. Selling those bonds in the open market along the way would have incurred a huge loss in principal from the original cost.

The inflation-adjusted total return for U.S. Treasury bonds (with interest compounded) was just about zero ("0") from 1926 to 1981. No wealth accumulated whatsoever for 55 years. From 1926 through the end of 1996, the real return from the intermediate-term U.S. Treasury bond asset class was only 2.1% per year. The real returns from bonds as compared to stocks will be further illustrated in the next chapter.

High-Yield Bonds

History is Very Relevant

Most of the available data on high-yield bonds is quite favorable. The problem is reliability. In this case, it is not reliability of the data. The problem lies in the changing and evolving nature of high-yield bonds themselves.

High-yield bonds are technically defined as those bonds that are rated below investment grade by credit rating agencies, such as Moody's and Standard & Poor's. While this definition has been consistent, the bonds that fall within this definition have changed dramatically over the past two decades. There are three distinct periods in their evolution:

- Before the early 1980s
- Mid-1980s through 1990 (the Michael Milken era)
- 1991–Present

The high-yield bond market before the early 1980s was tiny in terms of market capitalization, but the total return on those high-yield bonds was quite favorable compared to U.S. Treasuries—even considering credit and default risks. These bonds produced a remarkably consistent default rate of approximately 2% annually but paid a much higher interest rate spread than 2% over U.S. Treasury bonds. Many of the issuers of high-yield bonds in that period were healthy—just small. Often their bonds were not rated because these small companies would not pay Moody's or Standard & Poor's to receive a rating.

Michael Milken, a bond trader with Drexel, Burnham and Lambert, took notice of this apparent inefficiency in the high-yield bond market (high returns for *relatively* low risks). Furthermore, he fully recognized its marketing potential. Milken knew more investors would buy these bonds once they were made aware of their risk/reward characteristics.

The problem facing Milken was the tiny size of this market. There was not enough supply to satisfy much new investor demand. His solution was to generate more high-yield bonds. And that he did. Most of the newly created high-yield bonds were created to fund the leveraged buy-outs that stormed Wall Street in the 1980s. Unfortunately, these bond issuers have little resemblance to those of the earlier period that had created the attractive track record. High-leverage, low equity was the new guiding light for high-yield bond issues.

The day of reckoning came in 1989 when the pyramid of leveraged debt (high-yield bonds) began to unwind. Default rates skyrocketed. Worse still, many of these bonds suffered when their collateral was arbitrarily removed in the shuffling of corporate entities that ensued. The high-yield bond market collapsed in 1990.

☞ A new high-yield bond market emerged from the rubble beginning in early 1991. Characterized by super-high yields (demanded by investors) and uncertain collateral, it resembled a flea market more than a securities market. *Trash and treasure* would be an appropriate description.

Long-Term Value Uncertain

Today, the high-yield bond market has regained its equilibrium. Important changes have occurred in the industry. For one, liquidity has increased greatly since the '80s and early '90s. Junk-bond trader Michael Milken not only was the dominant dealer in high-yield securities, but one of the only ones making a market. Orders of $20 million were rare in those days, now they occur regularly.

These days there are hundreds of dealers, providing much more liquidity in a sector with $320 billion in debt outstanding. That's about one-fourth of the $1.2 trillion corporate debt market (1996).

The quality of new issues also has improved greatly. Issuers are bringing out more senior debt with first call on corporate assets than in the past.[5]

However, the history of high-yield bonds is too short and too erratic to instill confidence in their predictability going forward. High-quality indexes are only available beginning in 1985 and no high-yield bond index fund is readily available to the public. (In fact, it is somewhat difficult to isolate domestic high-yield bonds through the purchase of a high-yield mutual fund. Most such mutual funds regularly diversify into international, private placement and mortgage bond markets.) Lehman Brothers high-yield index does indicate interesting characteristics for the 1986-1996 time period: higher total returns than other domestic bond asset classes, low correlations with all other stock and bond asset classes and relatively mild risk. This will be an asset class well worth watching for consistency over the years to come.

At this stage, however, high-yield bonds appear more appropriate for value investors, traders and other short-term investors to sort through than for those investors seeking a high degree of reliability and long-term predictability from the asset classes they choose for their Wealth and Retirement Portfolios.

Conclusion

Cash is a necessary part of virtually every Wealth and Retirement Portfolio. However, its short-term positives must be carefully weighed with its long-term deficiencies when constructing a portfolio design.

U.S. Treasury bonds of five years to maturity have demonstrated superior characteristics of higher returns and lower volatility when compared to U.S. Treasury bonds of much longer maturity.

High-quality corporate bonds have produced higher returns than those of 5-year U.S. Treasuries, although their relative risk level is an issue to be explored in the chapters that follow.

High-yield bonds are, as yet, too unreliable an asset class to include in portfolios where predictability is desired.

Three of the asset classes discussed—cash, intermediate-term U.S. Treasury bonds and high-quality corporate bonds—appear to offer long-term investors attractive benefits for inclusion in their Wealth and Retirement Portfolio. These three asset classes will be further analyzed in the balance of this Section.

4

Domestic Stocks and Bonds: Real Returns in the Inflation Era (1960+)

Over the past 70 years, two major economic influences have significantly affected the nation's wealth: deflation and inflation. In order to evaluate the performance of the various asset classes that we might include in a Wealth and Retirement Portfolio, we look not to nominal returns but real returns adjusted for these two influences. Comparing various asset-class returns in the Inflation and Deflation Eras offers a number of counter-intuitive observations that debunk common investment maxims while providing many insights into our future investment alternatives.

"Bank on the long-term trends, and ignore the tremors."
— J. Paul Getty

Chapters 2 and 3 discussed the attractions and drawbacks of the major domestic asset classes. These asset classes represent most of the portfolio investments in wide use by American investors until relatively recently.

They possess a long, rich history that has been meticulously documented back to 1926 in SBBI.[*] Other researchers have recorded the fluctuations and returns on these asset classes back considerably further. This documented financial history is of immeasurable value to U.S. investors.

In this chapter, the modern period of American financial markets will be dissected into two eras: the **Deflation Era** and the **Inflation Era**. The results of each era will be analyzed. As the Inflation Era has more relevance to your investing today, the returns and fluctuations of this era will be presented in detail in Chapter 5. To thoroughly understand these results, you need a full appreciation of the grip inflation holds on the financial markets.

Nominal and Real Returns

We live in a world of *nominal returns*, returns that are not adjusted for inflation. Your bank quotes interest rates this way, mutual funds advertise performance nominally, the U.S. government offers Treasury bonds and T-bills at nominal rates and so forth.

 Yet *real returns*, those adjusted for inflation, are far more important to your Wealth and Retirement Portfolio. There is no creation or addition to wealth without increased purchasing power. And, in the same vein, the further in the future your proposed retirement is, the more the amount of your retirement income in nominal dollars becomes merely an abstraction. The purchasing power of those dollars is all that counts. (Even if you are currently retired, this is still a crucial distinction for your income for the remainder of your retirement.)

---

[*] Does not include High-Yield Bond index.

Inflation's Slow Burn

Inflation should be feared. Inflation is a particularly insidious financial disease. It attacks the corpus (principal) and the productive effort (yield or interest) at the same time. It is not only cumulative, it compounds like an interest-bearing account in reverse. After 30 years of retirement with inflation at 3%, you will need $250 to buy what $100 did when you retired. In other words, both your portfolio and retirement income must grow by 150% after taxes just to be even with inflation.

Unfortunately, inflation is not reflected on your brokerage statements. It grows unseen like a cancerous tumor. A graphic analogy of how inflation exacts its price is that of the proverbial "frog on the stove." As you have probably heard, if you place a frog in a pot of water on the stove and turn on the burner so that the water slowly heats to a boil, the frog will stay in the pot—even with full opportunity to hop out—until he boils to death. The slow incremental burn never rings an alarm to get out until it is too late.

Deflation Era & Inflation Era

Focusing on inflation-adjusted or real returns has another important advantage. It allows for an apples-to-apples comparison of different periods of financial history...those with very different inflationary—even deflationary—conditions.

Ibbotson's SBBI documents what may be called the modern financial period (1926-1996). There are some significant advantages and insights to be gained by dividing this period into two roughly equal, yet very distinctive, financial eras:

- **The Deflation Era** (the Great Depression and its grip: 1926-1959) and

- **The Inflation Era** (the Great Inflation, its build-up and its lingering effects: 1960+).

Two Great Anomalies of the 20th Century

SBBI data shows that inflation has averaged 3.1% for the entire modern period 1926-1996. This full period data hides the two great financial anomalies of the 20th century. The Great Depression's deflation of the 1930s and the great monetary inflation of the 1960s and 1970s.

In the first half of the 1930s, America suffered a severe deflationary shock. The price level *declined* between 6% and 10% each year in 1930, 1931 and 1932. Short-term interest rates fell from 4.7% in 1929 to 1% in 1932. After the deflation had run its course, interest rates continued to fall to a minuscule 0.2% annually on T-bills. Rates remained very low throughout the balance of the 1930s, the 1940s and well into the 1950s even though America never suffered deflation again and inflation returned to more normal levels between one and three percent. *Interest rates were stuck at low levels as a skeptical public feared a return of the depression.*

Beginning in the 1960s but really taking off in the 1970s, America suffered a severe inflationary shock. The consumer price level rose at least 8.8% in every year except two from 1973 through 1981. Short-term interest rates on cash equivalents increased from 3.8% in 1972 to 14.7% in 1981. Rates on 5-year Treasury bonds rose from 6.8% to 14.0% over that same period.

Inflation came down quickly in 1982 and averaged a more normal 3.6% for the 1982-1996 period. *However, interest rates have remained stuck at historically high levels since 1982 as a skeptical public fears a return of inflation.* The Inflation Era is likely to continue for many years to come.

Comparing the Two Eras

In comparing and contrasting the full modern financial period (1926-1996), the Deflation Era (1926-1959) and the Inflation Era (1960-1996), the following chart will be helpful.

	Average Annual Rates		
	Full Modern Period 1926-1996	Deflation Era 1926-1959	Inflation Era 1960-1996
Inflation	3.1%	1.5%	4.7%
Cash Returns (30-day T-bills)	3.7%	1.3%	6.1%
Real Returns (Inflation Adjusted)	0.6%	-0.2%	1.4%
Bond Returns (5-year Treasury bonds)	5.2%	2.8%	7.5%
Real Returns	2.1%	1.3%	2.8%
Stock Returns (S&P 500)	10.7%	10.3%	11.1%
Real Returns	7.6%	8.8%	6.4%

Source: © *Computed using data from* Stocks, Bonds, Bills & Inflation 1996 Yearbook™ *with data updated January 1997, Ibbotson Associates, Chicago*

CHART 4-1

Observations from the Comparison of Eras

- A general observation from this comparison is just how different the Deflation Era was from the Inflation Era with regard to inflation, interest rates and real returns in all three asset class families. The full period data (1926-1996) is simply an average of two distinctly different eras.

- The most counter-intuitive observation from this data is that the Deflation Era produced lower real returns for bond investors than the later Inflation Era. This is contrary to the conventional wisdom that inflation is bad for bonds.

- Large cap stocks (S&P 500) delivered consistent long-term nominal returns, 11.1% in the Inflation Era and 10.3% in the Deflation Era. However, the real returns from the two periods were at opposite ends of the range of real long-term returns discussed in Chapter 2. The Deflation Era, which included the Great Depression and World War II, produced significantly higher inflation-adjusted returns than the Inflation Era, 8.8% versus 6.4%. This also flies in the face of conventional wisdom regarding the two periods.

☞ • Perhaps the most significant observation from this data is that the Inflation Era has been a relatively poor one for stocks and a magnificent one for bonds and cash. Yet, stocks still more than doubled the real returns of bonds and more than quadrupled the real returns from cash.

Detailed Period for Stock Analysis: 1960-1996

☞ Studying the stock market's returns and fluctuations beginning with 1960 provides a good overview of the Inflation Era for any investor or investment professional. In many ways, it paints a worst-case scenario of what could unfold over any long-term period of stock ownership. In fact, the very *worst* 30-year period for stock ownership in the modern era is the 30 years beginning in 1960.

During this period, inflation skyrocketed, interest rates quintupled and price/earnings (P/E) multiples of stocks were sliced by two-thirds. If you can develop confidence in the stock market from the 1960-1996 period, you are well on your way to relying on the certainties that unfold over long periods of market experience.

High (P/E) Ratios: Past and Present

Many investors felt that the U.S. stock market was fully valued or even overvalued in 1991...and each year thereafter. Their primary cause for concern has been the relatively high P/E ratios of the major market averages. These investors will want to take special note of the P/E ratios in 1960 and for the decade that followed. The late 1950s through the late 1960s is the only extended period of relatively high and stable P/E ratios for the domestic stock market other than that which began in 1991 (see Chart 4-2). As this study of the 1960-1996 period attests, the U.S. stock market has provided excellent relative returns even beginning from periods with relatively high P/E ratios.

Large Company Stocks: S&P 500
P/E Ratios - 1960-1996

CHART 4-2

The Market Multiple (Review of a Basic Point)

What is the market multiple? Why is it important?

The best single expression of the current consensus outlook for the stock market is the market multiple. At any point in time, the U.S. stock market—as typically denoted by the S&P 500 Index—is selling at a multiple of the combined earnings of the companies that make up that index. [For example, if the S&P 500 index was currently at 685 and the combined per share earnings of the 500 companies in the index had added up to $43 for the past 12 months, the P/E ratio of the market is 685/43 = 16. The S&P 500 is selling for 16 times earnings or a market multiple of 16 in this instance.]

During this century, the market multiple for the U.S. stock market has normally ranged between 10 and 20 times earnings. The average has been about 15. The higher the current market multiple, the rosier the consensus view is about corporate earnings, inflation and interest rates ahead. But higher-than-average market multiples imply that the market has less room to rise based on the multiple itself going up further. It is less likely that investors are willing to pay still more per one dollar of earnings. It also implies that the market has more room to fall if the market multiple contracts. If investors are willing to pay less per dollar of earnings, it is indicative of a darker consensus view of corporate earnings, inflation and interest rates looking ahead.

Striking Similarities of Mid to Late 1990s and Late 1950s to Early 1960s

Another similarity (besides high P/E ratios) of the early 1960s and the mid-1990s is even more striking. Each period was preceded by a major bull market in stocks: 1949-1960+ and 1982-1996+. Each bull market saw a tripling of P/E ratios from 6 or 7 times earnings to 16 to 20 times earnings.

In 1959, the new investment firm of Donaldson, Lufkin and Jenrette introduced their firm through a small publication titled <u>Common Stocks and Common Sense</u>. This is an excerpt from that booklet:

> *"The most significant change in the position of the 1959 investor vis-à-vis the 1949 investor is in the multiple of earnings reflected in common stock prices today. Today's 'Favorite Fifty' stocks are selling at price-earnings ratios which are 21 times estimated 1959 earnings. Ten years ago these same stocks could have been purchased at prices averaging 7.7 times 1949 earnings."*

Almost this exact statement could have been written at any time in the 1990s, substituting 1982 for 1949 and the current year for 1959.

Yet another similarity of the two periods, both bull markets were led by large cap stocks. Despite the long-term advantage of micro cap stocks, large cap stocks outperformed by 2.5% annually in the 1950s bull market and by 2.5% annually in the 1980s/90s bull market.

Conclusion

☞ The stock market investor of the mid to late 1990s is in a very similar investment environment to the stock market investor of 1960. This makes January 1, 1960, an ideal date to begin a detailed analysis of the stock market that may provide guidance for today's investors. Studying the entire 1960-1996 period provides a wonderful insight into the long-term returns and the frequency and degree of any setbacks that will most likely unfold over the years ahead.

5

Comparing Risks and Rewards of Domestic Stocks and Bonds

The first three chapters of this section provided a discussion of the major domestic asset classes and how to evaluate them in light of inflation or deflation. This chapter will introduce a methodology for evaluating and measuring the long-term risks and rewards that each domestic asset class has offered. It will also address efficiency ratings by answering the question, *"How much reward has each domestic asset class delivered for the risks incurred?"*

"Nothing has really changed on Wall Street over the years. In fact, much of what happens in the financial world today has been played over in history many times before and has been captured in the cycles and trends of financial charts created over time. Understanding the movements within these charts provides a clearer perspective of today's market and can aid you in your investment decisions tomorrow."

— Ken Fisher, The Wall Street Waltz

Risk as Viewed by Four Blind Men

Like the story of the four blind men each describing the elephant differently by the part each felt… risk is not easily described by any one characteristic.

The Enigma of Risk

The long history of domestic asset classes reveals an important fact: *not one has ever sustained a permanent loss.* Eventually, every decline in value has been recovered. However, any decline in market value can be turned into a permanent loss. For example, many investors sold their equity mutual funds right after the 1987 crash. These investors were not properly prepared for the magnitude of that decline—even though it fell well within historic parameters.

The purpose of understanding the risks within each asset class is to be both intellectually and emotionally prepared for the intensity of its inevitable market declines. A special part of this preparation is to come to grips with the entirely random nature of these market declines. Neither the timing nor the intensity of the *next* decline can be predicted.

Therefore, the better an investor is prepared for the entire range of expected declines inherent in a particular asset class, the more likely his actions will serve his own best long-term interests. Either he will not invest in the asset in the first place or he will *stay the course* during declines.

The study of the risks within any particular asset class thus becomes the study of the severity, frequency and duration of its declines in market value. This is a daunting task since it requires measuring market declines in a variety of ways.

Standard Deviation as a Measure of Risk

The academic measurement of risk is standard deviation,* which is not an investor-friendly tool. It falls short of providing a real appreciation for the risk in owning a particular investment. In fact, standard deviation is not a measurement of market declines per se, it is a measurement of the annual volatility or degree of variance an investment experiences in producing a particular average rate of

---

* A complete explanation of the calculation of standard deviation is given in the Appendix, page 247.

return. Upside movements are as influential as downside movements in its calculation. Therefore, right from the beginning, standard deviation *fails* as a measurement of market *declines*.

Example of Standard Deviation "Predictions"

Suppose that the average of all the annual returns from an investment over a 20-year period of study is 10%[*]. Further assume that this investment produced a standard deviation of 18.5% for this 20-year period. The standard deviation for this investment predicts the following:

- **13** of the 20 annual returns likely fell within the range of **-8.5% to 28.5%**, the average annual return of 10% plus or minus one standard deviation

$$(10\% \pm 18.5\%)$$

- **19** of the 20 annual returns likely fell within the range of **-27% to 47%**, the average annual return of 10% plus or minus two standard deviations

$$[10\% \pm (2 \text{ times } 18.5\%)]$$

- **1** annual return may be lower than **-27.0% or higher than 47.0%**

Standard deviation has one distinctive advantage—its precision. Academics and market commentators like the fact that any historical set of returns can produce this precise, annual measurement of volatility to match up with an investment's annual return.

However, as pointed out by Harold Evensky in the December 1996 issue of Financial Planning magazine, "Modern research in investment theory and behavioral finance has demonstrated that standard deviation, even for normal distributions, is not necessarily an acceptable measure of risk. As many studies have demonstrated, return distributions of financial assets are not normally distributed. Thus, the mean variance does not reflect the action of real markets."

---

[*] This is not the compounded average annual return from this investment, it is simply the arithmetic *mean* of all 20 of its annual returns.

Standard Deviation's Limitations

From an investor's viewpoint, standard deviation does have several insurmountable shortcomings as the measure of an asset class's risk, i.e. the intensity of its market declines.

- **Omission of Worst Case.** In the eyes of many investors, the most significant risk of an investment is defined by, "What's the worst that can happen?" A major handicap of standard deviation is that it leaves out the worst case. Over the long term, the standard deviation calculation will not predict or illustrate the very worst "bear market" decline that the investor will likely face.

- **Annual Risks vs. Total Risk.** Standard deviation measures volatility in calendar year units. This has the effect of hiding or downplaying the real risks incurred. For example, in calculating the standard deviation for the S&P 500 index, a *positive* annual return is entered for 1987—the year of the crash! Is this an accurate portrayal of the risk that unfolded to investors in that year? Standard deviation also fails to prepare investors for the cumulative effect of back-to-back declines like 1973-1974. A better yardstick for the risk within asset classes would measure all major market declines from beginning to end, regardless of calendar year starts and stops, as this is what the investor feels as his monthly brokerage statements arrive.

- **Not Addressed: Period of Decline.** Standard deviation is not sensitive to the length of time over which a market decline unfolds. There is no way of telling from an investment's standard deviation whether the *average* decline is 6 months or 12 months long or if its worst period of decline was 13 months or 28 months. This is vital information to know about the risks of each asset class. Investors, particularly those who are unprepared, begin to see losses as permanent, not temporary, the longer they persist. It is the emotional trauma of the "unending decline" that causes unprepared investors to throw in the towel and turn temporary declines into losses.

- **Not Addressed: Recovery Period.** In the same fashion, standard deviation does not give any indication of the average period of recovery from a decline. One asset class that takes 18 months on average to recover from material declines, may have the same standard deviation of another asset class that takes only nine months to recover. Are these investments equally risky? When a major market decline is unfolding, no investor knows which new low point is the final bottom in market value. The confirmation that the risk of a new low is over often does not occur until the investor is back even, after recovering all that was temporarily lost in the decline. Therefore, the number of months until full recovery from the bottom of a major decline is an important characteristic of the risk of each asset class.

In summary, standard deviation may give a good insight into a normalized distribution of annual returns, but it fails to prepare investors for the intensity of the declines they will likely incur. (See page 193 for an example of how a standard deviation calculation can be misleading.) A more thorough and useful measurement of risk is required to fulfill the mission of preparing investors for the actual risks they face.

Bear Markets: Risk Characteristics and Measurements

Risk, the intensity of market declines, can be measured in a variety of ways. As this book takes a long-term perspective, it will focus on those major market declines that occur infrequently (about once every five years). These substantial setbacks in market value, often referred to as bear markets, tend to be the major concern of most investors.

Actually, the history of asset classes shows that there are two types of bear markets. First, there are the normal cyclical bear markets (*average* major declines) that tend to be sharp and short-term. Then there are the very infrequent mega bear markets (*worst-case* major declines) that tend to be much deeper and more prolonged. The worst-case market declines induce more than concern from investors, they instill real fear. Fortunately, such mega bear markets may only occur once in an entire investment lifetime (within each asset class). For example, the S&P 500 has endured two such worst-case market declines since 1925, the Depression Era crash of 1929 - '32 and the Inflation Era's monetary crisis of 1973-1974.

In order to gain a full sense of the risk that lies in wait within an asset class, an investor needs a complete picture of:

- The worst-case market decline, both the magnitude of the *temporary* loss in market value and the length of time over which it unfolded

- The average cyclical decline, again including both the magnitude of the *temporary* loss in market value and the length of time over which it unfolded and

- The average recovery period, i.e. how long it took to recover the market value temporarily lost during a major decline.

Chart 5-1 illustrates these risk characteristics and measurements for the S&P 500 over the 1960-1996 period.

Risk Characteristics	*Risk Measurements*
Worst-Case Decline*	43% (temporary loss) over 21 months
Average Cyclical Decline*	19% (temporary loss) over 7 months
Average Recovery Period	10 months

* Measured from high month-end market value to subsequent low month-end valuation.

CHART 5-1

The risk measurements are of great value when comparing different asset classes. Yet, it is often cumbersome to compare several asset classes with so many risk measures. Therefore, it would be helpful to compile these different risk measurements into a single risk grade.

Grading Quarterbacks

Whether you are a football fan or not, you probably have an appreciation for all of the skills required of the quarterback. His ability to throw the ball, run with the ball and operate the entire offensive team are all important to his success. Each of these skills can be measured in several ways. For example, his skill at throwing the ball can be measured by his pass completion percentage, his number of touchdown passes and his number of interceptions over the course of a season. How do you distill so many elements of a quarterback's skill into one number that can be used to compare his overall ability with that of his peers? Professional football came up with an answer. They developed a point system that assigned point values to every area of a quarterback's skills. Each quarterback earns points based on his performance in each skill. These points are then added up to provide a composite grade of his overall performance. This quarterback rating system proves of great value in comparing the performance of one quarterback versus another.

Grading Risk - A Composite Score

In a manner similar to the quarterback grading system, five risk measurements can be compiled to create one composite risk score.

One guiding principle of such a risk point system needs to be simplicity. It should be easy to implement and easy to remember. Another principle should be balance, each of the five risk measurements should have a meaningful impact on the final Composite Risk score. The following Composite Risk point system meets these tests. It assigns one "risk point" for each percentage point of major market declines, one "risk point" for each month of major market declines and one "risk point" for each month it takes to recover from major market declines. The following example, again using the S&P 500 in the 1960-1996 period, will illustrate this point system. (A full description begins on page 247 in the Appendix.)

Example:

Compiling Composite Risk Scores

Using the S&P 500 in the Inflation Era (1960-1996), a number of characteristics of risk are presented in Chart 5-2. This chart translates these risk characteristics into risk points.

S&P 500 (1960-1996)

Risk Characteristic	Risk Measurements	Risk Points
Worst Decline	43 %	43 points
	21 mo.	21
Average Decline	19 %	19
	7 mo.	7
Average Recovery Period	10 mo.	10
Composite Risk Score		**100 points**

CHART 5-2

Although not relevant to academicians, a Composite Risk score can be a useful tool for investors in comparing the overall risk of one asset class with another over the course of a set period of study. The Composite Risk Score of 100 for the S&P 500 reflected in Chart 5-2 means very little on its own, but becomes meaningful when compared to the Composite Risk scores of other asset classes over the same period of study.

Measuring Rewards

Financial performance is a combination of risk and reward. Whereas risk is multifaceted, the reward from investing is fairly easy to identify. Reward, as defined in Chapter 1, is a return above the riskless rate of 30-day U.S. Treasury bills.

Every investor can purchase a U.S. Treasury bill (the cash asset class) and receive the riskless return it offers. The return from cash therefore sets the base from which reward is measured. Your reward from an investment is only that extra return (above the riskless return of cash) for which you must incur some amount of risk.

**Reward = Rate of Return on Asset Class *less* the
Rate of Return on Cash (T-bills)**

For example, the Reward from owning the S&P 500 for the 1960-1996 period is 5.0%. This is simply the 11.1% rate of return of the S&P 500 for this period *less* the 6.1% return offered by Treasury bills (Chart 5-3).

Reward - S&P 500
(1960-1996)

Return (Annualized)	=	11.1%
Riskless Return (T-bills)	=	-6.1%
REWARD		**5.0%**

CHART 5-3

Efficiency Ratings — Reward Earned for the Risk Taken

Everyone wants to improve their investment results. For most investors, this means achieving the best return possible for the level of risk with which they are comfortable. This is all well and good, but just how does one quantify the trade-off or relationship between risk and reward. For long-term evaluation, the answer is an "efficiency rating," a measure of the reward earned for the risk taken.

The prior two parts of this chapter have discussed various measurements for both risk and reward. Efficiency is derived by dividing the best available measurement of reward by the best available measurement of risk:

$$\text{Efficiency Rating} = \frac{\text{Reward}}{\text{Risk}}$$

The efficiency rating of the S&P 500 for the Inflation Era may now be calculated as follows:

$$\frac{\text{Efficiency}}{\text{Rating}} = \frac{\text{Reward}}{\text{Composite Risk Score}} = \frac{5.0\,(\%)}{100\,(\text{points})} \times 1000 = 50$$

(The result is arbitrarily multiplied by 1000 so that the final result typically falls between 1 and 100.)

☞ The efficiency rating tells us how much reward was delivered for all of the risk the holder of this asset class experienced. The higher the efficiency rating of one asset class as compared to that of another—*for the same time period of analysis*—the more reward it has provided for the same degree of total risk within the same set of general market conditions.

Historical Risk/Reward - Putting It All Together

As stated earlier, "the purpose of understanding the risks within each asset class is to be both intellectually and emotionally prepared for the intensity of its inevitable market declines." The best preparation is to see and feel the major declines in market value each asset class has experienced over its history and then to envision living through those setbacks as if they were occurring in your own investment in the years ahead.

The Historical Risk/Reward chart allows you to do just that. On one page it walks you through the month-by-month history of the asset class segregated by periods of major market declines, recoveries and net new advancements. Spending just a few minutes studying a Historical Risk/Reward chart will greatly add to your appreciation of the relationship between the risks and reward within that asset class. It is a more complete picture of a long-term owner's experience with that asset class.

Historical Risk/Reward for S&P 500

Chart 5-4 is a Historical Risk/Reward chart of the S&P 500 for the Inflation Era. One hundred thousand dollars ($100,000) invested in the S&P 500 on December 31, 1959, grew to $4,840,300 by December 31, 1996. The equivalent return from cash (30-day T-bills) was $884,800. The S&P 500 more than quintupled the accumulated return from cash.

The computation of the Reward of owning the S&P 500 is shown on the bottom left side of this chart. The computation of its Composite Risk Score is shown on the bottom right side.

To achieve these superior results, an investor in the S&P 500 lived through periods of significant setbacks which are highlighted as the solid areas on the chart. These are the cyclical declines (bear markets) that long-term owners must take in stride.

As you can see, the magnitude of these declines varies widely both in terms of duration and percentage from as short as two months to as long as 21 months in length and from a mild 10% setback to an ugly 43% decline. The lightly shaded sections following each cyclical decline show how long it took to recover the temporary loss of that decline. These periods vary sharply too. The entire solid area plus the following lightly shaded area together indicate the total length of time an investor was underwater from a prior high in market value. The white areas denote major periods of net new advancement.

The combined lightly shaded areas (recovery periods) and the white areas (net new advancement) together represent the bull markets following the periods of decline (solid areas). The percentage gain and the number of months over which the bull markets unfolded are reflected in the numbers on the chart. These also varied widely in degree and duration. The smallest full bull market was up 42% over only eight months. The largest (so far) is the 282% bull market of 1982-1987 and the longest began November 1990.

The up and down arrows show whether that particular month-end value was up or down from the prior month. Directly below the chart, the standard deviation for the S&P 500 (15.4 for the period of 1960-1996) is also shown.

The then-current value of a $100,000 portfolio (beginning January 1, 1960) is shown at the end of each net new advancement and at the bottom of each major decline. This provides you an excellent view of where your month-end brokerage statements were heading in each major advance and each major decline. Visualize your own S&P 500 investment going through similar advances—and particularly declines—in the future. The intent is to prepare you today for what is likely to unfold in some random sequence in the decades ahead.

As you can see, the history of the S&P 500 is one of continuous progress punctuated by periodic setbacks of varying intensity.

Standard & Poor's 500
Growth of $100,000
(12/31/59 – 12/31/96)

Year	Jan	Feb	Mar	Apr	May	Jun	Jul	Aug	Sep	Oct	Nov	Dec	Annual Returns
1960	$100,000	↑	↓	↓	↑	+25% 26 mo.		↑	↓	↓	↑	↑	0.5
1961	↑	↑	↑	↑	↑	↓	↑	↑	↓	↑	↑	↑	26.9
1962	↓	$125,400	<21%> 4 mo.		$99,100		↑	↑	↓	↑	↑	↑	-8.7
1963	↑	↓	↑	↑	↑	↓	↓	↑	↓	↑	↓	↑	22.8
1964	↑	↑	↑	↑	↑	+88% 46 mo.		↓	↑	↑	↑	↑	16.5
1965	↑	↑	↓	↑	↓	↓	↑	↑	↑	↑	↓	↑	12.5
1966	↑	↓	↓	$186,000	<15%> 5 mo.				$158,900	↑	↑	→	-10.1
1967	↑	↑	↑	↑	↓	+47% 32 mo.		↓	↑	↓	↑	↑	24.0
1968	↓	↓	↑	↑	↑	↑	↑	↑	↑	↑	↑	↓	11.1
1969	↓	↓	↑	↑	$234,100	<27%> 13 mo.							-8.5
1970					$170,800	↑	↑	↑	↑	↑	↓	↑	4.0
1971	↑	↑	↑	↑	↓	↓	↑	↓	↓	↓	↑	↑	14.3
1972	↑	↑	↑	↑	+76% 30 mo.		↑	↑	↓	↑	↑	$300,000	19.0
1973	<43% 21 mo.												-14.7
1974									$172,100	↑	↓	↓	-26.5
1975	↑	↑	↑	↑	↑	↑	↓	↓	↓	↑	↑	↓	37.2
1976	↑	↓	↑	↓	↓	↑	↓	↑	↑	↓	↓	↑	23.8
1977	↓	↓	↓	↑	↓	+124% 65 mo.		↓	→	↑	↑	↑	-7.2
1978	↓	↓	↑	↑	↑	↓	↑	↑	↓	↑	↑	↑	6.6
1979	↑	↓	↑	↑	↓	↑	↑	↑	↑	↓	↑	↑	18.4
1980	↑	$398,800	<10%> 1 mo.	↑	↑	↑	+42% 8 mo.			↑	↑	$512,300	32.4
1981	<17% 20 mo.												-4.9
1982							$425,600	↑	↑	↑	↑	↑	21.4
1983	↑	↑	↑	↑	↓	↑	↓	↑	↓	↑	↑	↓	22.5
1984	↓	↓	↑	↑	↓	↑	↓	↑	↑	↑	↓	↑	6.3
1985	↑	↑	↑	↓	↑	↑	+282% 61 mo.		↓	↑	↑	↑	32.2
1986	↑	↑	↑	↓	↑	↑	↓	↑	↓	↑	↑	↓	18.5
1987	↑	↑	↑	↑	↑	↑	$1,623,700	<30%> 3 mo.		$1,144,200	↑		5.2
1988	↑	↑	↓	↑	↑	↑	↓	↓	↑	↑	↓	↑	16.8
1989	↑	↓	↑	↑	+71% 31 mo.		↑	↑	↓	↓	↑	↑	31.5
1990	↓	↑	↑	↓	$1,958,900	<15%> 5 mo.				$1,670,900	↑	↑	-3.2
1991	↑	↑	↑	↑	↑	↓	↑	↑	↓	↑	↓	↑	30.5
1992	↓	↑	↓	↑	↑	↓	↑	↓	↑	↑	↑	↑	7.7
1993	↑	↑	↑	↓	↑	+190% 74 mo.		↑	↓	↑	↓	↑	10.0
1994	↑	↓	↓	↑	↑	↓	↑	↑	↓	↑	↓	↑	1.3
1995	↑	↑	↑	↑	↑	↑	↑	↑	↑	↑	↓	↑	37.4
1996	↑	↑	↑	↑	↑	↑	↓	↑	↑	↑	↑	$4,840,300	23.1%

Total Return: Includes reinvested dividends and capital gains   **Standard Deviation: 15.4**

Source: © Computed using data from Stocks, Bonds, Bills & Inflation 1996 Yearbook™ with data updated January 1997, Ibbotson Associates, Chicago

↑ ↓ Up or Down Month   ⬛ Cyclical Declines   ▨ Recovery (to pre-decline level)   ⬭ Net New Advancement

REWARD*		RISK	
Total Return (1960-1996)	11.1%	Worst Decline	43 % / 21 mo.
Riskless Return (T-bills)	<6.1%>	Average Decline	19 % / 7 mo.
AVERAGE ANNUAL REWARD OF STANDARD & POOR'S 500	**5.0%**	Average Recovery	10 mo.
		COMPOSITE RISK	**100 points**

EFFICIENCY RATING = 50
(Reward ÷ Composite Risk x 1,000)

*Annualized

CHART 5-4

Rewards, Risks and Efficiency Ratings of Major Domestic Asset Classes

Historical Risk/Reward charts for the Total U.S. Stock Market, Large Cap Stocks, Mid/Small Cap Stocks, Micro Cap Stocks, U.S. Treasury Bonds (5-year) and Long-Term Corporate Bonds are presented in Charts A5-1 through A5-6 in the Appendix. A summary of the Rewards, Composite Risk Scores and Efficiency Ratings for these domestic asset classes, as well as the S&P 500, is presented in Chart 5-5.

Domestic Asset Classes in the Inflation Era

The rate of return from cash is the base from which the rates of return from all other asset classes are measured. Cash is truly the riskless, rewardless asset class. After inflation and taxes, money invested in cash is dead money—just treading water. Real wealth stands still in cash.

In the family of domestic, high-quality bond asset classes, there is but one long-term winner: 5-year U.S. Treasury bonds. In Chapter 3, long-term U.S. Government bonds were discarded as a potential asset class for the model portfolios to be developed in Section III. In more than 70 years, long-term U.S. Government bonds did not match the returns of the less volatile 5-year Treasuries. Now, long-term corporate bonds also can be safely eliminated from consideration for your Wealth and Retirement Portfolio. As shown in Chart 5-5, intermediate-term Treasury bonds outperformed their corporate counterparts in *every* measurement of risk and reward in the Inflation Era.

Domestic stocks do not offer such a lopsided comparison. True to the findings of the "size effect" discussed in Chapter 2, the large cap stocks' reward of 4.5% was outdone by the mid/small cap stocks' reward of 6.7%, which was topped by the outstanding reward of 8.4% from micro cap stocks. As each asset class's risk profile displays, however, the extra reward was earned with extra risk.

Domestic Asset Classes – Risks, Rewards & Efficiencies – 1960-1996

	Cash (30-Day T-Bills)	Bonds (5-Year Treasuries)	Bonds (Long-Term Corporate)
REWARD			
Return (Annualized)	6.1%	7.5%	7.4%
Riskless Return (T-bills)	-6.1%	-6.1%	-6.1%
REWARD	**0%**	**1.4%**	**1.3%**
RISK			
Worst Decline	0	9 %	22 %
	0	15 mo.	27 mo.
Average Decline	0	5 %	9 %
	0	6 mo.	8 mo.
Average Recovery	0	4 mo.	6 mo.
COMPOSITE RISK SCORE	**0**	**39 points**	**72 points**
EFFICIENCY RATING	**N/A**	**36**	**18**

	Total U.S. Stock Market	S&P 500 Stocks	Large Cap Stocks	Mid/Small Cap Stocks	Micro Cap Stocks
REWARD					
Return (Annualized)	11.0%	11.1%	10.6%	12.8%	14.5%
Riskless Return (T-bills)	-6.1%	-6.1%	-6.1%	-6.1%	-6.1%
REWARD	**4.9%**	**5.0%**	**4.5%**	**6.7%**	**8.4%**
RISK					
Worst Decline	45 %	43 %	44 %	50 %	58 %
	21 mo.	21 mo.	21 mo.	22 mo.	72 mo.
Average Decline	20 %	19 %	19 %	25 %	23 %
	9 mo.	7 mo.	8 mo.	7 mo.	8 mo.
Average Recovery	10 mo.	10 mo.	10 mo.	11 mo.	10 mo.
COMPOSITE RISK SCORE	**105 points**	**100 points**	**102 points**	**115 points**	**171 points**
EFFICIENCY RATING	**47**	**50**	**44**	**58**	**49**

Sources: © Computed using data from Stocks, Bonds, Bills & Inflation 1996 Yearbook™ with data updated January 1997, Ibbotson Associates, Chicago; Center for Research in Security Prices (CRSP) University of Chicago

CHART 5-5

Whereas owners of mid/small cap stocks endured a sizable increase in risks—higher Composite Risk (115 points) versus large cap stocks (102 points)—the risks in owning micro cap stocks jumped enormously (171 points). This is due to their worst-case decline of 58% over a stomach-churning 72 months in 1969-1974.

Note: Under the methodology for determining a Composite Risk score, a market decline cannot be considered over until there is a subsequent recovery to a market value higher than the highest month-end market value that was achieved before the decline began. Whereas all of the other domestic stock asset classes did recover to new highs after the 1969-1970 bear market, micro cap stocks never did. Therefore, the 1969-1970 and 1973-1974 bear markets became but one, long bear market for this asset class.

Even the extraordinary risk of owning micro caps was not enough to lower their Efficiency Rating (49) below that of large cap stocks (44) because of the huge differential in their rewards. **Nevertheless, mid/small caps are the true winner of the Inflation Era with their superior efficiency rating of 58 due to the best combination of risk and reward.**

It is interesting to compare the individual domestic stock asset classes with the total U.S. stock market. As would be expected, the risks, rewards and efficiency ratings of the entire market fall between those of the large cap stocks and mid/small cap stocks. Large cap stocks have the greatest influence because they represent such a large portion of the whole market on a market capitalization basis (72%). Now compare the S&P 500 with the Total U.S. Stock Market and with Large Cap Stocks. Whereas the Rewards and Composite Risks of all three are fairly close to one another, the S&P 500 is actually closer to the Total Stock Market than to Large Cap Stocks.

The S&P 500 is a "large company index," yet as these numbers demonstrate, the S&P 500 is an excellent gauge of the entire U.S. market. In fact, this is Standard and Poor's goal according to their own description of the index.[6] The S&P 500 has produced somewhat less risk than the Total U.S. Stock Market while delivering a slightly greater reward. No wonder the S&P 500 is so hard to beat when investing in large-cap-oriented mutual funds.

Historical Risk/Reward - A Powerful Predictor and Preparer

Long-term investors who have armed themselves with Historical Risk/Reward charts have a powerful advantage—they know what types of risks and rewards they are likely to incur in the years ahead. The choice as to which asset classes to own is intentional. They understand all of the major risks of ownership.

Know the risks and rewards of the asset classes in which you invest. What you see on any asset class's Historical Risk/Reward chart is a peek into its future. All of the declines shown on these charts will likely unfold again—only in some unforeseen and random sequence. The good news is that the reward, too, is likely to repeat over a long haul.

☞ The primary focus of studying asset classes should be their efficiency ratings. The most profitable and predictable portfolios will be assembled from the most efficient asset classes. Ultimately, all that matters is the balance of risk and reward within your entire Wealth and Retirement Portfolio, which will be discussed in detail in Section III. Our purpose will be to achieve the desired rate of return for your Wealth and Retirement Portfolio with the least amount of portfolio risk.

Conclusion

The Historical Risk Reward charts introduced in this chapter are designed to give you a thorough understanding of both the risks and rewards that each asset class has offered in the Inflation Era.

The clear winner in the bond family is 5-year U.S. Treasury bonds. Long-term quality corporate bonds were only half as efficient. On the other hand, domestic stocks provided no clear-cut winner among the three asset classes—large cap, mid/small cap and micro cap. However, the S&P 500 does appear to be a better choice than a pure large cap focus.

6

Misconceptions of International Investments

International stock and bond asset classes do not share the advantages cited for domestic securities in Chapter 2. International securities also lack meticulously recorded historical data such as that provided by CRSP and SBBI for U.S. securities back to 1926. In addition, to an American investor a foreign stock or bond reflects the gains and losses of the currency of its home country relative to the U.S. dollar. Currency fluctuation is a major ingredient in short- to intermediate-term performance. All of these factors add a degree of uncertainty in utilizing international asset classes.

Nevertheless, investing in foreign securities offers the advantage of diversification, so it is important to evaluate the potential of direct global investments versus only participating in foreign markets through major domestic companies that derive large portions of their revenue from sales and operations abroad.

"International investing involves a whole set of risks
that investors are not necessarily compensated for."
— John Bogle, Chairman, Vanguard Funds

Innocents Abroad

Long known for our parochial, stay-at-home investing habits, Americans in the 1990s burst onto the scene of international investing. One major catalyst was the crash of 1987. Many financial observers noticed that the major international stock indexes did not suffer nearly the decline of the major U.S. stock indexes during the crash. (As it turns out, most of this better performance was due to one country—Japan.)

A second factor was the tear down of the Berlin Wall and the crumbling of Communism. The world and all of its stock markets began to appear less menacing, less risky than before. A third impetus to diversifying into international stocks has been the wide circulation of an elliptical curve that showed how Americans could get higher returns with less risk by adding international stocks to their current portfolios (see chart 6-3 on page 82). As so often happens, the reality of international investing—particularly in the 1990s—has not lived up to the expectation. Direct international investing has both unique attributes and thorny problems which need to be understood and evaluated by the American investor.

International Stocks: Similar But Different

Virtually all of the discussion of domestic stock markets in the first part of Chapter 2 is applicable to international stock markets in that they share these characteristics:

- Long-term rationality, short-term irrationality

- Long-term rewards far in excess of their domestic cash and bond markets and

- Size effect: smaller companies have produced superior long-term returns relative to their home-based large companies.

In addition, rough data available on two international markets (England and Germany) back to 1926 (the modern period for security analysis) indicates similar—if somewhat lower—performance for international stocks.[7]

All of this would imply that there is a universality to stock performance that cuts across country borders, that business is business in whatever language it is conducted and that the owners of common shares are treated equally in every culture.

There are two reasons why this conclusion cannot be reached. The first is the limitation of available data and the second is the effect of currencies.

The Lack of Data

CRSP has provided meticulously compiled information on every publicly traded security of operating companies in America back to 1926. (Some of this information is accessed through reference guides like Ibbotson's SBBI.) This allows for in-depth research of every aspect of the risk and rewards of stock ownership in America.

Unfortunately, no such detailed long-term database is available for other countries. Therefore, conclusions built on the evaluation of international stocks are less reliable than with domestic stocks.

Detailed analysis of international stocks begins with 1970, which means that virtually all of the study of international stocks as an asset class for American investors is conducted in the historically "new era" of *floating* currencies discussed next.

The Importance of Currencies

International trade and commerce has been conducted for as long as history itself has been recorded. Businessmen want to trade, and no country can produce all the raw materials and finished goods it needs and wants within its own borders. One impediment to international trade has always been the establishment of a common unit of value that both sides could rely upon. For most of history, gold has served the purpose of a common commodity of equal acceptance in all countries. Any country could participate in world trade if it would declare at what rate its currency was fully convertible to one ounce of pure gold. A gold standard was more or less in effect from the beginning of the modern period of security analysis 1926 through 1971 when President Nixon closed the "gold window" by declaring the U.S. dollar no longer convertible to gold. From that year forward, the currencies of the world have *floated* against one another with no common anchor for business to rely upon. A change in a foreign currency's value will have the same impact on an American's investment abroad as it does on his/her travel abroad — a direct and immediate impact on cost and value.

The Currency Effect

A U.S. investor considering direct investment in international mutual funds will have two elements to her returns and two elements to her risks. She will have all the risks and rewards of underlying international stocks and additionally have the risks and rewards brought about by the changes in currency values as the foreign market's currencies are converted back into U.S. dollars.

The primary index of international stocks for U.S. investors is Morgan Stanley's EAFE Index (Europe, Australia and Far East). Chart 6-1 illustrates the performance of both the EAFE Index — *converted into U.S. dollars* — and the S&P 500 Index from the beginning of 1970 through the end of 1996.

For the entire period, the S&P 500 index delivered a 2,175% (12.3% annualized) total return, while the EAFE index outperformed the U.S. index with a total return of 2,541% (12.9% annualized) for the American investor.

Chart 6-2 also compares the EAFE Index to the S&P 500, but this chart compares *only* the returns from the stocks themselves; the EAFE Index is shown in local currencies — *not* converted into U.S. dollars.

As Chart 6-2 illustrates, the portfolio of international stocks (in local currencies) substantially underperformed the S&P 500 stock index producing a return of just 1,404% (10.6% annualized) for the period.

Source: Morgan Stanley Capital International; Standard & Poor's

CHART 6-1

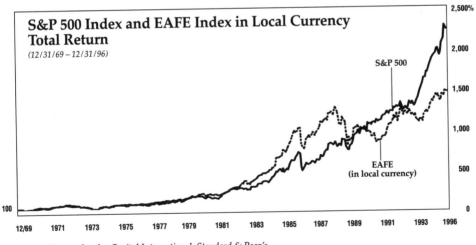

Source: Morgan Stanley Capital International; Standard & Poor's

CHART 6-2

International stocks substantially underperformed U.S. stocks, but international currencies substantially outperformed the U.S. dollar. You lost ground on your *investment* in international stocks—but if your portfolio did not hedge your currency risk—you made money on your *currency speculation*!

This result shows up in the performance of international mutual funds. For example, George Murnaghan, a vice president at T. Rowe Price International Fund, reported that this fund had an annualized gain of 14.7% on average for the 15½ years ending in December 1996. Currency gains contributed about 1.3% per year and the underlying securities 13.4%. (The Wall Street Journal, February 11, 1997)

☞ With perfect hindsight, the big winner of this period maintained a 100% U.S. stock portfolio (to achieve the better stock returns) and purchased futures contracts on the international currencies, which outperformed the U.S. dollar during the post-gold-standard period.

Brief History of U.S. Dollar (Post World War II)

Before going further, a brief look at why the gold standard fell apart will be helpful in understanding the miserable performance of the U.S. dollar since 1971. The post-World War II gold standard was arrived at by establishing the price of gold to $35 per ounce in U.S. dollars and then pegging other countries' currencies to the U.S. dollar. The U.S. dollar would become the reserve currency of the world, de facto gold.

This was the Bretton Woods Agreement that provided the post-WW II world with a stable means of exchange to allow for the massive reconstruction that was desperately needed. Unfortunately, the inflation pressures that would normally be reflected in the price of gold were shifted to the U.S. dollar—because of gold's fixed price (by government decree).

For its part, the U.S. exacerbated the problem in the 1960s by financing both the Vietnam War and the Great Society social programs with printing press dollars, not taxes. Other countries recognized that U.S. gold reserves were increasingly inadequate to maintain convertibility to gold at $35 per ounce because of the expanding supply of U.S. dollars. These countries began shipping inflated U.S. dollars back to the U.S. to redeem them in gold. It was the dramatic call on its gold supply and the inability to maintain the conversion that finally forced the closing of the gold window by President Nixon.

In other words, by 1971, the U.S. dollar was vastly overvalued at $35 per ounce of gold. If the member nations to the Bretton Woods could have agreed upon a devaluation of the U.S. dollar, allowing for the convertibility at some higher number like $70 per ounce or more, then perhaps the fixed system of exchange could have survived. (Of course, a method of controlling the U.S. printing press would also have been needed, but this means giving up complete sovereignty with regard to internal monetary policy.)

This is an oversimplified view of the maze of post-World War II events, policies and actions that influenced world currencies. What this history provides is a context for understanding the long devaluation of the U.S. dollar that occurred after 1971 relative to the currencies of our main trading partners. From 1971 through 1996, the U.S. dollar lost approximately 60% to 70% of its value versus the Japanese yen, Swiss franc and German mark. (At its low point in April 1995, the U.S. dollar had lost a full 75% of its value versus these currencies.)

No Free Lunch

Many proponents of international investing ignore or downplay the role of currencies. As mentioned at the beginning of this chapter, they package international stocks as a *free lunch* for Americans — higher returns with lower risks. Chart 6-3 is a common illustration they use to support their argument.

☞ This chart shows that adding international stocks to a U.S. stock portfolio both lowered volatility and increased returns.

When projecting the *future* risks and rewards of international stocks, this chart sends the wrong message. This chart is based on a unique period of world history in which currencies were removed from the gold standard and the U.S. dollar undertook a long unwinding of excessive valuation. The so-called free lunch was from the weakening U.S. dollar (or strengthening foreign currencies), *not* from international stocks.

Hypothetical U.S./International Equity Diversification Chart

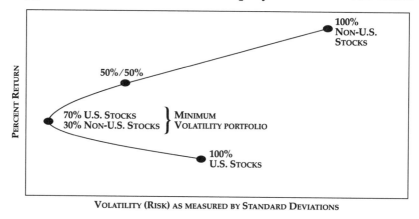

CHART 6-3

Hedging Currency Risk

Currency risks (and rewards) can be neutralized today in the futures markets. Many mutual fund managers, such as Michael Price of Mutual Series Funds and Chris Browne of Tweedy Browne Funds, hedge all of their currency exposure. This eliminates currency as a part of the investing equation and places the entire focus of the equity manager on picking stocks.

Is hedging the answer? Perhaps not. Hedging currency exposure is not free. The out-of-pocket costs are a direct reduction to the return from the underlying portfolio of securities. In addition, hedging may often be counterproductive based on the relationship of stock performance and currencies. Many economists believe that a devaluation of a country's currency will often make the businesses within that country more competitive internationally and thus benefit local share prices. **This means that you cannot simply strip away the currency effect to get at the real performance of the underlying stocks—one directly impacts the other!**

The Advantage of International Stocks

There is one very powerful advantage to investing in foreign equities: diversification. According to Jeremy Siegel's Stocks for the Long Run (1994), "Diversification will increase investor's expected compound returns while reducing risk even if expected returns on foreign equities do not exceed those of U.S. stocks." Siegel elaborated on the diversifying impact of foreign stocks in a conversation I had with him. He concluded that the long-term expected returns from unhedged foreign equities are about the same or slightly lower than from U.S. stocks. As he expects the returns from foreign equities to remain uncorrelated with U.S. equities, combining U.S. and international stocks will be particularly worthwhile in reducing the volatility of a U.S.-only stock portfolio. In his view, "global investment is best viewed as an extension of domestic diversification." (The impact of foreign stocks within a portfolio will be demonstrated in Chapter 10.)

Emerging Markets

Emerging markets are a new and credible asset class of international investing. Emerging markets are those countries with stock markets that are not considered mature or developed. They may be roughly grouped into four geographic areas: Far East, Latin America, Central Europe/Russia, and Africa.

Can a fundamental case be made for dedicating a portion of a U.S. investor's stock portfolio to these stocks? The basic draw of investing in emerging markets boils down to this, *that's where the growth is!* Fueled by cheap labor and varying country or regional-specific advantages, the economies of many emerging countries are growing much faster than the 2–3% growth pace of developed economies like the U.S. With such high growth in these economies, their companies and stock markets must outperform those of the more sluggishly growing developed countries, right?

Wrong! According to Morgan Stanley, returns from emerging markets have lagged those of both the U.S. and non-U.S. developed equity markets by an average of approximately 5% per year in the

21 years ending 1996. This is definitely not what most investors perceive to be the case.

Stock returns do not necessarily follow economic growth in developed countries either. In roughly the same 21-year period cited above, the British stock market greatly outperformed that of Japan, yet the English economy grew at barely half the rate of Japan.[8]

The lure of emerging markets appears to be not only the "growth story" but also the nature of their boom and bust cycles. When emerging markets boom, they explode to the upside. The dizzyingly high returns so easy to achieve during these periods are hard to ignore. From mid-1992 through the end of 1993 was such a period. **However, in this case, as with most such experiences, after the boom comes the bust. The bottom line is that this asset class has proved both unrewarding and highly volatile to long-term investors.**

Global Investing from the Safety of Home

 Investing internationally has become synonymous with investing in foreign-based corporations. It is not the only way to invest overseas, and may not be the best way.

When renowned investor Warren Buffett made his one and only decision to invest in an offshore company (Guiness, English beverage company), *he* made the decision to invest internationally. On the other hand, when he made the most significant investment decision of his career (Coca Cola, U.S. beverage company), Buffett in effect yielded to Coke's management the decision to invest internationally.

Actually, both Coca Cola and Guiness are *global companies*. Guiness transacts a significant share of its business in America. And Coca Cola may call America home, yet consider these calendar year 1995 statistics on Coke:

- 71% of revenues were from outside the U.S.

- 80% of profits were from outside the U.S.

- 67% of new capital investment was outside the U.S.

Coca Cola is a premier global growth company that would have peaked out long ago if it was only a premier American growth company.

American multinational companies, like Coca Cola and hundreds of others, are the most thoroughly globalized companies in the world. They produce about twice as much outside their borders as European and Japanese multinationals.[9]

Such geographic diversification helps U.S. companies smooth out the ups and downs internally. This is particularly true of investing in emerging markets. U.S.-based global companies are well positioned to invest in these countries and take advantage of their strategic production advantages and their rising consumer spending. U.S. companies' investment abroad is having a significant impact on their bottom lines and consequently their stock prices.

The U.S. led the world in competitiveness for the third year in a row in 1995 according to the World Competitiveness Yearbook, and 1996 promises to be more of the same. Published annually by the Lausanne, Switzerland-based Institute for Management Development, the study measures and compares the competitiveness of 46 countries. It defines competitiveness in terms of the mechanisms that help create wealth within a nation. In 1995, the United States strengthened its lead in the world, coming out on top in the areas of economic strength, new technology and financial services, and placing second in international trade.[10]

Investing in the U.S. large company asset class _is_ investing internationally with all of the major advantages of domestic investing intact.

Conclusion: Investing in International Stocks is Not Necessary for Top Notch Returns

For Americans, the transition from investing mainly at home to becoming full participants in the international markets has been relatively short and bittersweet.

The conventional wisdom of the 1990s is that a dedicated portion of almost every American's portfolio should be invested abroad. Two of America's most respected investors do not agree.

Both Warren Buffett, America's most successful investor, and Peter Lynch, the highly regarded mutual fund manager, are on record against such a dedicated allocation to overseas investments. In 1993, Lynch wrote, "Let me put my two cents in about foreign investing....From all my trips abroad, I've concluded that the U.S. still has the best companies and the best system for investing in them."[11] And Buffett admitted he would have no interest in purchasing a foreign company, primarily because communication between companies and their foreign shareholders tends to be much weaker than that between companies domiciled in the same country as their owners.[12]

Both of these great investment managers made exceptions. Lynch occasionally invested Fidelity Magellan's assets abroad when he perceived significant and incomparable investment opportunities there. Buffett made but one foreign investment in his entire 40-year career, Guiness, as previously cited.

Buffett and Lynch are not alone. Many of today's cream-of-the-crop investment professionals have never left or seldom left our shores in search of better opportunities. These include Foster Friess (Brandywine Fund), Gary Pilgrim (PBHG Growth Fund), Shelby Davis (New York Venture Fund), Bill Ruane (Sequoia Fund), Bill Nasgovitz (Heartland Value Fund), Bob Rodriguez (FPA Capital Fund) and many, many others.

Of course, many successful investment professionals, from Sir John Templeton (Templeton Funds) to Michael Price (Mutual Series Funds), have been very successful blending U.S. and international stock investments.

The bottom line is that it has not been *necessary* to invest in foreign equities in order to achieve outstanding performance, and it is likely that it will not become necessary any time soon for long-term investors. Nevertheless, introducing international stock mutual funds into a U.S. portfolio may lower volatility and produce somewhat higher risk-adjusted rewards. This will be further evaluated in Chapter 8 and in Section III.

International Cash and Bonds

The role of currencies is much more direct and immediate for the foreign holders of a country's money market or bond investments. Any depreciation of a country's currency will directly reduce the value of its bonds or cash equivalents in the hands of a foreign national without the potential for an offsetting benefit as illustrated in the discussion of foreign stocks. The reverse is also true. The appreciation of a country's currency is a direct benefit to the foreign holders of that country's bonds and cash.

Therefore, the long unwinding of the value of the U.S. dollar was a huge and direct—if irregular—benefit to American holders of international cash and bonds between 1971 and 1995. Will this continue? It seems unlikely. Perhaps the U.S. dollar's strength since April of 1995 signals a change of fortune going forward.

In the mid-1990s, the economic conditions and relative competitive positions between the U.S. and Japan, Germany, France and Switzerland have changed considerably from 1971. It is Europe and Japan that now have relatively overvalued currencies (on a purchasing power parity basis), higher government debt and deficits as a percentage of their GNP (domestic economies), more intrusive governments, larger welfare and unfunded social security commitments, easier monetary policy and higher unit labor costs.

In addition, Lowell Bryan and Diana Farrell in Market Unbound: Unleashing Global Capitalism (1996) argue that global integration of bond markets is substantially completed. In other words, the bond yield in every country is approximately equal when adjusted for their individual inflation rates and country-specific risks.

This is evident from how closely world bond yields now tend to track U.S. bond interest rates. After 25 years of slightly negative correlation, U.S. and global interest rates have been 79% correlated since 1993.[13]

More importantly, all of the major trends in international markets such as...

- more currencies directly or indirectly tied to the U.S. dollar,

- integration of monetary policies by developed nations,

- global village of multi-national companies and

- exceptional cross-border trading and currency flows

...suggest that the high correlation in world bond returns will persist for some time. Given this leveling of relative yields worldwide, and considering currency risks associated with international investing, international bonds are not well positioned to enhance a portfolio's long-term returns. As Bryan and Farrell suggest, a dollar-based investor who is investing in bonds to reduce overall risks should stick to U.S. Treasury bonds.

7

Tangible Investments: Metals and REITs

The performance of precious metals tends to be extremely volatile while providing returns that typically just match inflation over the long-run. The other tangible investment considered in this chapter, real estate investment trusts (REITs), offers a combination of risk and reward that can be a valuable addition to your Wealth and Retirement Portfolio. REITs, however, come with a caveat with regard to their documented history, and different REIT indexes are miles apart.

"All that glisters is not gold."
— William Shakespeare, <u>The Merchant of Venice</u>

Common stocks, bonds and cash equivalents are by far the most widely held financial investments by Americans, either directly or through mutual funds.

There is, however, one other group of asset classes that are often included in portfolios recommended by financial advisors and the media. These are the tangible asset classes. The two most widely available for Wealth and Retirement Portfolios that are easily bought and sold are:

- Precious metals and
- REITs

Precious Metals

Gold and silver are speculations, not investments. Investments are made in income-producing assets. Speculations produce no income and therefore must rely on changes in either supply and demand or public perception to effect a change in price.

Speculative commodities tend to make sharp moves up and down in the short run, yet often just match prevailing inflation over long periods of time. Gold is no exception.

In our period of study, 1960-1996, gold produced an average annualized return of approximately 6.5%. This result appears to compare favorably with the 6.1% average return on cash equivalents for this period, but is well below the returns of bonds and stocks.

The reality is that even this return for gold was artificially produced. By U.S. government decree, gold's price was held constant at $35 an ounce from 1935 to 1971. From the end of 1935 to the beginning of 1960, the inflation rate averaged 3.2% per year. Had gold's price been allowed free-market pricing, instead of being held down by government decree, it is likely that its price would have been closer to $77 per ounce at the beginning of 1960. From that price to the $366 per ounce gold was priced at the end of 1996, the average annual appreciation rate for gold would be 4.3% — very close to the 4.7% inflation rate for the same period. This is entirely consistent with gold's long history as an inflation hedge—or store of stable value.

> "Consider three ounces of silver: The first is a four-drachma piece from Greece, from about 425 BC. The second, a U.S. silver dollar, dated 1898. The third, a U.S. Eagle silver coin, dated 1989.

> "Each of these contains about one ounce of silver. Historians tell us that the one ounce of silver in 400 BC was about a week's wage for a skilled worker. About 100 years ago, a dollar, or its equivalent ounce of silver, was a day's wage. ('Another day, another dollar' is a slogan that survives from that era.) Today, a teenager working at a fast-food outlet can earn enough to buy an ounce of silver in an hour or two.

> "So, in terms of the value of labor, an ounce of silver has lost about 95% of its value over the past 2,400 years. Had our Greek worker hoarded his week's pay in silver and hidden it, he'd be very disappointed if he were reincarnated and dug it up today!

> "But suppose he had invested his week's pay in financial assets and earned a 3% annual return. Suppose that a week's pay in today's dollars is worth about $400. Since money doubles every 24 years at 3%, and since there have been one hundred 24-year periods since 400 BC, our worker (assuming he could avoid inheritance taxes and other forms of government confiscation) would have an account worth $400 times two to the 100th power. That's an 8 with 103 zeros after it."[14]

> *—Charles Carignan in* Barron's

Precious metals are a poor asset class choice for your Wealth and Retirement Portfolio. Their long-term returns are only expected to match inflation, at best, yet their volatility is very high. According to studies by the Wall Street firm of Morgan Stanley, since 1971 gold has generated less than a third of the returns small company stocks have, while experiencing as much or more fluctuation in market value.

REITs

Real estate investment trusts (REITs, pronounced "reets") are securitized real estate—listed securities that pool investors' money in all forms of real estate development, operations and lending. Typically the properties held by REITs are commercial real estate such as shopping centers and office buildings.

A REIT is like a mutual fund of real estate properties, typically offering investors a diversified portfolio with professional management. They are traded on stock exchanges and thereby offer "liquidity" to an otherwise illiquid market.

Created by legislation passed in 1960, a REIT is essentially a corporation with special tax treatment. As investment companies, they can avoid income tax by distributing out 95% of their taxable income to their shareholders as do mutual funds. Most REITs generate substantial depreciation, so their cash flow is much higher than the taxable income they distribute. This allows many REITs to grow their asset base via new construction or new purchases over time. Still, it is the high yields from the distribution of their taxable income that characterizes investment in this asset class.

REITs have produced a checkered history of overall returns in somewhat the same fashion as high-yield bonds. In their early years, REITs became a desirable source of capital for new realty development. A burst of enthusiasm in the late 1960s and early 1970s sent the microscopic base of REIT stocks soaring. In the early 1970s, the real estate market went through a devastating crash that went from one geographical area to another and one property type to the next. As real estate is typically highly leveraged—and REIT developments in the 1970s were no exception—the entire REIT industry was hit hard. Those most significantly impacted were those REITs referred to as mortgage REITs, which primarily lend money for commercial real estate development.

Chastened by this experience, most investors have focused on equity REITs which own the properties in the portfolio, although mortgage REITs and other specialized varieties continue to operate.

The National Association of Real Estate Investment Trusts (NAREIT) publishes several REIT indexes. From 1972 through 1996, the NAREIT equity index has outperformed the S&P 500 index. Incredibly, this performance was also delivered with less volatility than that of the stock market. However, the NAREIT index for all REITs (including mortgage and specialized REITs) has delivered substantially poorer performance. Therefore, only equity REITs will be evaluated for possible inclusion in the predictable portfolios assembled in Section III.

Note: The equity REIT performance is subject to qualification. In the REIT indexes published by NAREIT, "Only those REITs listed for the entire period are used in the Total Return calculation." In other words, delisted, bankrupt or merged REITs disappear from the index *without* accounting for their performance in the last month of their existence. How much impact this has had on performance is impossible to calculate.

The Rapid Growth of Equity REITs

The amount of publicly traded real estate is growing rapidly. The REIT asset class is quite small, totaling only about $75 billion at the end of 1996, yet it has grown substantially from a mere $9 billion base at the end of 1991. As the market has grown, so has the liquidity. About $200 million in REITs trade each day, almost 10 times as much as in 1992.

For years, large pension plans have allocated a portion of their investment portfolios to real estate. Increasingly, these pension plans are turning to REITs to fill out this allocation. This not only fuels demand for REITs but also helps stabilize the market as large pension plans tend to be patient, long-term holders of their investment assets.

The Maturing Public Real Estate Industry

From inception until the early 1990s, most equity REITs were little more than securitized ownership of specific properties. After a severe downturn in 1989 and 1990, the REIT has reinvented itself.

Today, most are bigger, stronger and deeper than earlier models. The new model is that of a fully integrated real estate company. These companies have developed talented organizations that can acquire, manage, lease and develop commercial real estate. The new model has opportunities to add value and increase cash flow from each activity within the organization. As the industry grows, it is also consolidating around ever bigger entities. (In late 1996, 10 REITs exceed $1 billion in capitalization.) Larger REITs are taking advantage of economies of scale and lower cost of capital.

The future of REITs looks quite promising. The real estate market in America alone is huge, roughly equivalent in size to the stock market. Yet it is still largely in private hands. Over time, a large portion of commercial real estate may find its way into public REITs. This is good for investors, too. Publicly traded real estate securities offer ordinary investors access to real estate investment on terms that are typically more economical and favorable than direct property investment partnerships. When evaluating publicly traded real estate securities for inclusion in portfolios with the most predictable characteristics, however, the checkered history of REITs and their relatively new operating model needs to be taken into consideration. Model portfolios in Section III will be developed both with and without representation of equity REITs.

8

Comparing Risks and Rewards of All Asset Classes

The risks, rewards and efficiency ratings of major *domestic* asset classes for the period 1960-1996 were presented in Chapter 5. These domestic asset classes enjoy a meticulously maintained monthly database that goes back to 1926, which validates the reliability of their long-term performance. International stocks and bonds, equity REITs and U.S. high-yield bonds do not enjoy such a long historical database. Most databases on these asset classes begin after 1970.

In this chapter, we compare the risks, rewards and efficiencies of *all* asset classes (except high-yield and international bonds) for the past quarter century (1972-1996). This comparison demonstrates clearly that some asset classes have been more efficient than others. More importantly, the stability of efficiency ratings over different time periods and over varied market conditions leads to the conclusion that these efficiency characteristics can be relied upon to position asset classes within portfolios that maximize returns and reduce risk.

> *"At heart, America is a nation of careful gamblers. The contradictions in that description are rooted in our national character as a people who know instinctively that no gain is achieved without both risks and costs....The secret of our success, indeed the key to democracy itself, is in striking the balance between risk and rewards...."*
> — Senator Nancy Kassebaum (retired),
> The Wall Street Journal, December 26, 1996

In selecting the most efficient asset classes to include in your Wealth and Retirement Portfolio, the various asset classes must be compared on an apples-to-apples basis.

All of the asset classes to be evaluated (except U.S. high-yield bonds and international bonds) have index-quality data back to January 1, 1972, or earlier (Chart 8-1). Therefore, January 1, 1972, through December 31, 1996, is the longest period for which all of these asset classes can be compared on an apples-to-apples basis—comparing their risks and rewards during the same market conditions. This 25-year period of market history was rich in variation—major bull and bear markets, rising and falling inflation, high and low interest rates and stagnant and growing periods for the world economy. This is, therefore, an excellent quarter century to use as the basis of comparison.

Asset Class	Index Source	Beginning Date
Large Cap Stocks	CRSP	1/1/26
Mid/Small Cap Stocks	CRSP	1/1/26
Micro Cap Stocks	CRSP/DFA	1/1/26
Intermediate Bonds (5-year U.S. Treasuries)	Ibbotson	1/1/26
Long-Term Bonds (Long-Term Investment Grade Corporate)	Ibbotson	1/1/26
Cash (30-day U.S. T-bills)	Ibbotson	1/1/26
International Stocks (EAFE)	Morgan Stanley	1/1/70
International Bonds	Salomon Brothers	1/1/86
Equity REITs	NAREIT	1/1/72
Gold	Federal Register	1/1/72
U.S. High-Yield Bonds	Merrill Lynch	1/1/85

CHART 8-1

Index-quality data has been produced for international bonds and high-yield bonds for a relatively short period of time. Periods of less than 20 years are not thought to be statistically relevant for predictable planning purposes, and periods under 15 years are not even considered long-term for evaluation of asset classes. So, these asset classes would not be appropriate for the portfolios to be developed in Section III. Moreover, they would fail to make the cut for more fundamental reasons discussed previously, such as the currency effect on international bonds and the checkered history of high-yield bonds.

Historical Risk/Rewards

A Historical Risk/Reward chart covering the period 1972-1996 is presented for each of the following asset classes in the special burgundy supplement at the end of this chapter (Charts S-1 through S-8).

- Total U.S. Stock Market
- S&P 500 Index (Domestic Large Cap equivalent)
- Domestic Mid/Small Cap Stocks
- Domestic Micro Cap Stocks
- 5-Year U.S. Treasury Bonds
- International Stocks (in U.S. Dollars)
- Equity REITs
- Gold

The risks, rewards and efficiencies of these asset classes and others are summarized in Chart 8-2 and Chart 8-3.

Evaluating the Asset Classes

A primary goal of this book is to develop the best portfolios composed of the most reliable and efficient asset classes. Charts 8-2 and 8-3 distill 25 years of head-to-head competition among these candidates for your Wealth and Retirement Portfolio. It shows the reward each provided and the risk endured to achieve that reward. The results are quite revealing.

Financial Asset Classes – Risks, Rewards & Efficiencies – 1972-1996

	Cash (30-Day T-Bills)	Bonds (5-Year Treasuries)	Bonds (Long-Term Corporate)
REWARD			
Return (Annualized)	7.0%	8.7%	9.5%
Riskless Return (T-bills)	-7.0%	-7.0%	-7.0%
REWARD	**0%**	**1.7%**	**2.5%**
RISK			
Worst Decline	0	9 %	22 %
	0	15 mo.	27 mo.
Average Decline	0	6 %	11 %
	0	6 mo.	9 mo.
Average Recovery	0	4 mo.	6 mo.
COMPOSITE RISK SCORE	**0**	**40 points**	**75 points**
EFFICIENCY RATING	**N/A**	**43**	**33**

	Large Cap Stocks	Mid/Small Cap Stocks	Micro Cap Stocks	Total U.S. Stock Market	S&P 500 Stocks
REWARD					
Return (Annualized)	12.1%	14.1%	15.5%	12.4%	12.5%
Riskless Return (T-bills)	-7.0%	-7.0%	-7.0%	-7.0%	-7.0%
REWARD	**5.1%**	**7.1%**	**8.5%**	**5.4%**	**5.5%**
RISK					
Worst Decline	44 %	50 %	50 %	45 %	43 %
	21 mo.	22 mo.	34 mo.	21 mo.	21 mo.
Average Decline	17 %	23 %	28 %	18 %	18 %
	7 mo.	6 mo.	5 mo.	9 mo.	8 mo.
Average Recovery	11 mo.	9 mo.	11 mo.	11 mo.	11 mo.
COMPOSITE RISK SCORE	**100 points**	**110 points**	**128 points**	**102 points**	**101 points**
EFFICIENCY RATING	**51**	**65**	**66**	**53**	**54**

CHART 8-2

The relationship between long-term risk and long-term rewards is a loose one — some asset classes clearly deliver more reward for the risks taken.

	International Stocks (Local Currencies)	International Stocks (U.S. $)	Equity REITs	Gold
REWARD				
Return (Annualized)	11.0%	13.2%	12.8%	9.1%
Riskless Return (T-bills)	-7.0%	-7.0%	-7.0%	-7.0%
REWARD	4.0%	6.2%	5.8%	2.1%
RISK				
Worst Decline	40 %	42 %	37 %	56 %
	31 mo.	18 mo.	27 mo.	62 mo.
Average Decline	20 %	20 %	17 %	33 %
	13 mo.	8 mo.	6 mo.	21 mo.
Average Recovery	15 mo.	19 mo.	11 mo.	62 mo.
COMPOSITE RISK SCORE	119 points	107 points	98 points	234 points
EFFICIENCY RATING	34	58	59	9

CHART 8-3

Asset Class "Awards" for the Quarter Century Ending December 1996

Best-in-Class:	Mid/Small Caps due to their superior efficiency rating in both periods of study (this one and full Inflation Era)
Highest Reward:	Micro Caps blew away the competition
Least Risky:	5-Year Treasury Bonds, winning four out of five risk measurements
Most Efficient:	Micro Caps offered big risks but an even bigger reward
Most Pitiful:	Gold served up stratospheric risks with a puny reward
Best Up and Comer:	Equity REITs for posting both the lowest worst-case decline and lowest Composite Risk score outside of bonds
Most Confusing:	S&P 500 for mimicking the risks and rewards of the Total Stock Market more closely than Large Cap Stocks (this index's presumed target asset class)
Biggest Surprise:	Micro Caps had the shortest period of average market decline (5 months)

CHART 8-4

Bonds

The *relative* efficiency of long-term corporate bonds (33 Efficiency Rating) did not improve from their poor showing in the full Inflation Era. This is additional verification that long-term corporate bonds are undesirable for inclusion in the best and most efficient portfolios.

Five-year U.S. Treasury bonds are the outstanding bond asset class (43 Efficiency Rating). Yet even these bonds were still *less* efficient than any domestic stock asset class.

Domestic Stocks

The domestic stock asset classes demonstrate the same relative risk and reward characteristics in the period since 1972 as they had in the analysis of the full Inflation Era in Chapter 5. This provides some confidence that *relative* efficiency ratings between asset classes are fairly constant over varying long-term periods.

For comparison purposes, the risk, reward and efficiency ratings of the domestic stock asset classes for both periods of study are summarized in Chart 8-5.

The Composite Risk scores were also quite similar for the two periods—except for micro cap stocks. This asset class enjoyed a material improvement in its risk profile when the 1960-1971 period is removed from the full Inflation Era. If you will recall from Chapter 5, the outsized risk of this asset class was primarily due to its worst case market decline covering the 72-month period from 1969 through 1974. The 1972-1996 period cuts off half of this mega decline and consequently improves its risk score.

The relationship of efficiency ratings among the domestic stock asset classes does not change in comparing the two periods, except again for the improved efficiency of micro cap stocks.

Domestic Stock Asset Classes
Comparison of 1972-1996 Period with 1960-1996 Period

	Large Cap Stocks	Mid/ Small Cap Stocks	Micro Cap Stocks	Total U.S. Stock Market	S&P 500
Reward ('72-'96)	5.1%	7.1%	8.5%	5.4%	5.5%
Reward ('60-'96)	4.5%	6.7%	8.4%	4.9%	5.0%
Composite Risk ('72-'96)	100	110	128	102	101
Composite Risk ('60-'96)	102	115	171	105	100
Efficiency Rating ('72-'96)	51	65	66	53	54
Efficiency Rating ('60-'96)	44	58	49	47	50

CHART 8-5

☞ As Chart 8-5 shows, domestic stocks have been highly consistent performers. Comparing the full 1960-1996 period with the one-third shorter 1972-1996 period shows very little change in the risks, rewards and efficiencies of these asset classes on either a nominal basis or on a relative basis (the differences separating these asset classes). This chart also verifies the added risks and rewards of investing in progressively smaller domestic stocks.

International Stocks

Chapter 6 provided a detailed presentation of the problems in evaluating international stocks based on the 1970-1996 period even though this is the longest period of index-quality data. As you will recall, this period matches the "new era" of floating currencies fairly closely, and a prime characteristic of this period has been the unwinding of an overvalued U.S. dollar. This raises questions that are not possible to answer. For example, how would a long-term period of U.S. dollar stability—or strength—change the risks and rewards of international stock investing?

The longest period of index-quality data (1970-1996) indicates that international stocks in their own currencies have underperformed U.S. stocks. The reward they offered was a little less than that of large cap U.S. stocks, but their risks (particularly in terms of the duration of declines and recoveries) were far greater. Therefore, international stocks in their own currencies have not yet proved themselves as a valuable addition to long-term portfolios.

On the other hand, international stocks in U.S. dollars (unhedged) have been desirable for this period of analysis. They offered both rewards and risks that fell between domestic large cap stocks and domestic mid/small cap stocks. Therefore, international stocks in U.S. dollars will be considered acceptable for inclusion in model portfolios. (As our enthusiasm is tempered by the uncertainties cited, our model portfolios will be built both with and without international stocks in Section III.)

Referring back to the conclusions reached in Chapter 6, international stocks are not a necessary ingredient for profitable long-term portfolios, yet their less-than-perfect correlation with domestic stock markets should, in fact, reduce the overall risk within a portfolio. Both of these conclusions—and the concept of correlation—will be explored in more detail in Section III.

REITs

Equity REITs offer a scenario very similar to that of international stocks. The reward of equity REITs also fits just between domestic large cap stocks and mid/small cap stocks while the risk of equity REITs was less than either. The efficiency ratings of REITs and international stocks (in U.S. $) were close to identical. Because equity REITs offer similar efficiency to domestic stocks, but with less than perfect correlation of returns, adding equity REITs to a portfolio should lower the Composite Risk of a long-term portfolio without reducing the expected long-term reward.

As with international stocks, there is a significant caveat to this conclusion. In the discussion of REITs in Chapter 7, it was pointed out that the equity REIT of today is far different than its 1970s and 1980s counterparts. This is an asset class of rising importance and integrity, yet still somewhat in its infancy. Therefore, the model portfolios in Section III will be assembled both with and without this asset class.

Gold

In Chapter 6, it was stated that gold is not an investment, it is a speculation. Its Historical Risk/Reward Chart S-8 vividly demonstrates that gold is indeed in a class by itself. This precious metal generated fantastic risks, yet only produced a small reward. This asset class will obviously *not* be included among the asset classes used to develop the best model portfolios in Section III.

Note: Stocks of gold mining companies have far different characteristics than the metal. These stocks, like all operating companies, are included within the domestic asset classes.

Each Asset Class is Its Own "Market"

As you look through the Historical Risk/Reward charts for each asset class in the special burgundy supplement at the end of this chapter, take special notice of when major cyclical declines occurred. You will quickly notice that *there is no general market cycle*. Each asset class marches to its own drummer, each asset class is in effect a market unto itself.

Certainly periods like 1973-'74 and 1987 caught all of the common stock asset classes in their down draft, but not bonds or gold. And over the balance of the past quarter decade, each asset class—even each equity asset class—advanced and declined in its own unique rhythm.

And yet, most market commentators try to force round pegs into square holes by assuming there is but one market and but one market cycle. It ain't so...

Conclusions

Section II began with the proposition that all of the major asset classes would be reviewed and analyzed as to their inherent risks and rewards using the best available *long-term* databases. A major point of comparison is the efficiency with which each asset class has produced its reward. This is consistent with one of the central objectives of this book—to build portfolios assembled from only the most efficiently rated asset classes in order to provide a desired rate of return with the least possible risk.

With these evaluations completed, the following asset classes did not make the cut:

- Long-Term U.S. Treasury Bonds
- Long-Term U.S. Corporate Bonds
- High-Yield Bonds
- International Bonds
- Emerging Market Stocks
- Gold

In addition, two asset classes were sub-divided into two more narrowly defined asset class categories. One category of each asset class also failed to meet the desired criteria of reliability or efficiency:

- Non-Equity REITs
- International Stocks in Local Currencies

This leaves the following asset classes as the most appropriate long-term, dedicated asset class positions for your Wealth and Retirement Portfolio:

- 30-Day U.S. Treasury Bills
- 5-Year U.S. Treasury Bonds
- Domestic Large Cap Stocks or S&P 500
- Domestic Mid/Small Cap Stocks
- Domestic Micro Cap Stocks
- International Stocks in U.S. Dollars (with caveats noted)
- Equity REITs (with caveats noted)

These will be the asset classes used in Section III to build the most reliable and the most efficiently rated portfolios.

Total Domestic Stock Market
Growth of $100,000
(12/31/71 – 12/31/96)

Year	Jan	Feb	Mar	Apr	May	Jun	Jul	Aug	Sep	Oct	Nov	Dec	Annual Returns
1972	$100,000	↑	↑	↑	↑	+17% 12 mo.		↑	↓	↑	↑	$116,900	16.9
1973					<45%> 21 mo.								-18.1
1974									$64,000	↑	↓	↓	-27.2
1975	↑	↑	↑	↑	↑	↑	↑	↓	↓	↑	↑	↓	38.7
1976	↑	↑	↑	↓	↑	↑	↓	↓	↓	↓	↑	↑	26.7
1977	↓	↓	↓	↑	↓	+158% 65 mo.		↓	↑	↓	↑	↑	-4.2
1978	↓	↓	↑	↑	↑	↓	↑	↑	↓	↓	↑	↑	7.5
1979	↑	↓	↑	↑	↓	↑	↑	↑	↑	↓	↑	↑	23.0
1980	↑	$141,000	<11%> 1 mo. ↑	↑	↑	↑	↑	+44% 12 mo.		↑	↑	↓	32.7
1981	↓	↑	$210,200										-3.7
1982			<16%> 16 mo.			$177,200		↑	↑	↑	↑	↑	20.8
1983	↑	↑	↑	↑	↑	↑	↑	↑	↑	↓	↑	↓	22.0
1984	↓	↑	↑	↑	↓	↑	↓	↑	↑	↑	↑	↑	4.3
1985	↑	↑	↓	+257% 61 mo.		↑	↓	↑	↓	↑	↑	↑	32.2
1986	↑	↑	↑	↓	↑	↑	↓	↑	↓	↑	↑	↓	16.1
1987	↑	↑	↑	↓	↑	↑	↑	$632,000	<30%> 3 mo.	$444,000	↑		1.8
1988	↑	↑	↓	↑	↑	↑	↓	↓	↑	↑	↓	↑	18.0
1989	↑	↓	↑	↑	↑	+68% 30 mo.		↑	↓	↑	↑	↑	28.9
1990	↑	↑	↑	↓	$743,600	<17%> 5 mo.				$618,500	↑	↑	-5.9
1991	↑	↑	↑	↑	↑	↓	↑	↑	↓	↑	↓	↑	34.7
1992	↓	↑	↓	↑	↑	↓	↑	↓	↑	↑	↑	↑	9.8
1993	↑	↑	↑	↓	↑	+200% 74 mo.		↑	↑	↑	↓	↑	11.1
1994	↑	↓	↓	↑	↑	↓	↑	↑	↓	↑	↓	↑	-0.1
1995	↑	↑	↑	↑	↑	↑	↑	↑	↑	↓	↑		36.8
1996	↑	↑	↑	↑	↑	↓	↓	↑	↑	↓	↓	$1,856,800	21.3%

Total Return: Includes reinvested dividends and capital gains   **Standard Deviation: 16.9**

Source: Center for Research in Security Prices (CRSP) University of Chicago

↑ ↓ *Up or Down Month*   ▬ *Cyclical Declines*   ▭ *Recovery (to pre-decline level)*   ⬭ *Net New Advancement*

REWARD*		RISK	
Total Return (1972-1996)	12.4%	Worst Decline	45 % 21 mo.
Riskless Return (T-bills)	<7.0%>	Average Decline	18 % 8 mo.
AVERAGE ANNUAL REWARD OF TOTAL DOMESTIC MARKET	5.4%	Average Recovery	11 mo.
		COMPOSITE RISK	103 points

EFFICIENCY RATING = 52
(Reward ÷ Composite Risk x 1,000)

*Annualized

CHART S-1

Standard and Poor's 500

Growth of $100,000

(12/31/71 – 12/31/96)

Year	Jan	Feb	Mar	Apr	May	Jun	Jul	Aug	Sep	Oct	Nov	Dec	Annual Returns
1972	$100,000	↑	↑	↑	↑	+19% 12 mo.	↑	↓		↑	↑	$119,000	19.0
1973				<43%> 21 mo.									-14.7
1974									$68,300	↑	↓	↓	-26.5
1975	↑	↑	↑	↑	↑	↑	↓	↓	↓	↑	↑	↓	37.2
1976	↑	↓	↑	↓	↓	↑	↓	↑	↑	↓	↓	↑	23.8
1977	↓	↓	↓	↑	↓	↓	+124% 65 mo.		→	↓	↑	↑	-7.2
1978	↓	↓	↑	↑	↑	↓	↑	↑	↓	↓	↑	↑	6.6
1979	↑	↓	↑	↑	↓	↑	↑	↓	↑	↓	↑	↑	18.4
1980	↑	$158,200	<10%> 1 mo.	↑	↑	↑	+42% 8 mo.		↑	↑	$203,200		32.4
1981													-4.9
1982			<17%> 20 mo.				$168,800	↑	↑	↑	↑	↑	21.4
1983	↑	↑	↑	↑	↓	↑	↓	↑	↓	↑	↑	↓	22.5
1984	↓	↓	↑	↑	↓	↓	↓	↑	↑	↑	↓	↑	6.3
1985	↑	↑	↑	↓	↑	+282% 61 mo.		↓	↓	↑	↑	↑	32.2
1986	↑	↑	↑	↓	↑	↑	↓	↑	↓	↑	↑	↓	18.5
1987	↑	↑	↑	↓	↑	↑	↑	$644,000	<30%> 3 mo.	$453,800	↑		5.2
1988	↑	↑	↓	↑	↑	↑	↓	↑	↑	↑	↓	↑	16.8
1989	↑	↓	↑	↑	↑	+71% 30 mo.		↑	↓	↓	↑	↑	31.5
1990	↓	↑	↑	↓	$777,000	<15%> 5 mo.			$662,700	↑	↑		-3.2
1991	↑	↑	↑	↑	↑	↓	↑	↑	↓	↑	↓	↑	30.5
1992	↓	↑	↓	↑	↑	↓	↑	↑	↑	↑	↑	↑	7.7
1993	↑	↑	↑	↓	↑	↑	↓	↑	↓	↑	↓	↑	10.0
1994	↑	↓	↓	↑	↑	+190% 74 mo.		↑	↓	↑	↓	↑	1.3
1995	↑	↑	↑	↑	↑	↑	↑	↑	↑	↓	↑	↑	37.4
1996	↑	↑	↑	↑	↑	↑	↓	↑	↑	↑	↑	$1,919,600	23.1%

Total Return: Includes reinvested dividends and capital gains

Standard Deviation: 16.4

Source: © Computed using data from Stocks, Bonds, Bills & Inflation 1996 Yearbook™ *with data updated January 1997, Ibbotson Associates, Chicago*

↑ ↓ *Up or Down Month* ⬛ *Cyclical Declines* ◼ *Recovery (to pre-decline level)* ◻ *Net New Advancement*

REWARD*

Total Return (1972-1996)	12.5%
Riskless Return (T-bills)	<7.0%>
AVERAGE ANNUAL REWARD OF STANDARD AND POOR'S 500	5.5%

RISK

Worst Decline	43 % 21 mo.
Average Decline	18 % 8 mo.
Average Recovery	11 mo.
COMPOSITE RISK	**101 points**

EFFICIENCY RATING = 54

(Reward ÷ Composite Risk x 1,000)

*Annualized

Historical Risk/Reward

Mid/Small Cap Stocks

Growth of $100,000
(12/31/71 – 12/31/96)

Year	Jan	Feb	Mar	Apr	May	Jun	Jul	Aug	Sep	Oct	Nov	Dec	Annual Returns
1972	$100,000	↑	↑	→	↓	+9% 11 mo.		↑	↓	↓	$108,900		7.8
1973						<50%> 22 mo.							-28.5
1974									$54,900	↑	↓	↓	-25.4
1975	↑	↑	↑	↑	↑	↑	↓	↓	↓	↑	↑	↓	57.7
1976	↑	↑	↑	↓	↓	↑	↓	↓	↑	↓	↑	↑	42.2
1977	↓	↓	↑	↑	+225% 47 mo.		↓	↓	↑	↓	↑	↑	7.5
1978	↓	↑	↑	↑	↑	↓	↑	$178,100	<17%> 2 mo.		↑	↑	12.5
1979	↑	↓	↑	↑	↓	↑	↑	↑	↑	↓	↑	↑	37.1
1980	↑	↓	↓	↑	↑	↑	↑	+115% 31 mo.		↑	↑	↓	31.9
1981	↑	↑	↑	↑	$317,600	<19%> 14 mo.							3.5
1982							$259,800	↑	↑	↑	↑	↑	26.0
1983	↑	↑	↑	↑	↑	↑	↓	↓	↑	↓	↑	↓	28.7
1984	↓	↓	↑	↓	↓	↑	↓	↑	↑	↑	↓	↓	-1.2
1985	↑	↑	↓	↓	+265% 61 mo.		↑	↓	↓	↓	↑	↑	31.8
1986	↑	↑	↑	↑	↑	↑	↓	↑	↓	↑	↑	↓	13.3
1987	↑	↑	↑	↓	↑	↑	↑	$926,300	<31%> 3 mo.	$635,800	↑		-1.5
1988	↑	↑	↑	↑	↓	↑	↓	↓	↑	↑	↓	↑	22.6
1989	↑	↑	↑	↑	↑	↑	+65% 30 mo.		↓	↓	↑	↑	23.1
1990	↓	↑	↑	↓	$1,045,800	<24%> 5 mo.				$792,300	↑	↑	-12.9
1991	↑	↑	↑	↑	↑	↓	↑	↑	↓	↑	↓	↑	44.3
1992	↑	↑	↓	↑	↑	↓	↑	↓	↑	↑	↑	↑	16.7
1993	↑	↓	↑	↓	↑	↑	↑	↑	↑	↑	↓	↑	16.9
1994	↑	↓	↓	↑	↓	+242% 74 mo.		↑	↓	↑	↓	↑	-2.2
1995	↑	↑	↑	↑	↑	↑	↑	↑	↑	↓	↑	↑	32.3
1996	↑	↑	↑	↑	↑	↓	↓	↑	↑	↓	↓	$2,709,600	17.5%

Total Return: Includes reinvested dividends and capital gains   **Standard Deviation: 20.6**

Source: Center for Research in Security Prices (CRSP) University of Chicago

↑ ↓ *Up or Down Month*   ⬛ *Cyclical Declines*   ⬤ *Recovery (to pre-decline level)*   ⬭ *Net New Advancement*

REWARD*		**RISK**	
Total Return (1972-1996)	14.1%	Worst Decline	50 % 22 mo.
Riskless Return (T-bills)	<7.0%>	Average Decline	23 % 6 mo.
AVERAGE ANNUAL REWARD OF MID/SMALL CAP STOCKS	7.1%	Average Recovery	9 mo.
		COMPOSITE RISK	110 points

EFFICIENCY RATING = 65
(Reward ÷ Composite Risk x 1,000)

*Annualized

CHART S-3

Micro Cap Stocks
Growth of $100,000
(12/31/71 – 12/31/96)

Year	Jan	Feb	Mar	Apr	May	Jun	Jul	Aug	Sep	Oct	Nov	Dec	Annual Returns
1972	$100,000 +15% 2 mo.	$114,600											4.4
1973					<50%> 34 mo.								-30.9
1974												$57,800	-19.9
1975	↑	↑	↑	↑	↑	↑	↓	↓	↓	↓	↑	↓	52.8
1976	↑	↑	↓	↓	↓	↑	↑	↓	↑	↓	↓	↑	57.4
1977	↑	↑	↑	↑	↓	↑ +352% 44 mo.↓		↓	↓	↓	↑	↑	25.4
1978	↓	↑	↑	↑	↑	↓	↑	$261,100	<25%> 2 mo.		↑	↑	23.5
1979	↑	↓	↑	↑	↑	+70% 15 mo.		↑	↓	↑	↑	↑	43.5
1980	$334,300	<20%> 2 mo.		↑	↑	↑	↑	↑	↑	↑	↑	↓	39.9
1981	↑	↑	↑	↑	↑	↑	↓	↓	↓	↑	↑	↓	13.9
1982	↓	↓	↓	↑	↓	↓	↓	↑	↑	↑	↑	↑	28.0
1983	↑	↑	↑	↑	↑	↑	↓	↓	↑	↓	↑	↓	39.7
1984	↓	↓	↑	↓	↓ +423% 89 mo. ↓			↑	↑	↓	↓	↑	-6.7
1985	↑	↑	↓	↑	↑	↑	↑	↓	↓	↑	↑	↑	24.7
1986	↑	↑	↑	↑	↑	↑	↓	↑	↓	↑	↑	↓	6.9
1987	↑	↑	↑	↓	↓	↑	↑	$1,396,300	<33%> 3 mo.	$941,800	↑		-9.3
1988	↑	↑	↑	↑	↓	↑	↓	↓	↑	↓	↓	↑	22.9
1989	↑	↑	↑	+54% 22 mo.		↓	↑	↑	$1,454,300				10.2
1990					<32%> 13 mo.					$987,600	↑	↑	-21.6
1991	↑	↑	↑	↑	↑	↓	↑	↑	↑	↑	↓	↑	44.6
1992	↑	↑	↓	↑	↓	↑	↑	↓	↑	↑	↑	↑	23.3
1993	↑	↓	↑	↓	↑	↓	↑	↑	↓	↑	↓	↑	21.0
1994	↑	↓	↓	↑	↓	+275% 74 mo.		↑	↑	↑	↓	↑	3.1
1995	↑	↑	↑	↑	↑	↓	↓	↑	↑	↓	↓	↓	34.5
1996	↑	↑	↑	↑	↑	↓	↓	↑	↑	↓	↓	$3,702,900	17.6%

Total Return: Includes reinvested dividends and capital gains   **Standard Deviation: 22.8**

Source: © Computed using data from Stocks, Bonds, Bills & Inflation 1996 Yearbook™ with data updated January 1997, Ibbotson Associates, Chicago

↑ ↓ Up or Down Month   ⬤ Cyclical Declines   ◖ Recovery (to pre-decline level)   ◗ Net New Advancement

REWARD*

Total Return (1972-1996)	15.5%
Riskless Return (T-bills)	<7.0%>
AVERAGE ANNUAL REWARD OF MICRO CAP STOCKS	8.5%

RISK

Worst Decline	50 % 34 mo.
Average Decline	26 % 7 mo.
Average Recovery	11 mo.
COMPOSITE RISK	128 points

EFFICIENCY RATING = 66
(Reward ÷ Composite Risk x 1,000)

*Annualized

Government Bonds (5-Year Treasury)
Growth of $100,000
(12/31/71 – 12/31/96)

Year	Jan	Feb	Mar	Apr	May	Jun	Jul	Aug	Sep	Oct	Nov	Dec	Annual Returns
1972	$100,000	↑	↑	↑	↑	↑	↑	↑	↑	↑	↑	↑	5.2
1973	↓	↓	↑	↑	↑	+11% 26 mo.	↑	↑	↑	↑	↑		4.6
1974	↑	$110,500	<4%> 2 mo.		↑	↓	↑	↓	↑	↑	↑	↑	5.7
1975	↑	↑	↓	↓	↑	↑	↓	↓	↑	↑	↓	↑	7.8
1976	↑	↑	↑	↑	↓	↑	↑	↑	↑	↑	↑	↑	12.9
1977	↓	↑	↓	↑	↑	+47% 62 mo.	↑	↑	↓	↑	↓		1.4
1978	↑	↑	↑	↑	→	↓	↑	↑	↑	↓	↑	↑	3.5
1979	↑	↓	↑	↑	↑	$156,600	<9%> 8 mo.						4.1
1980	$142,700	+19% 3 mo.		$170,000	<9%> 15 mo.								3.9
1981								$155,600	↑	↑	↑	↓	9.5
1982	↑	↑	↑	↑	↑	↓	↑	↑	↑	↑	↑	↑	29.1
1983	↑	↑	↓	↑	+59% 29 mo.		↓	↑	↑	↑	↑	↑	7.4
1984	$248,100	<4%> 4 mo.			$239,400	↑	↑	↑	↑	↑	↑	↑	14.0
1985	↑	↓	↑	↑	↑	↑	↓	↑	↑	↑	↑	↑	20.3
1986	↑	↑	↑	↓	↓	↑	↑	↓	↓	↑	↑	↓	15.1
1987	↑	↓	↓	↓	↓	↑	↑	↓	↓	↑	↑	→	2.9
1988	↑	↑	↓	↓	↓	↑	↑	↓	↑	↑	↓	↓	6.1
1989	↑	↓	↑	↑	↑	+205% 116 mo.	↓	↑	↑	↑	↑		13.2
1990	↓	↑	↑	↑	↑	↑	↓	↑	↑	↑	↑	↑	9.7
1991	↑	↑	↓	↑	↑	↑	↓	↑	↑	↑	↑	↑	15.5
1992	↓	↑	↓	↑	↑	↑	↑	↑	↓	↓	↓	↑	7.2
1993	↑	↑	↑	↑	↓	↑	↑	↑	↑	↑	↓	↑	11.2
1994	$729,500	<7%> 10 mo.								$678,900	↑		-5.1
1995	↑	↑	↑	↑	↑	↑	↓	↓	↑	↑	↑	↑	16.8
1996	↑	↓	↓	↓	↓	↓	+20% 25 mo.		↑	↓	↓	$813,900	2.1%

Total Return: Includes reinvested interest   Standard Deviation: 7.0

Source: © Computed using data from Stocks, Bonds, Bills & Inflation 1996 Yearbook™ with data updated January 1997, Ibbotson Associates, Chicago

↑ ↓ Up or Down Month   ⬛ Cyclical Declines   ⬛ Recovery (to pre-decline level)   ⬜ Net New Advancement

REWARD*		RISK	
Total Return (1972-1996)	8.7%	Worst Decline	9 % 15 mo.
Riskless Return (T-bills)	<7.0%>	Average Decline	6 % 6 mo.
AVERAGE ANNUAL REWARD OF GOVERNMENT BONDS (5-YEAR TREASURY)	1.7%	Average Recovery	4 mo.
		COMPOSITE RISK	**40 points**

EFFICIENCY RATING = 43
(Reward ÷ Composite Risk x 1,000)

*Annualized

CHART S-5

International Stocks – EAFE (U.S. $)

Growth of $100,000
(12/31/71 – 12/31/96)

Year	Jan	Feb	Mar	Apr	May	Jun	Jul	Aug	Sep	Oct	Nov	Dec	Annual Returns
1972	$100,000	↑	↑	↑	↑	+53% 15 mo.		↑	↓	↑	↑	↑	37.6
1973	↑	↑	$152,600		<42%> 18 mo.								-14.2
1974									$89,200	↑	↑	↓	-22.1
1975	↑	↑	↓	↑	↓	↓	↓	↓	↓	↑	↑	↑	37.1
1976	↑	↓	↓	↓	↓	↑	↓	↑	↓	↓	↑	↑	3.7
1977	↓	↑	↑	↑	↓	↑	↓	↑	↓	↑	↓	↑	12.5
1978	↑	↑	↑	↑	↑	+201% 79 mo.		↑	↑	↑	↓	↑	34.3
1979	↑	↓	↑	↓	↓	↑	↑	↑	↑	↓	↑	↑	6.2
1980	↑	↓	↓	↑	↑	↑	↓	↑	↑	↑	↓	↑	24.4
1981	↓	↓	↑	$270,500	<19%> 17 mo.								-1.0
1982									$218,700	↑	↑	↑	-0.9
1983	↓	↑	↑	↑	↓	↑	↑	+68% 18 mo.		→	↑	↑	24.6
1984	↑	↑	$368,400	<13%> 4 mo.			$304,600	↑	↓	↑	↑	↑	7.8
1985	↑	↓	↑	↑	↑	↓	↑	↑	↓	↑	↑	↑	56.8
1986	↑	↑	↑	↑	↓	+327% 37 mo.		↑	↓	↓	↑	↑	69.9
1987	↑	↑	↑	↑	↑	↓	↓	$1,300,800	<15%> 2 mo.		↑	↑	24.9
1988	↑	↑	↑	↑	↓	↑	↑	↓	↑	↑	↑	↑	28.6
1989	↑	↑	↓	↑	+48% 26 mo.		↑	↓	↑	↓	↑	$1,632,500	10.8
1990				<31%> 9 mo.					$1,133,200	↑	↓	↑	-23.2
1991	↑	↑	↓	↑	↑	↓	↑	↓	↑	↑	↓	↑	12.5
1992	↓	↓	↓	↑	↑	↓	↓	↑	↓	↓	↑	↑	-11.9
1993	↑	↑	↑	↑	↑	↑	↑	↑	↓	↑	↓	↑	32.9
1994	↑	↓	↓	↑	↓	+87% 75 mo.		↑	↓	↑	↓	↑	8.1
1995	↓	↓	↑	↑	↓	↓	↑	↓	↑	↓	↑	↑	11.6
1996	↑	↑	↑	↑	↓	↑	↓	↑	↑	↓	↑	$2,118,500	6.3%

Total Return: Includes reinvested dividends and capital gains **Standard Deviation: 22.1**

Source: Morgan Stanley Capital International

↑ ↓ *Up or Down Month* ■ *Cyclical Declines* ▨ *Recovery (to pre-decline level)* ⬭ *Net New Advancement*

REWARD*		**RISK**	
Total Return (1972-1996)	13.0%	Worst Decline	42 % 18 mo.
Riskless Return (T-bills)	<7.0%>	Average Decline	20 % 8 mo.
AVERAGE ANNUAL REWARD OF INTERNATIONAL STOCKS	6.0%	Average Recovery	19 mo.
		COMPOSITE RISK	107 points

EFFICIENCY RATING = 56
(Reward ÷ Composite Risk x 1,000)

*Annualized

CHART S-6

Historical Risk/Reward

Equity REITs
Growth of $100,000
(12/31/71 – 12/31/96)

Year	Jan	Feb	Mar	Apr	May	Jun	Jul	Aug	Sep	Oct	Nov	Dec	Annual Returns
1972	$100,000	↑	↓	+14% 9 mo.		↑	↑	↓	$113,800				8.0
1973					<37%> 27 mo.								-15.5
1974												$71,700	-21.4
1975	↑	↑	↑	↑	↑	↑	↓	↓	↓	↓	↑	↑	19.3
1976	↑	↑	↑	↓	↑	↑	↑	↑	↑	↑	↑	↓	49.9
1977	↑	↑	↑	↑	↑	+246% 56 mo.		↑	↑	→	↑	↑	20.5
1978	↓	↑	↑	↑	↓	↓	↑	↑	↓	↓	↑	↑	10.3
1979	↑	↑	↑	↑	↓	↓	↑	$248,300	<13%> 2 mo.		↑	↑	35.9
1980	↑	↑	↓	↓	↑	↑	↑	↑	↓	↑	↓	↓	24.4
1981	↑	↑	↑	↑	↓	↑	↓	↓	↓	↑	↑	↓	6.0
1982	↓	↓	↓	↑	↓	↓	↑	↑	↑	↑	↑	↑	21.6
1983	↑	↓	↑	↑	↑	+324% 93 mo.		↓	↓	↑	↑	↑	30.6
1984	↑	↑	↑	↓	↓	↓	↓	↑	↑	↑	↑	↑	20.9
1985	↑	↑	↑	↑	↑	↑	↑	↓	↓	↓	↑	↑	19.1
1986	↑	↑	↑	↓	↓	↑	↓	↑	↓	↑	↓	↑	19.2
1987	↑	↑	↑	↓	↓	↑	$919,600	<18%> 3 mo.		$754,900		↑	-3.6
1988	↑	↑	↑	↑	↓	↑	↑	↑	↓	↓	↓	↑	13.5
1989	↑	↓	↑	↑	+37% 22 mo.		↑	$1,032,400	<24%> 14 mo.		↑	↓	8.8
1990									$785,900		↑	↓	-15.4
1991	↑	↑	↑	↑	↑	↓	↑	↑	↑	↓	↑	↑	35.7
1992	↑	↓	↓	↓	↑	+135% 36 mo.		↑	↑	↓	↑	↑	14.6
1993	↑	↑	↑	↓	↓	↑	↑	↑	↑	$1,853,500	<16%> 2 mo.		19.7
1994	↑	↑	↓	↑	↑	↓	↓	↑	↓	↓	↓	↑	3.2
1995	↓	↑	↓	↓	↑	↑	↑	↑	↑	↓	↑	↑	15.3
1996	↑	↑	↓	↑	↑	+61% 36 mo.		↑	↑	↑	↑	$2,511,300	35.3%

Total Return: Includes reinvested dividends and capital gains   **Standard Deviation: 16.6**

Source: National Association of Real Estate Investment Trusts (NAREIT)

↑ ↓ *Up or Down Month*   ⬛ *Cyclical Declines*   ⬛ *Recovery (to pre-decline level)*   ⬭ *Net New Advancement*

REWARD*		**RISK**	
Total Return (1972-1996)	13.7%	Worst Decline	37 % 27 mo.
Riskless Return (T-bills)	<7.0%>	Average Decline	18 % 5 mo.
AVERAGE ANNUAL REWARD OF		Average Recovery	13 mo.
EQUITY REITS	6.7%	**COMPOSITE RISK**	100 points

EFFICIENCY RATING = 67
(Reward ÷ Composite Risk x 1,000)

*Annualized

CHART S-7

Gold
Growth of $100,000
(12/31/71 – 12/31/96)

Year	Jan	Feb	Mar	Apr	May	Jun	Jul	Aug	Sep	Oct	Nov	Dec	Annual Returns
1972	$100,000	↑	↑	↑	↑	↑	↑	↑	↓	↑	↓	↑	83.9
1973	↑	↑	↑	↑	↑	+343% 38 mo.		↓	↓	↓	↓	↑	66.8
1974	↑	↑	↑	↑	↓	↓	↓	↑	↑	↑	↑	↑	70.9
1975	↓	$513,700				<38%> 18 mo.							-23.9
1976								$316,900	↑	↑	↑	↑	-3.8
1977	↑	↑	↑	↓	↑	↓	↑	↑	↑	↑	↑	↓	19.9
1978	↑	↑	↑	↓	↑	+509% 49 mo.		↑	↑	↑	↓	↑	29.2
1979	↑	↑	↓	↓	↑	↑	↑	↑	↑	↑	↓	↑	122.3
1980	↑	↓	↓	↓	↓	↑	↑	↓	$1,930,600				28.6
1981				<53%> 21 mo.									-31.2
1982						$899,700	↑	↑	↑	↓	↓	↑	8.6
1983	↑	+39% 11 mo.		↑	$1,250,600		<32%> 21 mo.						-12.8
1984													-17.7
1985		$854,900	↑	↑	↓	↑	↑	↑	↓	↑	↓	↓	1.0
1986	↑	↓	↑	↑	+63% 34 mo.		↑	↑	↑	↑	↓	↓	21.6
1987	↑	↓	↑	↑	↑	↓	↑	↑	↓	↑	↑	$1,393,400	24.2
1988													-13.9
1989													-2.5
1990					<32%> 61 mo.								-7.3
1991													0.3
1992													-11.8
1993	$943,400	↑	↑	↑	↑	↑	↑	↓	↓	↑	↑	↑	14.8
1994	↑	↓	↑	↓	↑	+12% 47 mo.		↑	↓	↓	↓	↓	-1.1
1995	↓	↓	↑	↑	↓	↑	↓	↓	↓	↓	↑	↑	2.0
1996	↑	↑	↓	↓	↓	↓	↓	↑	↓	↓	↓	$1,053,800	-5.1%

Standard Deviation: 35.8

Source: Standard & Poor's Statistical Service, Metals Supplement

↑ ↓ Up or Down Month ⬛ Cyclical Declines ⬜ Recovery (to pre-decline level) ⬭ Net New Advancement

REWARD*		RISK	
Price Appreciation Return (1972-1996)	9.9%	Worst Decline	53 % 61 mo.
Riskless Return (T-bills)	<7.0%>	Average Decline	34 % 20 mo.
AVERAGE ANNUAL REWARD OF GOLD		Average Recovery	N/A
	2.9%	**COMPOSITE RISK**	**210 points**

EFFICIENCY RATING = 14
(Reward ÷ Composite Risk x 1,000)

*Annualized

Note: Gold has a unique attribute compared to all the other asset classes: it never has recovered to its 1980 valuation. To make gold's Historical Risk/Reward chart have similar characteristics to those of the other asset classes, the methodology was changed to allow for a decline to end at a subsequent low point even though there was no recovery to a new high in market value.

CHART S-8

Section III

Designing Reliable and Efficient Portfolios

Overview of Section III

Now that the most efficient asset classes have been determined, the next step is to find the most favorable combination of these asset classes (portfolio design) that will provide your targeted rate of return with the lowest level of Composite Risk.

This section begins by differentiating between broad portfolio designs (fixed commitments to asset class families) and structured portfolio designs (fixed commitments to individual asset classes). The pluses and minuses of each are explored. Structured portfolio designs are the more predictable.

Countless structured portfolio designs were evaluated over long time periods to discover which unique combination of asset classes provided a given rate of return with the least risk or, conversely, the highest rate of return for a given level of risk. The end result: the best model portfolio designs for each specific group of investors from conservative to aggressive.

9

Creating Predictable Long-Term Portfolios

A **broad** portfolio design (also call investment policy) establishes and maintains a specified weighting for each family of asset classes—stocks, bonds and cash. A **structured** portfolio design establishes *and maintains* a set weighting for each individual asset class. Once set, only a change in circumstances—*not* market conditions—should call for a reevaluation of a portfolio design. Adhering to a structured portfolio design over time provides the highest probability of achieving a targeted long-term rate of return and the least risk of falling short of the ultimate retirement objective.

> *"In investment management, the real opportunity to achieve superior results is not in scrambling to outperform the market, but in establishing and adhering to appropriate investment policies over the long term — policies that position the portfolio to benefit from riding the main long-term forces of the market."*
>
> — Charles D. Ellis, <u>Investment Policy</u> (1985)

Portfolio Design

Guiding Principles

A portfolio design is an intentional mix of asset classes which is maintained until a change of personal circumstances—*not* market conditions—necessitates an adjustment. The guiding principles of portfolio design are:

- **Diversification** - A cross-section of securities within an asset class is required in order to deliver the return associated with that asset class and to minimize the risk of opportunity loss (substantial underperformance).

- **Dedicated Asset Allocations** - 90% or more of long-term performance results from asset allocation decisions; less than 10% of performance is due to individual security selection.[15] (Ironically, many investors approach the investment process as if the exact opposite were true.)

- **Financial History is Rational and Repetitive (Over the Long-Term)** - The variation in returns from each asset class diminishes significantly with time. The longer an asset class is held, the more reliable its performance in relation to historical averages.

A portfolio design, once adopted, gives reliability and permanence to your long-term planning. It ends the search for the elusive magic black box system or set of indicators that will make substantial bets on relative short-term performance of one asset class versus another. A portfolio design provides long-term **predictability** for your Wealth and Retirement Portfolio.

Note: Within each asset class there is ample room for strategies and judgment to be exercised—if you so desire. This will be fully discussed in Section IV – Three Portfolio Strategies: Executing Your Portfolio Design.

Broad Portfolio Design (Investment Policy)

Portfolio designs may be broad in scope or more tightly defined. The broadest possible portfolio design is fulfilled by simply dividing your portfolio into the three families of asset classes: stocks, bonds and cash. An example of a broad portfolio design, also referred to as your investment policy, would be:

50%	dedicated to equity mutual funds
30%	dedicated to bond mutual funds
20%	dedicated to money market accounts
100%	Total Portfolio

This broad portfolio design allows you maximum latitude as to the make up of each asset class family. If you are so inclined, you could rotate or reapportion your equity commitment (50% of your portfolio in this example) among any of the major stock asset classes: domestic large cap, small/mid cap and micro cap or international. In other words, the whole world of equity mutual funds is available to you at any time—**as long as your total commitment to stocks is maintained at 50% of your Wealth and Retirement Portfolio.**

A broad portfolio design is a "wide track" that gives you maximum room to maneuver within each of the stock, bond and cash components of your portfolio. This is appropriate if you have the time, talent and desire to be actively involved in strategies for each asset class family. (In Chapter 14, a *benchmark* for your portfolio design will be developed to make sure you are on course.)

The benefit of a broad portfolio design is to eliminate two significant risks that would otherwise impact your Wealth and Retirement Portfolio:

- Market timing

- Company-specific risk

Market timing in all its many guises has been responsible for more portfolio loss than any other investing demon according to Peter Lynch, the widely celebrated former portfolio manager of the Fidelity Magellan Fund. Even a broad portfolio design enforces a discipline of a fixed commitment to each asset class family. Your focus is always, "Where in the universe of this asset class family are the best opportunities for my portfolio's allocation?"…instead of the market timer's constant credo, "Are stocks a good investment right now?"

Company-specific risk is eliminated by the principle of diversification. Diversification generally applies more to stocks than either bonds or cash. The fundamental premise of a diversified asset class is to own no single security that could, because of its unique company-specific risks, by itself cause substantial underperformance of your portfolio relative to a market benchmark (index). Most mutual funds limit the percentage that any single stock can represent within the fund's portfolio for this reason. Individuals may be overweighted with company-specific risk if a substantial portion of their Wealth and Retirement Portfolio is invested in their company's stock or an inherited block of stock (the sentimental hold), for example.

A portfolio built completely with mutual funds or similar diversified investments, such as 401(k) pooled accounts, rarely needs to be concerned with under-diversifying.

Setting a broad portfolio design will provide a wide but disciplined track for your Wealth and Retirement Portfolio. Somewhere between 50% and 90% of your long-term performance (returns and fluctuations) will be controlled by your strict adherence to a broad portfolio design, once set. This is a significant step in the direction of predictability, yet leaving you with great latitude within each asset class family.

A broad portfolio design implies ongoing evaluation and judgment as to how to divide stock and bond commitments between the various domestic, international and other asset classes. For many investors, this can be overwhelming.

Structured Portfolio Designs

The problem of too much latitude can be substantially reduced by crafting a portfolio design with more internal definition. An example of a structured portfolio design would be as follows:

Example of Structured Portfolio Design

Stocks	20%	dedicated to domestic Large Cap mutual funds
(50%)	10%	dedicated to domestic Mid/Small Cap mutual funds
	5%	dedicated to domestic Micro Cap mutual funds
	10%	dedicated to International Stock mutual funds
	5%	dedicated to equity REIT mutual funds
Bonds	25%	dedicated to Intermediate U.S. Treasury Bond mutual funds
(30%)	5%	dedicated to High-Yield Bond mutual funds
Cash	20%	allocated to a general Money Market account
(20%)		
	100%	Total Portfolio

CHART 9-1

A structured portfolio design such as this one provides a highly predictable track for your Wealth and Retirement Portfolio. Fully 90-95% of the ultimate performance of a structured portfolio will be determined by strict adherence to the design—regardless of the mutual funds purchased for each asset class.[16] This indicates how important both the selection of asset classes and the proportions decided upon are to final performance. *This is by far the most significant set of decisions with regard to your Wealth and Retirement Portfolio.*

With a structured portfolio design, switching between asset classes is eliminated. Mutual funds are only evaluated against other mutual funds within the same asset class; a domestic micro cap fund is only evaluated against other micro cap funds to fulfill that requirement of the portfolio design. (Strategies for evaluating and selecting mutual funds are thoroughly analyzed in Section IV.)

It should be readily apparent that you would not choose a structured portfolio design until you were completely committed to it. The balance of Section III is dedicated to creating and testing distinctive structured portfolio designs or model portfolios.

10

The Most Reliable and the Most Efficient Portfolios

The very best portfolio design is that combination of asset classes which will produce a desired long-term reward with the least possible risk. Four Domestic Model Portfolios and four Global Model Portfolios are introduced. The risk profiles of these model portfolios range from conservative to very aggressive (all-equity). These portfolio design models include only the most reliable and efficient asset classes. The specific proportion of the asset classes included in each model was arrived at by finding which combination squeezed the most risk out of a targeted rate of return. Any of these model portfolios offer the prospect of long-term predictability for your Wealth and Retirement Portfolio.

> *"Clients' expectations tend to err in an optimistic direction; they believe that higher returns are possible with less risk than is actually the case."*
> — Roger C. Gibson, <u>Asset Allocation</u> (1988)

Your Best Portfolio Design

What is the best structured portfolio design for your Wealth and Retirement Portfolio?

The most apparent answer would be to simply identify a portfolio design with a targeted rate of return that meets your financial goals while at the same time delivering risk characteristics consistent with your tolerance for market declines, assuming such a portfolio design exists. But what if your financial objective requires a rate of return that entails more risk than that with which you are comfortable? This is one of the common problems in structuring a portfolio.

Therefore, the best portfolio design for you may force a trade-off between your reward objective and your risk tolerance. You may have to "go for it" and choose a portfolio design that is closest to providing for your long-term financial security while exposing your portfolio to deeper and longer cyclical declines than you would otherwise accept. Or, you may choose a portfolio design based on the highest level of risk that you know you can stay with through its periodic cyclical declines even though its targeted rate of return will fall short of achieving your desired financial objectives. Either of these are intelligent choices if carefully thought through and made deliberately.

Until now, the desire to make such a knowledgeable choice may have been there, but you probably lacked a clear picture of the trade-off between risk and reward in structured portfolios. Don't feel alone. Thorough studies of complete portfolios over long periods of time based on the principles of portfolio design simply have not been available to the public. This is one of the motivations behind this book—to provide for this heretofore unfilled void.

Of course, you can still opt for the most common portfolio design—none at all. This is the hodge-podge portfolio discussed in Chapter 1 that never establishes nor adheres to a definite overall game plan and whose risks are all but unknown. Assuming you establish a structured portfolio design, you will build a much higher level of predictability into your long-term planning. This chapter will develop eight separate model portfolios (structured portfolio designs) for your review.

Each model portfolio's long-term historical characteristics of risk, reward and efficiency rating are established in this chapter. In the balance of this section, several of these models will be tested under the extreme conditions of the Great Depression, tested for their ability to pay out retirement income and evaluated for their individual appropriateness for short and intermediate time periods. One of these model portfolios may well be the best portfolio design for your Wealth and Retirement Portfolio.

Domestic Model Portfolios

The Most Reliable Asset Classes

Structured portfolio designs that employ only the most reliable asset classes will make the most predictable portfolios. For American investors, the most reliable asset classes are large cap stocks, mid/small cap stocks, micro cap stocks, 5-year Treasury bonds and cash (T-bills). This is one of the findings from Section II of this book. These five asset classes will be used to structure four Domestic Model Portfolios to be called: **Conservative, Moderate, Aggressive and All-Equity.**

Using the historical monthly data for each asset class (1960-1996), virtually every combination of these five asset classes was tested in order to determine either the very lowest risk for a given rate-of-return objective (reward) or the highest reward for a given level of risk. (A detailed description of the guidelines used is on page 255 in the Appendix.) A requirement for each model portfolio is that it be meaningful and realistic for the specific group of investors for whom it is intended.

Based on the guidelines set forth, the following four Domestic Model Portfolios are the most favorable combinations of the five *most reliable* asset classes. One of these model portfolios is likely to be the most reliable portfolio design for your Wealth and Retirement Portfolio.

Domestic Conservative Model Portfolio (30-50-20)

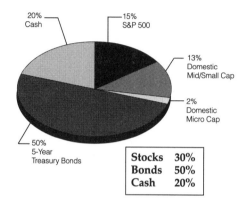

20%
Cash

15%
S&P 500

13%
Domestic
Mid/Small Cap

2%
Domestic
Micro Cap

50%
5-Year
Treasury Bonds

Stocks	**30%**
Bonds	**50%**
Cash	**20%**

Primary Objective: The portfolio design with the highest return that never incurred a decline in market value exceeding 10% (from any month-end high to a subsequent month-end low).

Performance Highlights: (1960-1996)

Rate of Return	8.9%
Riskless Rate (T-bills)	-6.1%
Reward	**2.8%**

Worst Decline: 10%

Domestic Moderate Model Portfolio (47-47-6)

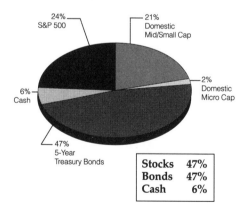

24%
S&P 500

21%
Domestic
Mid/Small Cap

2%
Domestic
Micro Cap

6%
Cash

47%
5-Year
Treasury Bonds

Stocks	**47%**
Bonds	**47%**
Cash	**6%**

Primary Objective: The portfolio design that achieves a 1.1% higher reward than that of the Domestic Conservative Model with the least risk.

Performance Highlights: (1960-1996)

Rate of Return	10.0%
Riskless Rate (T-bills)	-6.1%
Reward	**3.9%**

Worst Decline: 21%

Domestic Aggressive Model Portfolio (70-28-2)

35%
S&P 500

32%
Domestic
Mid/Small Cap

3%
Domestic
Micro Cap

2%
Cash

28%
5-Year
Treasury Bonds

Stocks	70%
Bonds	28%
Cash	2%

Primary Objective: The portfolio design that achieves a 2.1% higher reward than that of the Domestic Conservative Model with the least risk.

Performance Highlights: *(1960-1996)*

Rate of Return	11.0%
Riskless Rate (T-bills)	-6.1%
Reward	**4.9%**

Worst Decline: 32%

Domestic All-Equity Model Portfolio (100-0-0)

50%
S&P 500

45%
Domestic
Mid/Small Cap

5%
Domestic Micro Cap

Stocks	100%
Bonds	0%
Cash	0%

Primary Objective: To provide the maximum return without regard to risk.

Performance Highlights: *(1960-1996)*

Rate of Return	12.2%
Riskless Rate (T-bills)	-6.1%
Reward	**6.1%**

Worst Decline: 46%

All-Equity Model Portfolio

The Domestic All-Equity Model Portfolio emphasizes mid/small cap and micro cap stocks by giving them a significantly increased weighting compared to their normal representation in the U.S. stock market. Consequently, large cap stocks are given a reduced representation in this model portfolio.

	Weightings	
	Domestic All-Equity Model	Total U.S. Stock Market
Large Caps (S&P 500)	50%	72%
Mid/Small Caps	45%	25%
Micro Caps	5%	3%

As will be shown later in this chapter, the Domestic All-Equity Model has produced a higher long-term return and a lower Composite Risk score than the U.S. stock market (normal weighting).

Balanced Model Portfolios & Correlation Benefits

The term "balanced" is an excellent descriptive term for portfolios made up of stocks, bonds and cash in that they bring together the growth from stocks, the higher income from bonds and the ready liquidity of cash equivalents.

As illustrated in Section II, the degrees of fluctuation are far different within these three U.S. asset class families. What may not have been so obvious, however, is that the *direction* of advances or declines within one asset class family may not correlate with those of another. Bonds may *zig* when stocks *zag*. This was clearly evident in the stock market crash of October 1987. Bonds went up in value as stocks went down. Cash was, of course, stable in market value. Asset classes that do not move up and down together are said to be uncorrelated. By combining them within your portfolio, you achieve the diversification necessary to smooth fluctuations and reduce overall risk.

Rebalancing Magic: 2 + 2 = 5

Academic research has proved that the more uncorrelated the returns from various asset classes, the less volatile will be the aggregate performance of a portfolio. Blending uncorrelated asset classes smoothes the ride of investing. In addition, balanced portfolio designs generally provide higher long-term returns than the underlying asset classes. How's that possible... it sounds like 2 + 2 = 5?! It's made possible by rebalancing the portfolio annually to maintain its dedicated asset class representations.

Rebalancing enforces a discipline of BUY LOW/SELL HIGH, selling off a little of those asset classes that have done well and adding to those that have underperformed. The historical performance of the Domestic Model Portfolios, each portfolio was rebalanced at the end of every calendar year to bring it back into alignment with its fixed allocation. For example, if at the end of a year, Mr. Smith's Domestic Conservative Portfolio values are 35% stocks, 47% bonds and 18% cash, he will shift his investments so that they once again reflect his chosen 30-50-20 weightings.

The *free* or enhanced returns for the balanced model portfolios from rebalancing in the Inflation Era were as follows:

Conservative	0.3% annually
Moderate	0.5% annually
Aggressive	0.4% annually

This is the difference between the actual compounded annual performance of these models (rebalanced annually) and simply adding up the individual compounded annual returns of the underlying asset classes (by their weighting within the model portfolio).

For example, the Domestic Moderate Model delivered a 10.0% compounded rate of return for the Inflation Era, yet simply adding up the returns from the component asset classes during that same period (by their weighting within the portfolio) results in a total rate of return of just 9.5%. The 0.5% difference is the magic of rebalancing within this portfolio model.

In addition, balanced portfolio designs can lessen volatility for the same return. This is illustrated in Chart 10-2 by comparing the

performance of the S&P 500 and the Domestic Aggressive Model
for the period from 1960 to 1996.

	Inflation Era (1960-1996)			
	Return	Worst Decline	Average Decline	Composite Risk
S&P 500	11.1%	43%	19%	100 points
Aggressive Model Portfolio	11.0%	32%	16%	82 points

CHART 10-2

☞ This is a remarkable result—*approximately the same return and far
lower risk*! Not all balanced portfolios are created equal, however.
Each specific portfolio design delivers unique long-term rewards
and shorter-term risks. This is evident in the Risk/Reward data of
each Domestic Model Portfolio. A summary is provided in Chart
10-3.

Note: All of the results of the portfolios presented in this chapter
may be duplicated using the databases cited in Chart 8-1.

Domestic Model Portfolios – Risks, Rewards & Efficiencies – 1960-1996

	Conservative (30-50-20)	Moderate (47-47-6)	Aggressive (70-28-2)	All-Equity (100-0-0)
REWARD				
Return (Annualized)	8.9%	10.0%	11.0%	12.2%
Riskless Return (T-bills)	-6.1%	-6.1%	-6.1%	-6.1%
REWARD	2.8%	3.9%	4.9%	6.1%
RISK				
Worst Decline	10 %	21 %	32 %	46 %
	21 mo.	21 mo.	21 mo.	21 mo.
Average Decline	7 %	10 %	16 %	22 %
	5 mo.	5 mo.	5 mo.	6 mo.
Average Recovery	5 mo.	6 mo.	8 mo.	9 mo.
COMPOSITE RISK SCORE	**48 points**	**63 points**	**82 points**	**104 points**
EFFICIENCY RATING	**58**	**62**	**60**	**59**

CHART 10-3

Evaluating the Domestic Model Portfolios

Rewards. The table below displays the *growth* on an initial investment of $100,000 in each domestic model as compared to cash in the Inflation Era.

Domestic Model Portfolio Growth - $100,000 (1960-1996)

Cash	Conservative	Moderate	Aggressive	All-Equity
$784,800	$2,265,200	$3,252,800	$4,697,900	$6,886,300

The return from a Conservative Model Portfolio nearly tripled the return from cash. This is nearly three times the principal, which provides nearly three times the retirement income. A Moderate Model Portfolio quadruples the return from cash, Aggressive is six times, and All-Equity is over eight times higher principal and income-generating capacity. The long-term rewards from adding more domestic stocks and 5-year Treasury bonds into your portfolio design are very significant indeed!

Another view of the performance of a Conservative portfolio is to compare it with that of a portfolio of bonds, 5-year Treasury bonds in this example (Chart 10-4).

Performance Comparison: Conservative Model vs. Bonds
1960-1996

	Reward	Composite Risk	Worst Decline	Efficiency Rating
Domestic Conservative	2.8%	48	10%	58
5-Year Treasury Bonds	1.4%	39	9%	36

CHART 10-4

The Conservative model doubled the reward from the bonds while not increasing risk proportionately. In fact, the exposure to worst-case declines in market value were nearly identical.

Risks. The domestic model portfolios provide widely different answers to the question, "What's the worst that can happen?" By evaluating each model, investors can become knowledgeable and be prepared for the largest decline likely within their Wealth and Retirement Portfolios.

For example, the Moderate Portfolio experienced a 21% worst-case decline during the Inflation Era, more than doubling the 10% worst-case decline from a Conservative Portfolio. The Aggressive Model suffered a 32% decline and the All-Equity a full 46% decline. Yet, their differences were far less pronounced when comparing their respective *average* cyclical declines of 7%, 10%, 16% and 22%. **This leads to the conclusion that the normal cyclical risks (approximately once every five years) between domestic models are far less than the worst-case risks (approximately once per 35 years) to which they are exposed.**

The duration of declines is remarkably similar from one Domestic Model Portfolio to another. Each domestic model's worst decline lasted 21 months; each model's average decline lasted five or six months. The Conservative and Moderate Portfolios did recover faster to their pre-decline market value. They fully recovered in five and six months respectively, while Aggressive and All-Equity Portfolios took eight months and nine months.

Efficiency Rating. All four Domestic Model Portfolios are very efficient. In this particular respect, they are much more alike than different. The Moderate Model was the most efficient, scoring a 62 efficiency rating, while the Conservative Model was the least efficient, scoring a 58 rating. **The *least* efficient Domestic Model Portfolio has the same efficiency rating (58) as the *most* efficient individual asset class (mid/small cap stocks) in the Inflation Era.**

This is yet another illustration of the magic of rebalancing less-than perfectly correlated asset classes. This may be the one and only free lunch of investing.

Global Portfolios

Second Period of Study (1972-1996)

A second set of structured portfolio designs will now be developed by adding international stocks (in U.S. dollars) and equity REITs to domestic stocks, 5-year Treasury bonds and 30-day T-bills. Although not possessing the very long-term reliable data of the other asset classes, international stocks (U.S. dollars) and REITs were found to be highly efficient asset classes in Chapter 8.

The Global Model Portfolios take further advantage of the lack of correlation between asset classes. A Global Conservative, Global Moderate, Global Aggressive and Global All-Equity Model Portfolio will be constructed. The objective of each global model is to improve on both the risks and rewards of its domestic model counterpart.

Due to the constraints of the available data for equity REITs and international stocks (as discussed in Chapter 8), the period of analysis for Global Model Portfolios will be the 25-year period of 1972 through 1996.

In order to compare the Global Model Portfolios to the Domestic Model Portfolios, the domestic models must first be recomputed for this new time period of analysis. As noted earlier, cross-comparisons between asset classes or portfolios are only valid if comparing the same time periods. Charts S-9 through S-12 in the special burgundy supplement are Historical Risk/Reward charts for the four Domestic Model Portfolios covering this new period of analysis (1972-1996). Chart 10-5 is a summary of the significant data from these charts. Notice that the riskless return from T-bills for the 1972-1996 period is 7.0%, almost one percent higher than the 6.1% riskless return of the 1960-1996 period. Therefore, 7.0% will be the base rate from which rewards are measured in the new period.

Domestic Model Portfolios – Risks, Rewards & Efficiencies – 1972-1996

	Conservative (30-50-20)	Moderate (47-47-6)	Aggressive (70-28-2)	All-Equity (100-0-0)
RETURNS (Annualized)				
Return	10.2%	11.2%	12.3%	13.5%
Riskless Return (T-bills)	-7.0%	-7.0%	-7.0%	-7.0%
REWARD	**3.2%**	**4.2%**	**5.3%**	**6.5%**
RISK				
Worst Decline	10 %	21 %	32 %	46 %
	21 mo.	21 mo.	21 mo.	21 mo.
Average Decline	7 %	10 %	14 %	20 %
	3 mo.	3 mo.	3 mo.	6 mo.
Average Recovery	5 mo.	6 mo.	9 mo.	9 mo.
COMPOSITE RISK SCORE	**46 points**	**61 points**	**79 points**	**102 points**
EFFICIENCY RATING	**70**	**69**	**67**	**64**

CHART 10-5

Chart 10-6 compares the results of the 1960-1996 analysis of the Domestic Model Portfolios with those of the 1972-1996 analysis.

Domestic Model Portfolios
Comparison of 1972-1996 Period with 1960-1996 Period

	Conservative	Moderate	Aggressive	All-Equity
Reward ('72-'96)	3.2%	4.2%	5.3%	6.5%
Reward ('60-'96)	2.8%	3.9%	4.9%	6.1%
Composite Risk ('72-'96)	46	61	79	102
Composite Risk ('60-'96)	48	63	82	104
Efficiency Rating ('72-'96)	70	69	67	64
Efficiency Rating ('60-'96)	58	62	60	59

CHART 10-6

While the risks, rewards and efficiency ratings changed somewhat from the prior period, the relationships *between* models were nearly identical from one period of analysis (1960-1996) to the next (1972-1996) period. This is a valuable confirmation that the Domestic Model Portfolios possess inherently reliable long-term characteristics.

Global Model Portfolios

The guidelines that were established when constructing the Domestic Model Portfolios are equally applicable to the Global Model Portfolios (see page 255). In addition, two new guidelines are appropriate.

- International stocks (in U.S. dollars) may not exceed 25% of the stock portion of any model portfolio.

- REITs may not exceed 5% of any model portfolio (approximately twice their normal weighting in the universe of all domestic stocks).

Many combinations of the seven participating asset classes were tested. Each combination was held constant by rebalancing at the end of each calendar year, selling some of that year's asset class winners and using the proceeds to buy more of that year's asset class losers to bring the portfolio back into alignment with its fixed allocation.

The Very Best Portfolio Designs - Efficiency Ratings

Based on the guidelines set forth, the following four Global Model Portfolios are the most favorable combination of all seven qualifying *efficiently rated* asset classes. One of these model portfolios is the most efficient portfolio design for your Wealth and Retirement Portfolio.

Global Conservative Model Portfolio (30-50-20)

Stocks	30%
Bonds	50%
Cash	20%

Primary Objective: To improve on the Domestic Conservative Model, that is to identify the most favorable combination of the seven efficient asset classes that equals or improves upon *both* the risk and reward of its domestic counterpart.

Performance Comparison:

	Global vs. Domestic	
Reward	3.2%	3.2%
Composite Risk	33	46
Efficiency Rating	97	70

(See Historical Risk/Reward Chart S-13)

Global Moderate Model Portfolio (50-40-10)

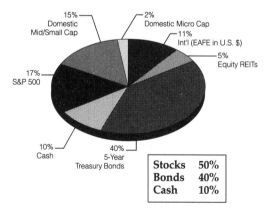

Stocks	50%
Bonds	40%
Cash	10%

Primary Objective: To improve on the Domestic Moderate Model, that is to identify the most favorable combination of the seven efficient asset classes that equals or improves upon *both* the risk and reward of its domestic counterpart.

Performance Comparison:

	Global vs. Domestic	
Reward	4.4%	4.2%
Composite Risk	57	61
Efficiency Rating	77	69

(See Historical Risk/Reward Chart S-14)

Global Aggressive Model Portfolio (70-25-5)

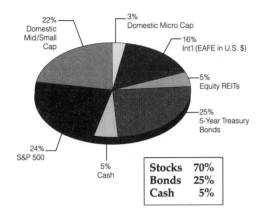

Stocks	70%
Bonds	25%
Cash	5%

Primary Objective: To improve on the Domestic Aggressive Model, that is to identify the most favorable combination of the seven efficient asset classes that equals or improves upon *both* the risk and reward of its domestic counterpart.

Performance Comparison:

	Global vs. Domestic	
Reward	5.4%	5.3%
Composite Risk	74	79
Efficiency Rating	73	67

(See Historical Risk/Reward Chart S-15)

Global All-Equity Model Portfolio (100-0-0)

Stocks	100%
Bonds	0%
Cash	0%

Primary Objective: To improve on the Domestic All-Equity Model, that is to identify the most favorable combination of the seven efficient asset classes that equals or improves upon *both* the risk and reward of its domestic counterpart.

Performance Comparison:

	Global vs. Domestic	
Reward	6.8%	6.5%
Composite Risk	96	102
Efficiency Rating	71	64

(See Historical Risk/Reward Chart S-16)

Global All-Equity Model Portfolio

The Global All-Equity Model is positioned with 76% in U.S. stocks (including a 5% position in equity REITs) and 24% in international stocks. The U.S. stock position (outside of REITs) is weighted identically to the Domestic All-Equity Model.

International stocks at 24% of the Global All-Equity Portfolio are represented by Morgan Stanley's EAFE Index in U.S. dollars. REITs are represented in the model by NAREIT's Equity REIT index.

Additional Correlation Benefits for the Balanced Global Models

For the three balanced Global Portfolio Models, the *free* or enhanced returns from combining these imperfectly correlated asset classes were as follows:

Global Conservative	0.5% Annually
Global Moderate	0.6% Annually
Global Aggressive	0.6% Annually

This is the difference between the actual compounded annual return of these models and simply adding up their individual compounded returns by their weighting within the model portfolio.

Charts S-13 through S-16 in the special burgundy supplement are Historical Risk/Reward charts for the four Global Model Portfolios covering the period 1972-1996. Chart 10-7 is a summary of the significant data from these charts.

Global Model Portfolios – Risks, Rewards & Efficiencies –
1972-1996

	Conservative (30-50-20)	Moderate (50-40-10)	Aggressive (70-25-5)	All-Equity (100-0-0)
REWARD				
Return (Annualized)	10.2%	11.4%	12.4%	13.8%
Riskless Return (T-bills)	-7.0%	-7.0%	-7.0%	-7.0%
REWARD	**3.2%**	**4.4%**	**5.4%**	**6.8%**
RISK				
Worst Decline	10 % 11 mo.	19 % 21 mo.	29 % 21 mo.	42 % 21 mo.
Average Decline	6 % 2 mo.	9 % 3 mo.	13 % 3 mo.	18 % 6 mo.
Average Recovery	4 mo.	5 mo.	8 mo.	9 mo.
COMPOSITE RISK SCORE	**33 points**	**57 points**	**74 points**	**96 points**
EFFICIENCY RATING	**97**	**77**	**73**	**71**

CHART 10-7

Global portfolio designs have *further* lessened the relatively low risk of the Domestic Model Portfolios while delivering the same or greater return. This greater efficiency is illustrated in Chart 10-8 by comparing the performances of the S&P 500, the Global Aggressive Model Portfolio and the Global All-Equity Portfolio in the 1972-1996 period.

Risks, Rewards and Efficiency Rating Highlights - 1972-1996
This accentuates the remarkable results illustrated earlier in this chapter – a much improved combination of risk and reward.

Model	Return	Worst Decline	Average Decline
S&P 500 Index	12.5%	43%	18%
Global Aggressive Model Portfolio	12.4%	29%	13%
Global All-Equity Model Portfolio	13.8%	42%	18%

CHART 10-8

Evaluating the Global Model Portfolios

Rewards, Risks and Efficiency Ratings. The Global Model Portfolios further improved the already outstanding performances of the domestic models.

Comparing the global models to each other, the difference in exposure to average declines is quite mild. The average declines in the global portfolios begin with Conservative at 6%, then move to Moderate at 9%, Aggressive at 13% and All-Equity at 18%. On the other hand, the rewards increase further within the Global Portfolios beginning with a reward of 3.2% for the Global Conservative Model, then moving to 4.4% for Global Moderate, 5.4% for Global Aggressive and 6.8% for Global All-Equity.

The Global Model Portfolios are extremely efficient, even more so than their Domestic Model counterparts. This is due to their lower Composite Risk scores for the same or higher reward. As stated earlier, assembling portfolios of reliable but uncorrelated asset classes improves efficiency ratings and lowers risk. This is the core element of the best and most efficiently rated portfolios.

The Wind at Your Back

Selecting and adhering to one of the most reliable Domestic Model Portfolios or most efficient Global Model Portfolios puts the wind at your back as you sail through the years with your Wealth and Retirement Portfolio. You have channeled all of the best information from the history of investing right into the structure of your portfolio. **You are squeezing a great deal of risk out of your portfolio while weighting the odds heavily in favor of your targeted long-term rate of return.** You also have a powerful ally in that you have a thorough insight into the major risks to which your own portfolio is exposed...*in advance.*

Just how good are the model portfolios? Look again at Charts 10-2 and 10-8. The S&P 500 is rightfully credited with outstanding performance, yet both the domestic and global portfolios with approximately 30% allocated to bonds and cash proved far superior to the S&P 500 over the past 37- and 25-year periods on a risk-adjusted basis. And the Global All-Equity Model provided a significantly higher rate of return than the S&P 500 with identical risk characteristics. **Merely indexing each component of these portfolios means you could outperform the S&P 500!** (Both index mutual funds and managed mutual funds will be evaluated in Section IV.)

This page left intentionally blank.

This page left intentionally blank.

Domestic Conservative Portfolio (30-50-20)
30% Domestic All-Equity – 50% Bonds (5-Yr Treasury) – 20% T-bills
Growth of $100,000
(12/31/71 – 12/31/96)

Year	Jan	Feb	Mar	Apr	May	Jun	Jul	Aug	Sep	Oct	Nov	Dec	Annual Returns
1972	$100,000	↑	↑	↑	↑	+7% 12 mo.		↑	↓	↑	↑	$107,300	7.3
1973					<10%> 21 mo.								-2.8
1974									$96,200	↑	↑	↑	-3.2
1975	↑	↑	↑	↑	↑	↑	↓	↓	↓	↑	↑	↑	19.2
1976	↑	↑	↑	↑	↓	+63% 48 mo.		↑	↑	→	↑	↑	17.6
1977	↑	↓	↑	↑	↑	↑	↓	↓	↑	↓	↑	↑	2.0
1978	↓	↑	↑	↑	↑	↓	↑	↑	$156,900 <5%> 1 mo. ↑		↑		6.2
1979	↑	↓	↑	↑	↑	+17% 15 mo.		↑	↑	↓	↑	↑	12.6
1980	$174,800	<6%> 2 mo.		↑	↑	↑	↑	↓	↑	↑	↑	↑	14.0
1981	↓	↓	↑	↓	↑	↑	↓	↑	↓	↑	↑	↑	7.7
1982	↓	↓	↑	↑	↑	↓	↑	↑	↑	↑	↓	↑	23.8
1983	↑	↑	↑	↑	↑	↑	↓	↑	↑	↓	↑	↓	13.3
1984	↑	↓	↑	↑	↓	+204% 89 mo.		↑	↑	↑	↑	↑	9.7
1985	↑	↓	↑	↑	↑	↑	→	↑	↓	↑	↑	↑	21.2
1986	↑	↑	↑	↑	↑	↑	↓	↑	↓	↑	↓	↓	13.5
1987	↑	↑	↑	↓	↑	↑	↑	$497,700	<10%> 3 mo.	$448,800		↑	3.0
1988	↑	↑	↓	↑	↓	↑	↓	↓	↑	↑	↓	↑	10.2
1989	↑	↓	↑	↑	↑	↑	↑	↓	↑	↑	↑	↑	16.3
1990	↑	↓	↑	↓	↑	↑	↑	↓	↓	↑	↑	↑	3.9
1991	↑	↑	↑	↑	↑	+99% 74 mo.		↑	↑	↑	↓	↑	20.1
1992	↓	↑	↓	↑	↑	↑	↑	↑	↑	↑	↑	↑	8.1
1993	↑	↑	↑	↓	↑	↑	↑	↑	↑	↑	↓	↑	10.3
1994	$894,200	<5%> 5 mo.				$847,200	↑	↑	↓	↑	↓	↑	-1.8
1995	↑	↑	↑	↑	↑	+32% 30 mo.		↑	↑	↑	↑		20.0
1996	↑	↑	↑	↑	↑	↑	↓	↑	↑	↑	↑	$1,120,000	8.2%

Total Return: Includes dividends, interest and capital gains reinvested   **Standard Deviation: 7.5**

↑↓ *Up or Down Month*   ⬤ *Cyclical Declines*   ⬤ *Recovery (to pre-decline level)*   ⬭ *Net New Advancement*

REWARD*

Total Return (1972-1996)	10.2%
Riskless Return (T-bills)	<7.0%>
AVERAGE ANNUAL REWARD OF DOMESTIC CONSERVATIVE PORTFOLIO	3.2%

RISK

Worst Decline	10 % / 21 mo.
Average Decline	7 % / 3 mo.
Average Recovery	5 mo.
COMPOSITE RISK	46 points

EFFICIENCY RATING = 70
(Reward ÷ Composite Risk x 1,000)

*Annualized

CHART S-9

Domestic Moderate Portfolio (47-47-6)
47% Domestic All-Equity – 47% Bonds (5-Yr Treasury) – 6% T-bills
Growth of $100,000
(12/31/71 – 12/31/96)

Year	Jan	Feb	Mar	Apr	May	Jun	Jul	Aug	Sep	Oct	Nov	Dec	Annual Returns
1972	$100,000	↑	↑	↑	↑	+9% 12 mo.		↑	↓	↑	↑	$108,900	8.9
1973					<21%> 21 mo.								-7.6
1974									$86,800	↑	↓	↓	-8.9
1975	↑	↑	↑	↑	↑	↑	↓	↓	↓	↑	↑	↑	26.2
1976	↑	↑	↑	↓	↓	↑	+84% 47 mo.		↑	↓	↑	↑	22.2
1977	↓	↓	↑	↓	↑	↑	↓	↓	↑	↓	↑	↑	1.5
1978	↑	↓	↑	↑	↑	↓	↑	$160,000	<8%> 2 mo.		↑	↑	6.8
1979	↑	↑	↑	↑	↑	+22% 15 mo.		↑	↓	↓	↑	↑	15.8
1980	$181,300	<9%> 2 mo.		↑	↑	↑	↑	↑	↑	↑	↑	↓	17.8
1981	↓	↓	↓	↓	↑	↓	↓	↓	↓	↑	↑	↓	5.2
1982	↓	↓	→	↑	↓	↓	↑	↑	↑	↑	↑	↑	25.5
1983	↑	↑	↑	↑	↑	↑	↓	↑	↑	↓	↑	↓	16.3
1984	↑	↓	↑	↑	↓	+251% 89 mo.		↑	↑	↑	↑	↑	8.3
1985	↑	↓	↑	↑	↑	↑	→	↑	↓	↑	↑	↑	24.9
1986	↓	↑	↑	↑	↓	↑	↓	↑	↓	↑	↑	↓	14.8
1987	↑	↑	↑	↓	↑	↑	↑	$581,300	<16%> 3 mo.	$490,500	↑		2.4
1988	↑	↑	↓	↑	↓	↑	↓	↓	↓	↑	↓	↑	12.5
1989	↑	↓	↑	↑	+42% 31 mo.		↑	↑	↑	↑	↑	↑	19.3
1990	↓	↑	↑	↓	↑	$698,900	<7%> 4 mo.			$649,000	↑	↑	1.1
1991	↑	↑	↑	↑	↑	↓	↑	↑	↑	↑	↓	↑	25.2
1992	↓	↑	↓	↑	↑	↓	↑	↓	↑	↓	↑	↑	9.5
1993	↑	↑	↑	↑	↑	↑	↑	↑	↓	↑	↓	↑	11.9
1994	↑	↓	↓	↓	↑	+120% 74 mo.		↑	↓	↑	↓	↑	-2.3
1995	↑	↑	↑	↑	↑	↑	↑	↑	↑	↓	↑	↑	24.7
1996	↑	↑	↑	↑	↑	↓	↓	↑	↑	↑	↑	$1,431,900	10.8%

Total Return: Includes dividends, interest and capital gains reinvested   **Standard Deviation: 10.1**

↑ ↓ *Up or Down Month*   ⬛ *Cyclical Declines*   ⬤ *Recovery (to pre-decline level)*   ⬭ *Net New Advancement*

REWARD*

Total Return (1972-1996)	11.2%
Riskless Return (T-bills)	<7.0%>
AVERAGE ANNUAL REWARD OF	
DOMESTIC MODERATE PORTFOLIO	4.2%

RISK

Worst Decline	21 % 21 mo.
Average Decline	10 % 3 mo.
Average Recovery	6 mo.
COMPOSITE RISK	61 points

EFFICIENCY RATING = 69
(Reward ÷ Composite Risk x 1,000)

*Annualized

CHART S-10

Domestic Aggressive Portfolio (70-28-2)
70% Domestic All-Equity – 28% Bonds (5-Yr Treasury) – 2% T-bills
Growth of $100,000
(12/31/71 – 12/31/96)

Year	Jan	Feb	Mar	Apr	May	Jun	Jul	Aug	Sep	Oct	Nov	Dec	Annual Returns
1972	$100,000	↑	↑	↑	↑	+11% 12 mo.		↑	↓	↑	↑	$110,800	10.8
1973					<32%> 21 mo.								-13.8
1974									$75,500	↑	↓	↓	-16.2
1975	↑	↑	↑	↑	↑	↑	↓	↓	↓	↑	↑	↓	35.4
1976	↑	↑	↑	↓	↓	↑	↓	↑	↑	↓	↑	↑	27.3
1977	↓	↓	↓	↑	+114% 47 mo.		↓	↓	↑	↓	↑	↑	1.2
1978	↓	↓	↑	↑	↑	↓	↑	$161,900	<11%> 2 mo.		↑	↑	8.2
1979	↑	↓	↑	↑	↓	+31% 15 mo.		↑	↓	↓	↑	↑	21.0
1980	$189,900	<11%> 2 mo.		↓	↑	↑	↑	↑	↑	↑	↑	↓	24.1
1981	↓	↑	↑	↓	↑	↓	↓	↓	↓	↑	↑	↓	2.8
1982	↓	↓	↓	↑	↓	↓	↑	↑	↑	↑	↑	↑	25.0
1983	↑	↑	↑	↑	↑	↑	↑	↑	↑	↓	↑	↓	20.6
1984	↓	↓	↑	↑	↓	+304% 89 mo.		↑	↑	↑	↑	↑	5.7
1985	↑	↑	↑	↓	↑	↑	↑	↓	↑	↑	↑	↑	28.0
1986	↑	↑	↑	↓	↑	↑	↓	↑	↓	↑	↑	↓	15.2
1987	↑	↑	↑	↓	↑	↑	↑	$684,700	<23%> 3 mo.	$529,900	↑		2.0
1988	↑	↑	↓	↑	↓	↑	↓	↓	↑	↑	↓	↑	15.7
1989	↑	↓	↑	↑	+52% 31 mo.		↑	↑	↓	↓	↑	↑	22.5
1990	↓	↑	↑	↓	↑	$807,700	<13%> 4 mo.			$708,300	↑	↑	-3.0
1991	↑	↑	↑	↑	↑	↓	↑	↑	↓	↓	↓	↑	30.7
1992	↑	↑	↓	↑	↑	↓	↑	↓	↑	↑	↑	↑	10.8
1993	↑	↑	↑	↓	↑	↑	↑	↑	↑	↑	↓	↑	12.8
1994	↑	↑	↓	↑	↑	+159% 74 mo.		↑	↓	↑	↓	↑	-1.5
1995	↑	↑	↑	↑	↑	↑	↑	↑	↑	↓	↑	↑	29.3
1996	↑	↑	↑	↑	↑	↓	↓	↑	↑	↑	↑	$1,836,300	14.9%

Total Return: Includes dividends, interest and capital gains reinvested   **Standard Deviation: 13.4**

↑ ↓ *Up or Down Month*   ⬤ *Cyclical Declines*   ⬭ *Recovery (to pre-decline level)*   ⬭ *Net New Advancement*

REWARD*		RISK	
Total Return (1972-1996)	12.3%	Worst Decline	32 % 21 mo.
Riskless Return (T-bills)	<7.0%>	Average Decline	14 % 3 mo.
AVERAGE ANNUAL REWARD OF		Average Recovery	9 mo.
DOMESTIC AGGRESSIVE PORTFOLIO	5.3%	COMPOSITE RISK	79 points

EFFICIENCY RATING = 67
(Reward ÷ Composite Risk x 1,000)

*Annualized

CHART S-11

Domestic All-Equity Portfolio (100-0-0)
100% Stocks (50% S&P 500/45% Mid/Small Cap/5% Micro Cap) – 0% Bonds – 0% T-bills
Growth of $100,000
(12/31/71 – 12/31/96)

Year	Jan	Feb	Mar	Apr	May	Jun	Jul	Aug	Sep	Oct	Nov	Dec	Annual Returns
1972	$100,000	↑	↑	↑	↑	+13% 12 mo.		↑	↓	↑	↑	$113,200	13.2
1973				<45%> 21 mo.									-21.7
1974									$61,800	↑	↓	↓	-25.6
1975	↑	↑	↑	↑	↑	↑	↓	↓	↓	↑	↑	↓	47.2
1976	↑	↑	↑	↓	↓	+158% 47 mo.		↓	↑	↓	↑	↑	33.8
1977	↓	↓	↓	↑	↓	↑	↓	↓	↑	↓	↑	↑	1.1
1978	↓	↓	↑	↑	↑	↓	↑	$159,500	<14%> 2 mo.		↑	↑	10.1
1979	↑	↓	↑	↑	+91% 31 mo.		↑	↑	↑	↑	↑		28.1
1980	↑	↓	↓	↑	↑	↑	↑	↑	↑	↑	↑	↓	32.5
1981	↓	↑	↑	↓	$261,800	<16%> 14 mo.							-0.2
1982		↑		↑		$219,900		↑	↑	↑	↑	↑	23.8
1983	↑	↑	↑	↑	↑	↑	↓	↓	↓	↓	↑	↓	26.2
1984	↓	↓	↑	↑	↓	↑	↓	↑	↓	↓	↓	↑	2.3
1985	↑	↑	↓	↓	↑	+267% 61 mo.		↓	↓	↑	↑	↑	31.6
1986	↑	↑	↑	↓	↑	↑	↓	↑	↓	↑	↑	↓	15.5
1987	↑	↑	↑	↓	↑	↑	↑	$806,100	<30%> 3 mo.	$560,400	↑		1.5
1988	↑	↑	↓	↑	↑	↑	↓	↓	↑	↑	↓	↑	19.7
1989	↑	↓	↑	↑	+67% 30 mo.		↑	↑	↓	↓	↑	↑	26.7
1990	↓	↑	↑	↓	$935,100	<20%> 5 mo.				$752,700	↑	↑	-8.5
1991	↑	↑	↑	↑	↑	↓	↑	↑	↓	↑	↓	↑	37.4
1992	↑	↑	↓	↑	↑	↓	↓	↓	↑	↑	↑	↑	12.5
1993	↑	↓	↑	↓	↑	↑	↑	↑	↑	↑	↓	↑	13.6
1994	↑	↓	↓	↑	↑	+217% 74 mo.		↑	↓	↑	↓	↑	-0.2
1995	↑	↑	↑	↑	↑	↑	↑	↑	↑	↓	↑	↑	35.0
1996	↑	↑	↑	↑	↑	↓	↓	↑	↑	↑	↑	$2,386,000	20.3

Total Return: Includes reinvested dividends and capital gains   **Standard Deviation: 17.9**

↑ ↓ *Up or Down Month*   ▉ *Cyclical Declines*   ▨ *Recovery (to pre-decline level)*   ◯ *Net New Advancement*

REWARD*		RISK	
Total Return (1972-1996)	13.5%	Worst Decline	46 % 21 mo.
Riskless Return (T-bills)	<7.0%>	Average Decline	20 % 6 mo.
AVERAGE ANNUAL REWARD OF		Average Recovery	9 mo.
DOMESTIC ALL-EQUITY PORTFOLIO	6.5%	**COMPOSITE RISK**	102 points

EFFICIENCY RATING = 64
(Reward ÷ Composite Risk x 1,000)

*Annualized

CHART S-12

Global Conservative Portfolio (30-50-20)

30% Stocks* (71% U.S./24% Intl/5% REITs) – 50% Bonds(5-Yr Treasury) – 20% T-bills
Growth of $100,000
(12/31/71 – 12/31/96)

Year	Jan	Feb	Mar	Apr	May	Jun	Jul	Aug	Sep	Oct	Nov	Dec	Annual Returns
1972	$100,000	↑	↑	↑	↑	+10% 22 mo.		↑	↓	↑	↑	↑	8.6
1973	↓	↓	↑	↓	↓	↑	↓	↑	↑	$109,800			-2.0
1974	<10%> 11 mo.			↑					$99,100	↑	↑	↑	-2.8
1975	↑	↑	↑	↑	↑	↑	↓	↓	↓	↑	↑	↑	17.2
1976	↑	↑	↑	↑	↓	↑	↑	↑	↑	↑	↑	↑	16.5
1977	↓	↑	↑	↑	↑	+77% 60 mo.		↑	↑	↓	↑	↑	3.7
1978	↓	↑	↑	↑	↑	↑	↑	↑	↑	↓	↑	↑	7.7
1979	↑	↓	↑	↑	↑	↑	↑	↑	$175,800 <5%> 1 mo.		+7% 3 mo.		11.6
1980	$178,300	<6%> 2 mo.		↑	↑	↑	↑	↑	↓	↓	↑	↑	13.0
1981	↓	↓	↑	↓	↑	↑	↓	↑	↓	↑	↑	↓	7.9
1982	↓	↓	↓	↑	↑	↓	↑	↑	↑	↑	↑	↑	22.1
1983	↑	↑	↑	↑	↑	↑	↓	↑	↑	↑	↑	↑	13.4
1984	↑	↓	↑	↓	+210% 89 mo.		↑	↑	↑	↑	↑	↑	10.9
1985	↑	↓	↑	↑	↑	↑	↑	↑	↑	↑	↑	↑	22.1
1986	↑	↑	↑	↑	↓	↑	↓	↑	↓	↑	↑	↓	17.0
1987	↑	↑	↑	↓	↓	↑	↑	$519,700	<8%> 3 mo.	$480,500	↑		4.2
1988	↑	↑	↓	↑	↓	↑	↑	↓	↑	↑	↓	↑	10.5
1989	↑	↓	↑	↑	↑	+32% 32 mo.		↑	↑	↑	↑	↑	14.4
1990	↓	→	↑	↓	↑	↓	$634,200	<4%> 2 mo.		↑	↑	↑	2.6
1991	↑	↑	↑	↑	↑	↓	↑	↑	↑	↑	↓	↑	18.4
1992	↓	↑	↓	↑	↑	↓	↑	↓	↑	↓	↑	↑	6.6
1993	↑	↑	↑	↑	↓	↑	↑	↑	↑	↑	↓	↑	11.8
1994	↑	↓	↓	↑	↑	+87% 75 mo.		↑	↓	↑	↓	↑	-1.2
1995	↑	↑	↑	↑	↑	↑	↑	↑	↑	↑	↑		17.6
1996	↑	↑	↑	↑	↑	↑	↓	↑	↑	↑	↑	$1,130,400	8.1%

Total Return: Includes dividends, interest and capital gains reinvested **Standard Deviation: 6.9**

U.S. Stocks=Domestic All-Equity Model; International Stocks=MSCI EAFE Index in U.S. $; REITs=NAREIT Equity REIT Index

↑ ↓ *Up or Down Month* ⬤ *Cyclical Declines* ⬤ *Recovery (to pre-decline level)* ⬭ *Net New Advancement*

REWARD**

Total Return (1972-1996)	10.2%	
Riskless Return (T-bills)	<7.0%>	
AVERAGE ANNUAL REWARD OF		
GLOBAL CONSERVATIVE PORTFOLIO	3.2%	

RISK

Worst Decline	10 % 11 mo.
Average Decline	6 % 2 mo.
Average Recovery	4 mo.
COMPOSITE RISK	33 points

EFFICIENCY RATING = 97
(Reward ÷ Composite Risk x 1,000)

**Annualized

CHART S-13

Global Moderate Portfolio (50-40-10)
50% Stocks* (71% U.S./24% Intl/5% REITs) – 40% Bonds (5-Yr Treasury) – 10% T-bills
Growth of $100,000
(12/31/71 – 12/31/96)

Year	Jan	Feb	Mar	Apr	May	Jun	Jul	Aug	Sep	Oct	Nov	Dec	Annual Returns
1972	$100,000	↑	↑	↑	↑	+12% 12 mo.		↑	↓	↑	↑	$111,500	11.5
1973					<19%> 21 mo.								-7.2
1974									$89,900	↑	→	↓	-9.1
1975	↑	↑	↑	↑	↑	↑	↓	↓	↓	↑	↑	↑	24.8
1976	↑	↑	↑	↑	↓	↑	↑	↑	↑	↓	↑	↑	20.0
1977	↓	→	↑	↑	↓	↑	+110% 64 mo.		↓	↓	↑	↑	3.9
1978	↓	↑	↑	↑	↑	↑	↓	↑	↑	↓	↑	↑	9.9
1979	↑	↓	↑	↑	↑	↑	↑	↑	↑	↓	↑	↑	14.7
1980	$188,900	<8%> 2 mo.		↑	↑	+30% 15 mo.		→	↑	↑	↑	↓	17.6
1981	↓	↓	↑	↓	↑	$224,600	<7%> 3 mo.	$209,400		↑	↑	↓	5.4
1982	↓	↓	↓	↑	↓	↑	↑	↑	↑	↑	↑	↑	21.7
1983	↑	↑	↑	↑	↑	↑	↓	↑	↑	↓	↑	↑	17.0
1984	↑	↓	↑	↓	↓	+205% 71 mo.		↑	↑	↑	↑	↑	9.3
1985	↑	→	↑	↑	↑	↑	↑	↑	↓	↑	↑	↑	26.9
1986	↑	↑	↑	↑	↑	↑	↓	↑	↓	↑	↑	↓	20.7
1987	↑	↑	↑	↓	↑	↑	↑	$639,000	<14%> 3 mo.	$552,300		↑	4.8
1988	↑	↑	↑	↑	↓	↑	↓	↓	↑	↑	↓	↑	13.6
1989	↑	↓	↑	↑	+38% 32 mo.		↑	↑	↑	↓	↑	↑	16.8
1990	↓	↓	↓	↓	↑	↑	$763,100	<8%> 2 mo.		↑	↑	↑	-1.6
1991	↑	↑	↑	↑	↑	↓	↑	↑	↑	↑	↓	↑	22.6
1992	↓	↑	↓	↑	↑	↓	↑	↓	↑	↓	↑	↑	6.8
1993	↑	↓	↑	↑	↓	↑	↑	↑	↑	↑	↓	↑	14.1
1994	↑	↓	↓	↑	↑	+112% 75 mo.			↓	↑	↓	↑	-0.7
1995	↑	↑	↑	↑	↑	↑	↑	↑	↑	↑	↑	↓	21.1
1996	↑	↑	↑	↑	↑	↑	↓	↑	↑	↓	↑	$1,485,000	10.7%

Total Return: Includes dividends, interest and capital gains reinvested   **Standard Deviation: 9.5**

U.S. Stocks=Domestic All-Equity Model; International Stocks=MSCI EAFE Index in U.S. $; REITs=NAREIT Equity REIT Index

↑ ↓ *Up or Down Month*   ⬛ *Cyclical Declines*   ⬤ *Recovery (to pre-decline level)*   ⬭ *Net New Advancement*

	REWARD**		**RISK**	
Total Return (1972-1996)	11.4%	Worst Decline	19 % / 21 mo.	
Riskless Return (T-bills)	<7.0%>	Average Decline	9 % / 3 mo.	
AVERAGE ANNUAL REWARD OF		Average Recovery	5 mo.	
GLOBAL MODERATE PORTFOLIO	4.4%	**COMPOSITE RISK**	57 points	

EFFICIENCY RATING = 77
(Reward ÷ Composite Risk x 1,000)

**Annualized

CHART S-14

Global Aggressive Portfolio (70-25-5)
70% Stocks* (71% U.S./24% Intl/5% REITs) – 25% Bonds (5-Yr Treasury)– 5% T-bills
Growth of $100,000
(12/31/71 – 12/31/96)

Year	Jan	Feb	Mar	Apr	May	Jun	Jul	Aug	Sep	Oct	Nov	Dec	Annual Returns
1972	$100,000	↑	↑	+14% 12 mo.		↓	↑	↑	↓	↑	↑	$114,400	14.4
1973				<29%> 21 mo.									-12.2
1974									$81,100	↑	↓	↓	-15.3
1975	↑	↑	↑	↑	↑	↑	↓	↓	↓	↑	↑	↑	32.3
1976	↑	↑	↑	↓	↓	↑	↑	↑	↑	↓	↑	↑	23.0
1977	↓	↓	↑	↑	↓	↑	↓	↑	↓	↓	↑	↑	4.2
1978	↑	↑	↑	↑	↑	+145% 64 mo.		↑	↑	↓	↑	↑	12.2
1979	↑	↓	↑	↑	↓	↑	↑	↑	↑	↓	↑	↑	18.0
1980	$198,400	<10%> 2 mo.		↑	↑	+37% 14 mo.		↑	↑	↑	↑	↓	22.6
1981	↓	↑	↑	↓	$243,700	<9%> 4 mo.			$221,600	↑	↑	↓	3.2
1982	↓	↓	↑	↑	↓	↓	↑	↑	↑	↑	↑	↑	20.3
1983	↑	↑	↑	↑	↑	↑	↓	→	↑	↓	↑	↑	20.6
1984	↑	↓	↑	↓	↓	+244% 71 mo.		↑	↑	↑	↑	↑	7.4
1985	↑	↑	↑	↑	↑	↑	↑	↑	↓	↑	↑	↑	31.1
1986	↑	↑	↑	↑	↑	↑	↓	↑	↓	↑	↑	↑	24.0
1987	↑	↑	↑	↑	↑	↑	↑	$762,800	<19%> 3 mo.	$618,500	↑		5.6
1988	↑	↑	↑	↑	↓	↑	↓	↓	↑	↓	↓	↑	16.8
1989	↑	↓	↑	↑	↑	+44% 31 mo.		↑	↑	↓	↑	↑	18.9
1990	↓	↓	↓	↓	↑	$893,000	<12%> 3 mo. $788,200		↑	↑	↑	↑	-5.8
1991	↑	↑	↑	↑	↑	↑	↑	↑	↑	↑	↓	↑	26.2
1992	↑	↑	↓	↑	↑	↓	↑	↑	↑	↓	↑	↑	6.9
1993	↑	↑	↑	↑	↑	↑	↑	↑	↑	↑	↓	↑	15.9
1994	↑	↓	↓	↑	+137% 75 mo.		↑	↑	↓	↑	↓	↑	0.3
1995	↑	↑	↑	↑	↑	↑	↑	↑	↑	↓	↑	↑	24.2
1996	↑	↑	↑	↑	↑	↓	↓	↑	↑	↑	↑	$1,868,500	13.5%

Total Return: Includes dividends, interest and capital gains reinvested   **Standard Deviation: 12.3**

U.S. Stocks=Domestic All-Equity Model; International Stocks=MSCI EAFE Index in U.S. $; REITs=NAREIT Equity REIT Index

↑ ↓ *Up or Down Month*   ⬤ *Cyclical Declines*   ◖ *Recovery (to pre-decline level)*   ◗ *Net New Advancement*

REWARD**

Total Return (1972-1996)	12.4%
Riskless Return (T-bills)	<7.0%>
AVERAGE ANNUAL REWARD OF	
GLOBAL AGGRESSIVE PORTFOLIO	5.4%

RISK

Worst Decline	29 % / 21 mo.
Average Decline	13 % / 3 mo.
Average Recovery	8 mo.
COMPOSITE RISK	74 points

EFFICIENCY RATING = 73
(Reward ÷ Composite Risk x 1,000)

**Annualized

CHART S-15

Global All-Equity Portfolio (100-0-0)
100% Stocks* (71% U.S./24% Intl/5% REITs) – 0% Bonds – 0% T-bills
Growth of $100,000
(12/31/71 – 12/31/96)

Year	Jan	Feb	Mar	Apr	May	Jun	Jul	Aug	Sep	Oct	Nov	Dec	Annual Returns
1972	$100,000	↑	↑	↑	↑	+19% 12 mo.		↑	↓	↑	↑	$118,800	18.8
1973		↑		<42%> 21 mo.									-19.6
1974									$68,500	↑	↓	↑	-24.6
1975	↑	↑	↑	↑	↑	↑	↓	↓	↓	↑	↑	↑	43.4
1976	↑	↑	↑	↓	↓	↑	↓	↓	↑	↓	↑	↑	27.4
1977	↓	↓	↑	↑	↓	+204% 64 mo.		↑	↓	↓	↑	↑	4.8
1978	↓	↑	↑	↑	↑	↑	↓	↑	↑	↓	↓	↑	15.9
1979	↑	↓		↑	↓	↑	↑	↑	↑	↓	↑	↑	23.2
1980	$208,400	<13%> 2 mo.		↑	↑	↑	+47% 13 mo.		↑	↑	↑	↓	30.2
1981	↓	↑	↑	$268,500	<15%> 15 mo.								-0.1
1982						$228,000	↑	↑	↑	↑	↑	↑	17.8
1983	↑	↑	↑	↑	↑	↑	↓	↓	↑	↓	↑	↑	26.0
1984	↑	↓	↑	↓	↓	↑	↓	↑	↑	↑	↓	↑	4.5
1985	↑	↑	↑	↓	↑	+317% 61 mo.		↑	↓	↑	↑	↑	37.0
1986	↑	↑	↑	↑	↑	↑	↓	↑	↓	↑	↑	↓	28.8
1987	↑	↑	↑	↑	↑	↑	↑	$951,700 <26%> 3 mo.		$706,100	↑		6.9
1988	↑	↑	↑	↑	↓	↑	↑	↓	↑	↑	↓	↑	21.6
1989	↑	↓	↑	+55% 30 mo.		↓	↑	↑	↑	↓	↑	↑	22.0
1990	↓	↓	↓	↓	$1,095,300	<18%> 4 mo.			$895,100	↑	↑	↑	-12.3
1991	↑	↑	↑	↑	↑	↓	↑	↑	↑	↑	↓	↑	31.4
1992	↑	↑	↓	↑	↑	↓	↑	↓	↑	↑	↑	↑	6.8
1993	↑	↑	↑	↑	↑	+179% 75 mo.		↑	↓	↑	↓	↑	18.6
1994	↑	↓	↓	↑	↑	↓	↑	↑	↓	↑	↓	↑	2.0
1995	↑	↑	↑	↑	↑	↑	↑	↑	↑	↓	↑	↑	28.4
1996	↑	↑	↑	↑	↑	↓	↓	↑	↑	↑	↑	$2,495,300	17.7%

Total Return: Includes reinvested dividends and capital gains   **Standard Deviation: 16.6**

U.S. Stocks=Domestic All-Equity Model; International Stocks=MSCI EAFE Index in U.S. $; REITs=NAREIT Equity REIT Index

↑ ↓ Up or Down Month   ⬛ Cyclical Declines   ⬤ Recovery (to pre-decline level)   ⬭ Net New Advancement

REWARD**		RISK	
Total Return (1972-1996)	13.8%	Worst Decline	42 % 21 mo.
Riskless Return (T-bills)	<7.0%>	Average Decline	18 % 6 mo.
AVERAGE ANNUAL REWARD OF		Average Recovery	9 mo.
GLOBAL ALL-EQUITY PORTFOLIO	6.8%	**COMPOSITE RISK**	96 points

EFFICIENCY RATING = 71
(Reward ÷ Composite Risk x 1,000)

**Annualized

CHART S-16

11

The Ultimate Test: The Great Depression

How would the Domestic Model Portfolios described in Chapter 10 perform in the event of a market crash or economic downturn of the magnitude of the Great Depression? Say you invested at the top of the market in 1929. You were convinced of the logic of maintaining a disciplined strategy, so you stayed the course with your chosen portfolio design (Domestic Model Portfolio) throughout the Great Depression. What then? Each Domestic Model Portfolio's performance is examined in both nominal and real U.S. dollars through the full market cycle from 1929 through 1937 with interesting and counter-intuitive results.

"In the main, therefore, slumps are experiences to be lived through... with as much equanimity and patience as possible."
— John Maynard Keynes (1938)

What is your greatest *fear* when it comes to your investments? For many investors, a possible replay of the Great Depression tops the list.

Investing a Million Before the Crash

Assume you inherit $1,000,000 in August 1929. The feel-good era of the Roaring '20s is still going strong. The U.S. has blossomed in the post-War years, and there is a general sense of pride in American industry—its strength and potential. Stock market investors in the U.S. are euphoric after years of sensational returns. The stocks leading the market are not speculative, they are industry leaders: Radio Corp. (RCA), General Electric, American Telephone, General Motors and United States Steel. These companies seemed irrevocably poised to deliver on America's bright promise.

Without hesitation, you invest your new wealth following the criteria of one of the Domestic Model Portfolios presented in Chapter 10. Unknowingly, you have just invested 100% of your portfolio at the very top of a major bull market! Disaster strikes with the stock market crash of October 1929, followed by the worst bear market of this century. A horrifying and debilitating period of relentlessly declining stock prices unfolds (see Chart 11-1).

Fortunately, you have a comprehensive understanding of portfolio designs. You stay the course and rebalance your stock, bond and cash allocations at the end of each calendar year to bring them back into alignment with your portfolio design. It certainly isn't easy; the gloom and doomers are out in force (as usual), and the voice of calm reason is scoffed at and even ridiculed. Yet you stick to your guns....How bad is it? What happens to your $1,000,000? Did you blow your inheritance?

A Complete Market Cycle

☞ The proper way to measure your results is over a full market cycle. Far too many market evaluations are hopelessly biased by either their starting date or ending date or both. The history of the U.S.

stock market is one of sustained overall upward progress in market prices, which unfolds in periods of general advancement (bull markets), punctuated by sharp setbacks (bear markets). The only fair evaluation of the stock market over spans of less than 15 to 20 years is to both begin and end at the exact same point in the market cycle. In other words, it makes the most sense to measure performance from one bull market peak to the next or one bear market trough to the following one.

As you entered the markets at the very peak in stock prices (September 1, 1929), the fair evaluation of your results would include the entire bear market (through June 1932) and the complete bull market that follows (through February 1937)—one full market cycle.

The Great Depression Market Cycle
(August 1929 through February 1937)
Annual Returns* from Stocks, Bonds, Cash and Inflation

Year	Inflation/ <Deflation>	U.S. Treasury Bills	U.S. 5-Year Treasury Bonds	Large Cap Stocks	Mid/ Small Cap Stocks	Micro Cap Stocks
1929**	-0.9%	1.6%	3.8%	-31.2%	-33.9%	-47.0%
1930	-6.0	2.4	6.7	-24.9	-35.2	-38.1
1931	-9.5	1.1	-2.3	-43.3	-46.5	-49.7
1932	-10.3	1.0	8.8	-8.2	-6.0	-5.4
1933	0.5	0.3	1.8	54.0	107.0	142.4
1934	2.0	0.2	9.0	-1.4	12.3	24.2
1935	3.0	0.2	7.0	47.7	43.8	40.2
1936	1.2	0.2	3.1	33.9	38.6	64.7
1937***	1.0	0.0	-0.2	5.9	8.2	20.1

Sources: © Computed using data from Stocks, Bonds, Bills & Inflation 1996 Yearbook™ with data updated January 1997, Ibbotson Associates, Chicago; Center for Research in Security Prices (CRSP) University of Chicago

* Total returns include interest, dividends and capital gains or losses.
** September through December
*** January through February

CHART 11-1

Historical Note:

The bull market of the 1920s peaked in August 1929. The worst bear market of this century began in earnest with the infamous crash of October that same year. It was not straight down as there were substantial rallies to the upside along the way. The market finally bottomed in the summer of 1932. From that very low point, the stock market turned around and began one of its most rewarding bull markets. This bull market experienced several steep setbacks on its way to a peak in February 1937.

In Chart 11-2 the progress of the four Domestic Model Portfolios is followed on a year-by-year basis from the very top of the Roaring '20s bull market, through the devastation of the Great Depression's vicious bear market and on through the completion of the awesome bull market that peaked in February 1937. This is one complete market cycle. Each domestic model begins with $1,000,000 as of September 1, 1929. Returns are reflected on both a nominal basis (what shows up on your brokerage statement) and on a real return basis (the change in your wealth).

Domestic Model Portfolios in the Great Depression
(September 1929 through February 1937)
$1,000,000 Portfolio: Change in Value Over the Market Cycle**

End of Year	Value of Sept. '29 U.S. $*	CONSERVATIVE (30-50-20)		MODERATE (47-47-6)		AGGRESSIVE (70-28-2)		ALL-EQUITY (100-0-0)	
		Nominal U.S. $	Real* U.S. $	Nominal U.S. $	Real* U.S. $	Nominal U.S. $	Real* U.S. $	Nominal $	Real* U.S. $
1929[†]	1.01	922,000	931,000	863,000	872,000	778,000	786,000	668,000	675,000
1930	1.07	875,000	936,000	769,000	823,000	629,000	673,000	466,000	499,000
1931	1.19	748,000	890,000	598,000	712,000	426,000	507,000	256,000	305,000
1932	1.33	767,000	1,020,000	603,000	802,000	416,000	553,000	238,000	317,000
1933	1.32	963,000	1,271,000	842,000	1,111,000	658,000	868,000	434,000	573,000
1934	1.30	1,024,000	1,331,000	901,000	1,171,000	702,000	913,000	460,000	598,000
1935	1.26	1,200,000	1,512,000	1,124,000	1,416,000	940,000	1,184,000	669,000	843,000
1936	1.24	1,354,000	1,679,000	1,339,000	1,660,000	1,195,000	1,482,000	921,000	1,142,000
1937[††]	1.23	1,384,000	1,702,000	1,386,000	1,705,000	1,258,000	1,547,000	991,000	1,219,000
Avg. Annual Returns:		4.4%	7.3%	4.4%	7.4%	3.1%	6.0%	-0.1%	2.7%
For Comparison: Returns from 1960-1996		8.9%	4.2%	10.0%	5.3%	11.0%	6.3%	12.2%	7.5%

* *Reflects Deflation/Inflation of Period*

** *Rebalanced Annually Utilizing Data from Chart 11-1*

[†] *September through December*

[††] *January and February*

Source: © *Computed using data from* Stocks, Bonds, Bills & Inflation 1996 Yearbook™ *with data updated January 1997, Ibbotson Associates, Chicago; Center for Research in Security Prices (CRSP) University of Chicago*

CHART 11–2

Deflation's Effect

There is one other factor that has an unusual bearing on this particular market cycle. As was discussed in Chapter 4, the bear market of September 1929 through the end of 1932 is perhaps as noteworthy for its sustained **deflation** as for its falling stock prices.

Deflation is the opposite of inflation, i.e. the value or purchasing power of a dollar goes *up*, not down. Take a close look at Chart 11-1. The deflation from August 1929 to the end of 1932 added one-third to the purchasing power of every U.S. dollar. In isolation, this is a wonderful experience. Unfortunately, the accompanying economic conditions that bring about and sustain a period of deflation are not pleasant at all. (Just look at Japan's experience with deflation in the early to mid-1990s to see that this is still true.)

As was also discussed in Chapter 4, *real* returns, those adjusted for a change in the value of the currency unit, are much more important than nominal returns as far as measuring increases or decreases in wealth. It is the purchasing power of your portfolio you wish to increase. The same principle applies during this unusual period of deflation. The real return (buying power) is still more important than the nominal return. However, for deflation, returns are adjusted upward to reflect the increased purchasing power of the U.S. dollar.

Moderate (Domestic) Portfolio Design: Step-By-Step

Assume your chosen portfolio design was **47% domestic stocks** (24% large cap, 21% mid/small cap and 2% micro cap), **47% bonds** (5-year U.S. treasuries) and **6% cash** (30-day T-bills) — the Domestic Moderate Model. Let's see how you navigated the full Great Depression cycle that unfolded after you invested your $1,000,000. The bottom-line results are shown in Chart 11-2 along with those of the other portfolio designs. [To see how these results were actually developed, Chart A11-1 on page 257 in the Appendix provides a detailed presentation of the year-by-year gains and losses of each asset class, as well as the year-end rebalancing to maintain the portfolio design.]

Starting with $1,000,000 at the beginning of September 1929, your Moderate Model Portfolio falls to $863,000 in just four months (a loss of almost 14% during the crash). In 1930, your portfolio falls to $769,000 — about 23% below where it was just 16 months before. The year 1931 is worse still; your rebalanced portfolio declines to $598,000 by year-end — down almost 40% from your original $1,000,000 in nominal terms. The vicious bear market reaches its low point at the end of May 1932. Your moderate portfolio is valued at $486,000, more than 51% below its beginning value. By the end of 1932, the bull market of 1932-1937 has begun, and your account is back up above where it began the year.

 Good news! (And you need it.) The value of the U.S. dollar has experienced a substantial bull market. The number on your year-end 1932 brokerage statement — $603,000 — will actually purchase in goods and services what $802,000 would have purchased in August 1929. Therefore, the real value of your portfolio has declined only a little over 19%.

The bull market for stocks, which began in the summer of 1932, now begins to significantly improve the numbers on your brokerage statement. By the end of 1933, your portfolio is up to $842,000, while your wealth (purchasing power) now exceeds that of your original inheritance. The year 1934 sees further improvement, and 1935 is a truly banner year. Even your brokerage statement now shows your account to be above your initial investment. The year 1936 and the first two months of 1937 provide more big returns for your portfolio. By the end of February 1937, your brokerage statement reads $1,386,000…a 38% nominal gain from September 1929.

Taking into consideration the deflation/inflation for the entire 7½-year cycle, your wealth in August 1929 dollars stands at $1,705,000 — a 70% real gain — or 7.4% compounded annually! In an inflationary environment similar to the 1990s, it would take a 10.5% compounded annual return to produce this result. (This adds a 3.1% inflation rate to the 7.4% real return). This outcome is probably much better than most people would believe possible for the market cycle that included the worst stock market conditions of this century.

Observations and Lessons

Economic Tragedy

The Great Depression was the worst economic period of this century. The financial dislocations reached much further and deeper than the stock market alone. Joblessness reached 25 percent. The size of the American economy shrunk by *one-third*. Much of the confidence in the new American dream of perpetual prosperity was greatly eroded.

There is no one source to blame for a tragedy of such immense proportions. The relatively new Federal Reserve made serious mistakes, both in the boom period of the late 1920s and in the first few years of the Depression (shrinking the money supply by over 30%). Congress thought it could dictate trade rules to the world (Smoot-Hawley Tariff). The unsupervised stock market (the Securities and Exchange Commission and the National Association of Securities Dealers did not yet exist) encouraged highly speculative commodities-style stock trading. Stocks could be bought with as little as 10% of the purchase price paid in cash (margin) and 90% borrowed from the broker. Therefore, a minimal 10% decline in the value of a stock would force additional principal to be paid in (margin call) or the whole position would be lost. Thankfully, much has changed since that unfortunate period in U.S. history.[17]

Stock Market Lessons

For long-term investors (as opposed to speculators or traders), the stock market's ebb and flow in this period should provide important lessons and confirmations.

> **Bull markets**, no matter how apparently sound the underpinnings, no matter how good the economic conditions, are followed by bear markets.

Bear markets, no matter how pernicious the economic conditions, no matter how deep the damage, are followed by bull markets.

There are no guarantees. Even a full market cycle does not guarantee that stocks will always be the best portfolio investment. It takes a period of 20 years for history to prove stocks are *always* the better investment over bonds and cash.

Do not buy stocks on margin. Buying stocks on margin leaves you vulnerable to complete loss during periods of major market declines. It robs you of your ability to stay the course with your plan.

Stocks were truly devastated by the bear market of 1929-1932. Even the following bull market (1932-1937) did not quite restore the full loss in nominal dollars. Fortunately, this was a one-of-a-kind event so far in this century.

Balanced Portfolio Designs....More Magic

The conventional wisdom is that the Great Depression virtually wiped out all investors and that there was no clear path to avoid the destruction in paper assets. This leaves many investors with a deep-seated, gripping fear of a repeat of 1929. The facts from the full period paint a somewhat different picture. The balanced portfolio designs performed remarkably well in the full market cycle and, if applied at the time, would have successfully dampened the volatility of stocks during this worst-of-its-kind period. In fact, the 4.4% average annual nominal returns from both the Conservative and Moderate Models were substantially better than the 0.9% average annual riskless return from T-bills and not too much below the 5.0% annual return from 5-year U.S. Treasury bonds. Even the Aggressive Portfolio's 3.1% average annual return was substantially better than that of cash. Balanced portfolios more than held their own—even in the worst market cycle of the modern financial era.

☞ This performance from balanced portfolio designs is one of the least known attributes of investment history. Balanced portfolios have wonderful risk-squelching characteristics that can serve the long-term investor.

12

The Right Portfolio
For You

The model portfolio designs in Chapter 10 provide a wide cross-section of risks and rewards. One of those models is likely a sound choice to serve as the fundamental structure of your Wealth and Retirement Portfolio. You may already know which one is right for you. If you are uncertain as to a choice, there are three very important factors to consider: your personal financial situation, your likely reaction to market setbacks of varying intensity and the specific time horizon over which your investment portfolio will be held.

"Know thyself"
— Socrates

Before You Finalize Your Selection of a Portfolio Design

As stated in the introduction, this is not a book about financial planning, as important as that area is. Therefore, you need to undertake the following, either by yourself or with the help of a financial planning expert.

- **Analyze your financial situation.** Put your Wealth and Retirement Portfolio on paper (or on computer).

- **Determine your major financial objectives.** Partial or full retirement? Early or later retirement? The idea is to estimate how many years of growth and new investment you anticipate versus the number of years you will be taking an income from your Wealth and Retirement Portfolio.

- **Prepare a retirement budget.** A realistic projection of your expenses that provides for your basic needs and a separate calculation of the non-essentials that will make your retirement enjoyable.

Charts A1-1 through A1-6 in the Appendix (pages 240-245) will help you evaluate the other side of your ledger—the maximum sustainable income that your current portfolio and your current percentage of compensation set aside into 401(k)-type programs will provide you during retirement. These charts illustrate varying average annual returns on your investments. Determine the retirement income that is possible from the portfolio designs you are considering. This may influence your commitment to additional savings as well as your selection of a portfolio design.

Before you finalize the critical decision as to which portfolio design is most appropriate for your Wealth and Retirement Portfolio, take the following into consideration:

- **Diversification.** The model portfolios set forth in Chapter 10 assume broad diversification within each stock asset class. However, your particular portfolio may not make this possible. For example, you may have a substantial commitment to your company's stock. A single stock has an undiversifiable risk that results from factors unique to a particular company. You may want to reduce risks in the balance of your portfolio to offset any such unavoidable and unique risks.

- **Income.** Once your Wealth and Retirement Portfolio begins to distribute income for your retirement, a greater prudence must be taken in implementing your portfolio design.

  As will be discussed thoroughly in Chapter 13, the maximum level of income you can take from your retirement portfolio—as a percentage of the portfolio—is subject to several assumptions including market conditions.

Simple "Formulas" That Don't Work

Regrettably, there is no black box we can plug some numbers into and produce the right portfolio design for you. One-size-fits-all formulas should be ignored.

For instance, one such formula in the popular media is to establish a portfolio in which the percentage allocated to bonds is equal to your current age, with the balance to be put in stocks. This implies that it is appropriate for every 40-year-old to hold 40% in bonds. And, likewise, that every 60-year-old should allocate 60% to bonds.

Such a naïve formula would result in substantial and needless opportunity loss in wealth or retirement income for most of its followers.

For those 40-year-olds and even 60-year-olds who understand and accept market fluctuations, both emotionally and intellectually, the much higher long-term returns of Aggressive or All-Equity Model Portfolios may be more appropriate choices for many years to come in their lives.

After all, 40-year-olds should be building retirement portfolios planned to last for 50 years! This combines their remaining wealth building years (before retirement) and income distribution years (after retirement). And those who are 60 years of age should plan for a time horizon of 30 years for their retirement portfolios.

The Voice of Experience

And what about Phil Carret? This legendary investor turned age 100 in November 1996. He is truly the most experienced investment manager in America. He started the Pioneer Mutual Fund in 1928 and has managed client funds ever since—from the 1929 crash to the 1987 crash and every bull and bear market in between.

In his 55-year tenure as manager of the Pioneer Fund, a $10,000 investment in the fund would have grown to $28.3 million. By contrast, the same investment in the Dow Jones Industrial Average would have grown to only $3.8 million. (This record inspired market wizard Warren Buffett to praise Carret as having "the best long-term investment record of anyone in America.") Should Carret avoid stocks altogether because of his age? Let's hear what he had to say at age 98 on "Wall $treet Week With Louis Rukeyser," April 28, 1995.

> RUKEYSER: "What would be your (portfolio design) advice to some kid of, say, 65?"
>
> CARRET: "Buy 30% bonds and 70% common stocks." (Basically, the Aggressive Model Portfolios—domestic and global.)
>
> RUKEYSER: "And that would be the same (advice for someone of age) 75 and 85?
>
> CARRET: "Same thing."

☞ This has been a winning portfolio design for Carret *because* of his personal comfort with its risks and rewards. Even at age 100, he is not tempted to change a portfolio design that works for him. This is the level of commitment to a portfolio design to which every long-term investor should aspire.

Where is Your Threshold of Pain?

A basic premise of this book is that the more prepared you are for the inevitable setbacks that are cooked-in-the-mix of your portfolio design, the less likely you will be foiled by the great enemy of long-term investment success — fear.

> "Fear leads to panic, panic breeds the inability to distinguish between temporary declines and permanent losses. That, in turn, leads to the well-documented propensity of investors to be massive sellers of good investments near market bottoms.
>
> "Success is purely a function of two things: (1) recognition of the inevitability of major market declines; and (2) emotional/behavioral preparation to regard such declines as…non-events…"
>
> — *Nick Murray, Investment Advisor magazine, April, 1996*

Not every investor has the same threshold for pain. To some investors, a 10% decline in their Wealth and Retirement Portfolio is extremely painful—prepared or not. Others, once prepared, can treat 25% declines as non-events.

Where do you fit? Numbers on a page have a way of appealing to your left brain, your intelligence. If they appeal to your emotions at all, it is usually to the other emotion that drives investment decisions — greed.

Right (Brain) Choice

Right now, you need to fully activate your right brain, your feelings. Call up any of your investment fears.

Select the portfolio design that you think most closely matches your financial facts and objectives or is simply your intuitive choice. Open this book to that portfolio design's Historical Risk/Reward chart in the special burgundy supplement at the end of Chapter 10. Look at the setbacks that this portfolio has incurred on its way to delivering its long-term return. Your Wealth and Retirement Portfolio will more than likely last that many years—and randomly incur setbacks of that same magnitude.

How will you feel when these losses unfold over periods of up to 22 months in your Wealth and Retirement Portfolio? Stomach-turning reactions are normal. As Richard Thaler, the economist at the University of Chicago, has pointed out, "Losing $100 hurts about twice as much as winning $100 gives you pleasure." Could this feeling induce fear or panic that will cause you to take actions that are inappropriate for your long-term success?

"Successful investment management depends to a large extent on the emotional stability of the individual, particularly during periods of strain and stress, and on his ability to overcome the severe psychological hurdles present during crucial periods." —*Ragnar D. Naess, Readings in Financial Analysis and Investment Management*, 1963

Many financial plans are foiled by poor emotional planning. Don't let your plan be overturned during the next stressful market period. Choose a portfolio design you can truly live with through all its inherent ups and downs.

Time Horizon

It has been stressed that the principles of this book only apply to long-term portfolios, i.e. portfolios expected to see you throughout your retirement and perhaps to be left to your heirs. Not knowing how long your needs for retirement income will last, plan on your portfolio providing an inflation adjusted income well beyond the life expectancy of you and your spouse. Therefore, if you or your spouse are under 65 years of age, your Wealth and Retirement Portfolio is definitely long-term.

If you are older than 65 or are planning for a portfolio that will last less than 20 years, you should take into consideration the full range of possible returns from your selected portfolio design for the time period you have allocated.

The rewards for each model portfolio discussed in Chapter 10 are the historic averages toward which each model has gravitated over long time periods. However, the shorter the time period being evaluated, the higher the variance in average annual returns. This variance is highlighted in Charts 12-1 through 12-4 which illustrate the range of average annual returns from the domestic model portfolios for all 5-year, 10-year, 15-year and 20-year periods within the Inflation Era. A review of these charts offers the following insights for those whose investment time horizons better fit one of these time periods.

How Long is Your Investment Horizon?

5-Year Total Return Comparisons
Rolling 5-year periods – 1/1/60 – 12/31/96
(1/1/60 – 12/31/64; 1/1/61 – 12/31/65; etc.)

All Equity   Conservative
Aggressive   US Treasury Bills
Moderate

1960   1965   1970   1975   1980   1985   1990
1964   1969   1974   1979   1984   1989   1994

Each point on this graph represents the start of a 5-year investment period. The first point (1960-1964) is the 5-year total return (annualized) for each portfolio beginning 1/1/60.

CHART 12-1

- **5-Year Investment Horizon.** Each domestic model portfolio has provided a wide range of annualized returns over 5-year periods. The Conservative Model has provided average annual returns from as low as 4% to as high as 16% for the 32 5-year periods beginning with 1960. The range of annualized returns for 5-year periods from the other domestic model portfolios are as follows: 2% to 17% for Moderate, -1% to 18% for Aggressive and -4% to 20% for All-Equity. As you can see, there is nothing predictable in such a short investment period.

  Another way of looking at a 5-year horizon may be summed up by the question, "How often and by how much did each domestic model portfolio underperform the riskless return of cash equivalents (30-day U.S. Treasury bills)?" (The return from Treasury bills is included on each of these four charts.) Whereas each model portfolio underperformed Treasury bills in either four or five of the 32 5-year periods shown, the degree of underperformance is quite different among the four models. For *any* 5-year period in the Inflation Era, the maximum annualized percentage return *under* that of U.S. Treasury bills for the Conservative Model is only 1% annualized. By contrast, the Moderate Model has underperformed U.S. Treasury bills by as much as 4% per year in a 5-year period, while the Aggressive Model has underperformed cash by as much as 6% per year and the All-Equity Model by a whopping 10% per year.

With a 5-year time horizon, the Conservative Model is the only acceptable choice for a portfolio design. It provides both a low risk of underperforming cash (four periods out of 32) and a low degree of underperformance during such periods. Yet, on average, the Conservative Model has outperformed Treasury bills by an average of 3% over all 5-year periods.

Each of the other model portfolios should be approached much more cautiously for such a short investment horizon as five years. Although the risk of underperformance may be low, the degree of underperformance is substantial and may jeopardize the achievement of the goal for which the money is invested.

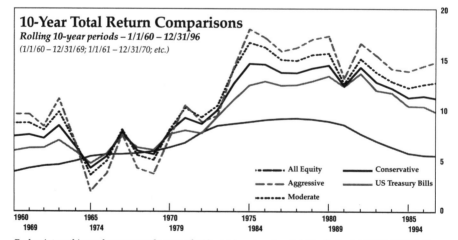

10-Year Total Return Comparisons
Rolling 10-year periods – 1/1/60 – 12/31/96
(1/1/60 – 12/31/69; 1/1/61 – 12/31/70; etc.)

All Equity   Conservative
Aggressive   US Treasury Bills
Moderate

Each point on this graph represents the start of a 10-year investment period. The first point (1960-1969) is the 10-year total return (annualized) for each portfolio beginning 1/1/60.

CHART 12-2

- **10-Year Investment Horizon.** The range of returns over the 28 10-year periods reflected on Chart 12-2 is still quite significant for the four domestic model portfolios. The Conservative Model ranges from a low 10-year return of 4% to a high of 14%, not that much different from its range of 5-year returns. The Moderate Model's 10-year average annual returns range from a low of 4% to a high of 16%. The Aggressive Model ranges from 3% to 17%, and All-Equity has a range of 2% to 18%. The most noticeable improvement at a 10-year time horizon over that of a 5-year horizon is the progressively better low-end of the range of returns as one moves from Conservative to All-Equity. The worst 10-year average annual return from an All-Equity Model (+2%) is a full 6% better than its worst average annual 5-year return (-4%). Yet the Conservative Model maintains the same worst-case return for both 5-year and 10-year periods at 4% annualized.

  As for the degree of underperforming cash, the Conservative Model just barely underperforms Treasury bills in two of the 28 10-year periods. The Moderate Model underperforms Treasury bills by as much as 1% per year in only one 10-year period. Even the Aggressive Model underperforms Treasury bills by more than 1% per year in only one 10-year period. By contrast, the All-Equity Model substantially underperforms cash in four 10-year periods, the worst being a full 3% average annual underperformance. (So much for stocks always being the best investment in a 10-year period.)

  Therefore, with a 10-year time horizon, it appears that either the Conservative or Moderate Model are quite acceptable and the additional risk of an Aggressive Model would not likely discourage investors who would normally choose the Aggressive Model based on all the other factors in their decision. On the other hand, the All-Equity Model in a 10-year time horizon carries substantial risk of underperforming Treasury bills and by a margin great enough to jeopardize the goals set for the portfolio based on a minimum return of at least that provided by cash equivalents.

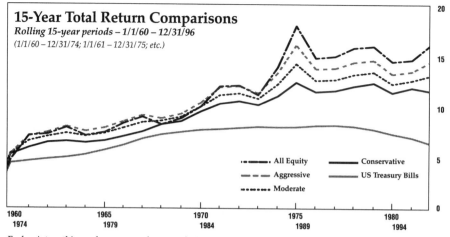

Each point on this graph represents the start of a 15-year investment period. The first point (1960-1974) is the 15-year total return (annualized) for each portfolio beginning 1/1/60.

CHART 12-3

- **15-Year Time Horizon.** The graph of 15-year returns (Chart 12-3) begins to smooth out considerably compared to the five-year and 10-year charts of annualized returns. Yet there is still a considerable range in the average 15-year returns delivered by each domestic model portfolio. The Conservative Model produces average annual returns over 15-year periods of between 5.5% at the low end and 11.5% at the high end. The range for the Moderate Model is between 5.5% and 14.0%. For the Aggressive Model it is between 5.5% and 16.0%, and for All-Equity the range is from 5.0% to 18.0%.

Fifteen years turns out to be a significant time horizon in two respects. All four domestic models outperform U.S. Treasury bills in each of the 23 15-year periods shown. In addition, at 15 years, the Aggressive Model always outperformed the Moderate Model, which in turn always outperformed the Conservative Model. However, the same cannot be said of the All-Equity Model whose 15-year rate of return dipped below that of the Aggressive Model—and even the Moderate Model—for extended periods.

 Whereas any of the four domestic models are acceptable with a 15-year investment horizon, the Aggressive portfolio appears to be a better choice than All-Equity.

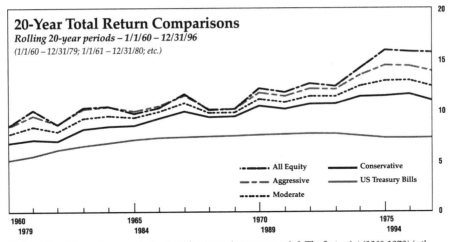

Each point on this graph represents the start of a 20-year investment period. The first point (1960-1979) is the 20-year total return (annualized) for each portfolio beginning 1/1/60.

CHART 12-4

- **20-Year Time Horizon.** Contrasting Chart 12-4 with the other three charts demonstrates why this book has chosen a 20-year time horizon or greater as the appropriate time horizon for long-term portfolios. By 20 years, the returns from the various model portfolios have flattened out considerably. And yet, there is still a fairly significant range of average annual returns for even the 20-year periods. If this is your time horizon, it may be wise to consider the *lowest* 20-year average return when doing your own planning.

 When planning for time periods of less than 20 years, perhaps a variation in an old saying is appropriate, "Plan for the worst, expect the average." In other words, you may want to prepare two retirement income calculations, one utilizing the long-term average annual rate of return from Chapter 10 and one utilizing the worst-case scenario as indicated by the bottom portion of the range for the time period nearest your end use of the funds within the portfolio.

13

Maximizing Your Retirement Income

How much income can your portfolio reasonably provide throughout your retirement? This is a critically important question to be able to answer *before* you begin taking out income. Certain choices will have a dramatic affect on the answer. Do you wish to leave a legacy to your heirs? Do you want to fully or partially increase your income to reflect changes in the cost of living? You should also take into consideration factors over which you have no control but still may significantly influence the amount that your portfolio can distribute during your full retirement. One such factor is the unfolding of worst-case market conditions early in your retirement. This chapter will explore the impact of each of these choices and factors on the four Domestic Model Portfolios.

"Nine-tenths of wisdom is being wise in time."
— Theodore Roosevelt

No Room for Error

Many retirees face the financial side of their retirement with an understandable touch of fear. Before retiring, employment income paid the bills. Investments were for the future, and there was time to make up for any mistakes. Suddenly, it's very different.

One of the biggest challenges for those contemplating retirement is to determine how much income they can comfortably take out of their portfolio. While there is no precise answer, a realistic approximation is far better than no estimate at all.

Four Considerations in Calculating Retirement Income

There are four major considerations in determining the maximum amount of income your retirement portfolio can provide.

- Your portfolio's expected long-term rate of return;

- The appropriate adjustment to your retirement income for inflation;

- Your intention with regard to maintaining or depleting the principal of your retirement portfolio; and

- Your life expectancy (or how long your portfolio will provide an income).

Notice that your expenses or spending level are not considered here. Although your retirement spending level is a critical, separate variable, it really does not influence what a portfolio *can* pay out over its full term.

Assumptions for Each Model Portfolio

In order to calculate the maximum percentage of income that each model portfolio could pay out annually during retirement, the following assumptions are made.

Expected Returns and Inflation. Both the performance of the model portfolios and the Consumer Price Index (CPI) in the Inflation Era (1960-1996) will form the basis of this study.

Life Expectancy. Each model portfolio is assumed to provide income for 30 years. (This is well beyond the average number of years a retiree takes income out of his/her portfolio.)

Principal: Maintain or Deplete. Each model portfolio is looked at both ways. A *Legacy Portfolio* in which principal is more or less maintained intact (adjusted for inflation) is presented, as well as a *Spendthrift Portfolio* (Spending My Children's Inheritance) in which principal is used to enhance income over 30 years before being depleted.

Based on these assumptions, Chart 13-1 below shows the maximum percentage that each model portfolio could pay out as retirement income and still satisfy all of the assumptions above. (Charts A13-1 through A13-8 in the Appendix illustrate the year-by-year calculations and results for the Domestic Moderate Model Portfolio that are summarized within this chapter.) Real returns for any long period of time are likely to approximate those of the Inflation Era, therefore these percentages of distributable income are likely appropriate for your own future planning.

Maximum Retirement Income – Full CPI Adjustment

Retirement income, once set, adjusts annually by the full change in CPI.

Domestic Model Portfolios	Spendthrift Portfolio (30 Years' Income)	Legacy Portfolio (Perpetual Income)
Conservative (30-50-20)	4.9%	3.2%
Moderate (47-47-6)	5.4%	3.9%
Aggressive (70-28-2)	6.0%	4.6%
All-Equity (100-0-0)	6.5%	5.3%

CHART 13-1

Example: A new retiree that has selected a Moderate (Domestic) portfolio design for her Wealth and Retirement Portfolio of $500,000 could take an income of $27,000 in her first year of retirement (500,000 x 5.4%) and adjust this income upward by the full change in the CPI index for 30 years before her principal is depleted. Or, she could take an income of $19,500 in her first year of retirement ($500,000 x 3.9%) and adjust this income upward by the full change in the CPI index in perpetuity. Under this last scenario, the full inflation-adjusted value of the $500,000 portfolio would be more or less maintained indefinitely.

Your Inflation Rate

Suppose you want a higher level of income from your portfolio than that shown by the model closest to your own portfolio design in Chart 13-1. One obvious choice would be to adopt a higher returning model for your retirement portfolio.

Another change of assumptions that may be appropriate is in the inflation adjustment. It is quite possible that the pay-out from your Wealth and Retirement Portfolio will not require an automatic raise by the full percentage increase in the CPI each year. Some of your expenses may be fixed, some may be stable, some may decline as your retirement unfolds. Obviously, you will gauge your actual expenses and raise your income accordingly. Perhaps your own personal inflation rate may only be two-thirds of the general rate *as registered by the CPI statistic.*

In addition, the CPI itself has come under criticism by noted economists; and even Alan Greenspan, the Chairman of the Federal Reserve, stated in testimony to congress in August 1996, "The (CPI) statistic is but an imprecise statistical proxy for inflation." He is also on record as stating that the reported CPI may overstate inflation by a full percentage point—about one-third of the projected 3.1% inflation rate. Therefore, estimating your personal inflation rate at two-thirds of the CPI rate may better recognize the U.S. economy's true rate of inflation and particularly your own.

Therefore, for each of the stated objectives above, a second set of maximum retirement incomes have been calculated assuming your retirement income need only increase at 67% of reported CPI. These numbers are reflected in Chart 13-2.

Maximum Retirement Income – Two-Thirds CPI Adjustment
Retirement income, once set, adjusts annually by two-thirds of the change in CPI.

Domestic Model Portfolios	Spendthrift Portfolio (30 Years' Income)	Legacy Portfolio (Perpetual Income)
Conservative (30-50-20)	5.8%	4.6%
Moderate (47-47-6)	6.4%	5.3%
Aggressive (70-28-2)	7.0%	6.0%
All-Equity (100-0-0)	7.5%	6.7%

CHART 13-2

For any Spendthrift Model Portfolio, this particular change in your long-term planning allows for a one percentage increase in the initial pay-out from your portfolio at retirement because you will not need as large an investment to maintain your living standard over 30 years. In our prior example, the new retiree with a portfolio of $500,000 can add $5,000 to her beginning income at retirement (from $27,000 to $32,000) if she adjusts this higher initial income by only two-thirds of the CPI index annually. However, she will want to carefully monitor her actual increase in expense level and determine if it is indeed only two-thirds of reported CPI over a reasonable period.

Worst-Case Market Conditions

One other consideration needs to be addressed. As pointed out, the calculations in this chapter follow the thesis presented in Chapter 4 that the year 1960 is perhaps the best representative year for beginning a long-term market analysis, i.e. normal market conditions relative to the 1990s. But what if it isn't?

A search of the data reveals that 1968 was the worst year to begin retirement in the Inflation Era. Not only was the stock market beginning one of its worst six-year periods ever, but inflation was just starting a long, dramatic rise. The impact of retiring at just the wrong time is calculated for each model portfolio in Chart 13-3. Like Chart 13-2, this chart assumes retirement income is adjusted by two-thirds of the annual change in CPI.

Maximum Retirement Income – Worst-Case Initial Market Conditions

Retirement income, beginning in the worst market conditions of the Inflation Era, adjusts annually by two-thirds of the change in CPI.

Domestic Model Portfolios	Spendthrift Portfolio (30 Years' Income)	Legacy Portfolio (Perpetual Income)
Conservative (30-50-20)	5.5%	4.5%
Moderate (47-47-6)	5.7%	4.9%
Aggressive (70-28-2)	5.7%	5.0%
All-Equity (100-0-0)	5.5%	5.0%

CHART 13-3

Comparing Chart 13-3 with Chart 13-2 vividly demonstrates the impact of *initial* market conditions on the amount of income a portfolio can afford to pay-out. Keep in mind that both sets of portfolios in these two charts experienced the poor market conditions of 1968-1974. The difference is that those portfolios in Chart 13-3 *began* with them.

Also notice the unevenness of the effect on the four model portfolios. As with Chapter 11's discussion of portfolios in the Great Depression, the less growth-oriented the portfolio design (percentage of stocks), the less damage inflicted by worst-case market conditions—inflationary or deflationary. For example, the Conservative Model's maximum pay-out was only reduced by three-tenths of one percent (5.8%→5.5%), while the All-Equity model suffered a full two percent reduction (7.5%→5.5%).

Considering the Choices

There is a good deal of information within this chapter that can help anyone in formulating their plans for retirement.

Model Portfolio Choice. These charts provide valuable additional input in choosing a model portfolio to emulate during retirement. Under normal market conditions, looking from one model portfolio to the next (as measured by a higher percentage dedicated to stocks) adds between 10% to 20% to your sustainable retirement income.

Inflation Adjustment. Planning for a retirement income that fully adjusts for annual changes in CPI has a big price tag. It may be worth it, but perhaps it isn't. In the 1960-1996 period and likely in any future period, adjusting your retirement income by 67% of the annual change in CPI (instead of 100%) allows for between 15% and 30% higher initial retirement income.

Legacy or Spendthrift. This decision has a substantial effect on your retirement income. For those who wish to leave an estate behind approximately equal to the real value of their portfolio at retirement, the reduction in the maximum retirement income that could be paid out in the 1960-1996 period was between 35% (from 4.9% to 3.2% in a Conservative Model Portfolio) and 18% (from 6.5% to 5.3% in an All-Equity Model Portfolio). This is also a likely consequence going forward.

Market Conditions. Market conditions are a more troubling topic. Certainly those who retired in 1968 did not know at the time that they were looking down a double-barreled shotgun of much higher inflation and extremely poor market performance for the next six years (as a whole). Those 1968 retirees, who were anticipating a continuance of market conditions similar to 1960, would face some unhappy choices if they paid out the maximum retirement income allowed by more normal market conditions. They would run out of retirement income well short of the 30 years anticipated.

The impact of poor market conditions diminishes the further in the future they unfold. The retirees of 1960 also experienced the 1968-1974 bear market and accelerating inflation of that period, yet were much less affected.

The best advice is **be prepared**. Know your worst-case scenario and be prepared to live within it. If extremely poor market conditions do unfold early in your retirement, you will be glad you were ready.

Section IV

Three Portfolio Strategies:
Executing Your Portfolio Design

Overview
of Section IV

You now have the most important piece of your investment gameplan in place—you have a **Portfolio Design** for your entire Wealth and Retirement Portfolio. This is the most reliable and/or efficient portfolio that will deliver your targeted rate of return.

Whereas your portfolio design provides the structure for your portfolio, you still need to choose a comprehensive strategy to implement it. The three primary strategies discussed in this Section are:

- *Passive Strategy* - employing index mutual funds (the most certain strategy of precisely fulfilling your portfolio design)

- *Active Strategy* - employing various *styles* of actively managed mutual funds (the most challenging yet potentially rewarding strategy) and

- *Managed Account Strategy* - employing your own money manager (the most disciplined strategy, removing emotionally motivated decisions).

Index funds need to be fully understood as to the exact asset class or combination of asset classes they are attempting to capture. Actively managed mutual funds need to be understood in terms of their ability to add value to the asset class(es) in which they invest. Money managers need to be evaluated on a host of important criteria to make sure they are both professionally competent and *right for you.*

14

The Certainty of Index Funds

Investing through mutual funds that hold a broad selection of almost all securities in an asset class, such as the S&P 500 Index, is the most certain strategy for meeting the results anticipated in the model portfolios. Index funds are designed to track an entire asset class. Offering low fees, index funds are suitable for individuals with limited investment time or interest who still want to assure the average return of their selected portfolio design. The appropriate combination of index funds also provides an excellent gauge or "benchmark" for the performance of any portfolio.

*"Simplicity or singleness of approach is a greatly
underestimated factor of market success."*
— Garfield Drew, <u>New Methods of
Profit in the Stock Market</u> (1941)

Simple and Certain Strategy

The simplest and most certain way to put your portfolio design in action is with **index mutual funds** of the asset classes that are included in your portfolio design. Indexing, or *passive* management, virtually guarantees that you will achieve results that closely parallel those of the portfolio design you have chosen as the years are tacked on in the future.

It's that simple! Whether your retirement portfolio is $10,000 or $10,000,000, you can put it all into index mutual funds allocated according to your chosen portfolio design and be done with it (except for annual rebalancing). You have achieved broad diversification within each of your chosen asset classes.

Is an index fund strategy right for you? Your orientation toward investing is the main determinant. A general profile of a good candidate for an index fund strategy is shown below:

Issues to Consider	Candidate for Index Fund Strategy
Time for Investments	"I want to spend as little time on my investments as possible."
Interest Level in Investing	"Investments are boring."
Stress Level	"Uncertainties of investing are stressful."
Goals for Investment Performance	"Capturing market returns with normal ups and downs is okay with me."
Attitude Toward Fees	"I don't like paying any more in fees than I absolutely have to."

CHART 14-1

If you choose this elegantly simple strategy of capturing average returns and average setbacks, you will never suffer below average performance! You will have completely harnessed the full long-term predictability of your portfolio design.

Benchmark Portfolio

☞ This leads into one of the most important observations of this book. Any other strategy you employ should add value to the performance of a pure index approach, otherwise, *What's the Point?!*

Therefore, if you do *not* choose to use an index fund strategy, assemble it on paper anyway. This will be your own benchmark to gauge the performance of your actual Wealth and Retirement Portfolio. (Benchmark portfolios for the portfolio designs developed in Chapter 10 are shown in Chart 14-2 utilizing Vanguard Index Funds.)

Your Benchmark Portfolio is now the track that your portfolio is following and attempting to improve upon. **It is the only valid yardstick by which to measure your Wealth and Retirement Portfolio's performance.** Every time you compute the total return of your portfolio, also compute the return over the same period for your benchmark portfolio. Compare the two. How are you doing? Now you know for sure. No wishful thinking. No inappropriate yardsticks.

Right and Wrong Yardsticks

Applying the wrong yardstick to portfolio performance is very common among individual investors and professionals alike.

By far the most common mis-measuring tool is the Dow Jones Industrial Average ("Dow"). When virtually anyone asks, "How did the market do today?" the appropriate response is the gain or loss in the Dow that day. In other words, the performance of the Giant Cap component (just 30 very large cap stocks) of the total domestic stock market is the expected answer.

This may seem innocent enough because everyone knows what is meant. Perhaps it would be safe if this were the end of it. Unfortunately, this is just the beginning, for the very next question is, "How are you doing vs. 'the market'?" This pits your portfolio's performance against that of the Dow.

Benchmark Portfolios - Using Vanguard Index Funds

Domestic Conservative (30-50-20)

15%	S&P 500 Trust
15%	Extended Market
50%	Intermediate-Term Treasury Bond
20%	Money Market
100%	Total Portfolio

Domestic Aggressive (70-28-2)

35%	S&P 500 Trust
35%	Extended Market
28%	Intermediate-Term Treasury Bond
2%	Money Market
100%	Total Portfolio

Domestic Moderate (47-47-6)

24%	S&P 500 Trust
23%	Extended Market
47%	Intermediate-Term Treasury Bond
6%	Money Market
100%	Total Portfolio

Domestic All Equity (100-0-0)

50%	S&P 500 Trust
50%	Extended Market
100%	Total Portfolio

Global Conservative (30-50-20)

10%	S&P 500 Trust
9%	Extended Market
6%	Total International
5%	REIT
50%	Intermediate-Term Treasury Bond
20%	Money Market
100%	Total Portfolio

Domestic Aggressive (70-25-5)

25%	S&P 500 Trust
24%	Extended Market
16%	Total International
5%	REIT
25%	Intermediate-Term Treasury Bond
5%	Money Market
100%	Total Portfolio

Global Moderate (50-40-10)

17%	S&P 500 Trust
17%	Extended Market
11%	Total International
5%	REIT
40%	Intermediate-Term Treasury Bond
10%	Money Market
100%	Total Portfolio

Global All Equity (100-0-0)

36%	S&P 500 Trust
35%	Extended Market
24%	Total International
5%	REIT
100%	Total Portfolio

CHART 14-2

Definitions – Chart 14-2

Vanguard 500 Index. This fund seeks investment results that correspond with the price and yield performance of the S&P 500 index, the most commonly used proxy for domestic large cap stocks. Similar S&P 500 index funds are widely available from mutual fund providers such as **Charles Schwab & Company, Inc., Fidelity, Dreyfus, Stagecoach** and many others.

Vanguard Extended Market Index. This fund seeks to replicate the performance of the Wilshire 4500 Index. Basically, this fund captures the performance of the entire mid/small cap and micro cap asset classes. (If overweighting the micro cap asset class is desired, Dimensional Fund Advisors' 9-10 Fund is the best representative index fund.)

Vanguard Total International Index. This fund seeks a broad balance of international equities designed to track the performance of the Morgan Stanley EAFE Index, including approximately 15% in Emerging Markets.

Note: For investors desiring a more conservative index to international equity markets, the **Schwab International Index** is a good alternative. In lieu of country weightings, the Schwab International Index fund primarily invests in the 350 largest companies outside of the U.S.

Vanguard Intermediate-Term U.S. Treasury. This managed fund invests exclusively in U.S. government securities and ordinarily maintains a weighted maturity of between five and ten years. An alternative fund that comes even closer to the 5-Year U.S. Treasury bond index used in this book is the **Dreyfus 100% U.S. Treasury Intermediate Term** fund.

Vanguard REIT Index. This index fund seeks to replicate the performance of the Morgan Stanley Equity REIT index (excluding healthcare properties). This index has closely paralleled the NAREIT equity index over its short existence.

This is appropriate only if your portfolio design (or the stocks portion thereof) is made up of but one asset class—the giant Dow stocks. With any other portfolio design, such a comparison is apples to oranges. Using the wrong yardstick leads to the wrong conclusions about your portfolio's performance and soon may lead you to make changes within your portfolio that are completely uncalled for.

S&P 500 Index Vs. General Equity Funds

An index—or index fund—is nothing more, nothing less than an average for the asset class being indexed. Can average be *better* than average? This question may sound nonsensical; yet, the S&P 500 Index is frequently touted (in the mid-1990s) as superior to 70-80% of all actively managed general equity mutual funds.

One obvious problem with such a comparison is that most mutual fund portfolio managers do not invest exclusively in domestic large cap stocks and many do not use the S&P 500 as their portfolio's benchmark (target asset class).

Many general equity mutual funds today invest in a range of equity asset classes including mid cap, small cap and micro cap stocks, as well as domestic large cap stocks. Many of these funds also establish a small commitment to foreign stocks and REITs. Therefore, if the S&P 500 is outperforming more than 50% of managed domestic stock portfolios, it is likely that the domestic large cap asset class is simply the best performing asset class for the period used for comparison.

And this was the case in the mid-1990s. As pointed out in Chapter 4, the bull market of 1982-1996+ has been led by domestic large cap stocks—those that dominate the S&P 500. This asset class outperformed the other three domestic asset classes and international stocks (disregarding currency effects) and REITs. **The average of the best performing asset class (whichever one it is for the time period being measured) will *always* outperform most money managers or mutual funds.**

A comparison of the S&P 500 Index with the average performance of all general equity funds for the full Inflation Era (1960-1996+) paints a truer picture. During that time period, there were periods when each one did far better than the other. However, in the end, each one's outperformance periods were canceled out by its underperformance periods. And, as might have been expected, the S&P 500 *average* just about equaled the equity fund *average* (Chart 14-3). There is no implicit guarantee that either is a better long-term choice based on performance alone.

Gus Sauter, principal at the Vanguard Group and manager of all the company's index funds had this to say in the February 18, 1997, issue of <u>Financial World</u> magazine, "Markets are a zero sum game. All investors are the market and by definition half will outperform and half will underperform—before fees. Once fees are added to the equation, the marginal outperformers will fall below average."

Your Domestic Stocks Can Beat the S&P 500 Index

Do you want 95% certainty that the domestic stocks portion of your Wealth and Retirement Portfolio will beat the S&P 500? Easy. Utilize only micro cap stocks in your portfolio design. Micro cap stocks have outperformed large cap stocks (S&P 500) in 48 out of a possible 51 20-year time periods since 1926 and hold a 2.0% annualized advantage for the whole time period (1926-1996).

Average performance for the micro cap asset class is easily attainable for many investors. DFA's Small 9-10 Fund is the micro cap asset class (since 1981) as used by Ibbotson Associates in their SBBI Yearbook. Before you opt for this solution, however, be sure to study the fluctuation pattern of micro caps in their Historical Risk/Reward [Chart A5-4 (1960-1996) and Chart S-4 (1972-1996) in the special supplement] and pay particular attention to their degree of temporary losses during setbacks. Micro cap stocks have been very volatile, which would make a portfolio comprised of only these very small stocks difficult to live with over time. (See pages 31 through 34 for more information on micro cap stocks.) *Either the Domestic All-Equity Model Portfolio or the Global All-Equity Model Portfolio has been a far less-risky choice for outperforming the mighty S&P 500.*

Mutual Fund Managers Versus S&P 500

Calendar Year	General Equity Funds (%)	S&P 500 Reinvested (%)
1996	19.5	23.1
1995	31.3	37.5
1994	-1.4	1.3
1993	13.0	10.1
1992	9.1	7.6
1991	35.9	30.4
1990	-6.0	-3.1
1989	24.9	31.6
1988	15.4	16.6
1987	0.9	5.2
1986	14.4	18.7
1985	28.1	31.7
1984	-1.2	6.3
1983	21.6	22.6
1982	26.0	21.6
1981	-0.6	-4.9
1980	34.8	32.5
1979	29.5	18.6
1978	11.9	6.6
1977	2.5	-7.1
1976	26.7	23.9
1975	35.0	37.2
1974	-24.2	-26.5
1973	-22.3	-14.7
1972	13.2	19.0
1971	21.3	14.3
1970	-7.2	3.9
1969	-13.0	-8.4
1968	18.1	11.0
1967	37.2	23.9
1966	-4.9	-10.0
1965	23.3	12.5
1964	14.3	16.5
1963	19.2	22.8
1962	-13.6	-8.7
1961	25.9	26.9
1960	3.6	0.5

AVERAGE ANNUAL RETURN PERFORMANCE (%)
1960-96   11.0%   11.1%

Source: Lipper Analytical Services, Inc.

CHART 14-3

Bottom Line

An index fund strategy is perfect for the investor who is interested in a simple, yet certain, method of capturing the average returns—and accepting the average setbacks—of his/her portfolio design. An added plus is the minimum amount of time required to maintain an index portfolio. Just don't be deceived into believing that an index strategy is better than average.

In fact, when viewed from the perspective of indexes other than the S&P 500 Index, the more appropriate question may be, "Can average be *worse* than average?" While mutual funds that specialize in domestic large cap stocks have in fact had difficulty in outperforming the S&P 500 (recently), there has been no such difficulty in virtually any other equity asset class.

Studies conducted by Morningstar Mutual Funds have found that actively managed mutual funds that target the other domestic equity asset classes or the broad based EAFE international stock index have enjoyed significantly better average performance than the indexes or comparable index funds. Figures from Lipper Analytical back this up: 74 percent of actively managed small-company funds beat their benchmark—the Russell 2000 Index—for the 10 years ended December 1996. In the international arena, 70 percent of actively managed funds beat the EAFE international index over the past five years.[18]

The capitalization weighted Vanguard Extended Market Index Fund, which invests in all U.S. companies except the S&P 500, is an ideal index of domestic mid/small and micro cap asset classes combined. This index has never (in the nine years of its existence through 1996) scored in the top 25% of Morningstar's Small Company Universe, and only twice has it been in the top half.

These time periods of comparison are too short to be conclusive. Until proved otherwise, it is best to assume that a stock index or equity index fund provides no more, no less than the average returns with the average setbacks of the underlying assets in that class and that half of all actively managed funds will improve on this average and half will underperform over long time periods.

Bond Indexing

Index mutual funds are also available to match various bond indexes prepared by Lehman Brothers, Merrill Lynch, Salomon Brothers and other Wall Street firms. Included in the diverse group of bond index funds are specific offerings that target a "constant maturity" U.S. Treasury bond.

Bond index funds are perhaps even more appropriate than equity index funds for the predictable portfolios developed with this book. Bonds offer fewer options to fund managers for "adding value" than do stocks, particularly in U.S. Treasury bonds of intermediate maturity. Therefore, the low level of fees within bond index funds (about one-fourth of broad-based bond funds) are more likely to impact final performance. The results appear to verify this observation. "Mutual funds linked to bond indexes have outperformed at least two-thirds of comparable non-indexed funds in seven of the last eight years."[19]

Other Attributes of Index Funds

Index funds are passively managed and, therefore, do not need the breadth and depth of personnel that actively managed funds require to be competitive. This shows up in much lower fund management fees. Trading securities is held to a minimum so brokerage costs are also held down. The total cost differential between an index fund and an actively managed fund can easily run between 0.5% and 1.0% per year. This is a head start with which index funds begin each year.

The lower fee structure of index funds provides a definite advantage to their long-term reward. Offsetting this reward advantage is the somewhat higher risk that index funds sport relative to the average managed fund. This is primarily due to the fully invested nature of index funds through all market declines.

Some comparisons also attribute tax savings to index funds in taxable accounts. This is due to their low turnover of securities creating little in the way of capital gains. However, recent studies, including one conducted by the <u>No-Load Fund Analyst</u> in 1995, have raised clouds over this issue, and many actively managed funds that produced superior returns to index funds have actually distributed less in taxable gains and dividends.

Asset Class Rotating

The index fund strategy for managing a portfolio is an ideal extension of the structured portfolio design developed in Chapters 9 and 10. Implementing a structured portfolio design with index funds offers market certainty, low costs and fees and the possibility of an average or lower tax bite.

These attributes of an index strategy disappear if you attempt to achieve short-term advantages by rotating among the asset classes. This adds an element of market timing even if the broad portfolio design is maintained.

This is not just a subtle change or enhancement; it is an entirely different strategy. The enforced discipline of rebalancing is rendered moot. As Gus Sauter was quoted as saying, "(Asset class) rotating is like betting, pure and simple. It's silly to choose a strategy that guarantees market returns and then use it in a way that risks (opportunity) loss."

Conclusion

Implementing your investment strategy with index mutual funds is the most reliable way to achieve your portfolio design's performance. From a long-term perspective, this is your most predictable portfolio.

15

Managed Funds: Adding Value to Your Portfolio Design

Like many investors, you may be invigorated by the challenge of outperforming the index averages. Assembling a portfolio of mutual funds with superior managers at the helm offers the potential of higher returns and/or lower risk than that of your benchmark (index) portfolio. This chapter lays out a unique approach to evaluating fund managers so as to identify those few who have demonstrated success at consistently outperforming the average returns for their asset class.

"It is impossible to produce superior performance unless you do something different from the majority."
— Sir John Templeton

Actively Managed Mutual Funds

The prior chapter examined a portfolio strategy built around the advantages and long-term predictability of index mutual funds. As pointed out, if index funds are not employed directly, every investor and investment professional should establish and monitor a benchmark portfolio of index funds that best fits his/her portfolio design. Your benchmark portfolio will be the guiding light—the appropriate yardstick—for your personal Wealth and Retirement Portfolio.

This chapter will focus on adding value to your benchmark portfolio with actively managed mutual funds. These mutual funds rely on the judgment of their portfolio manager to attempt to *improve on the performance of the asset class* or asset classes they are targeting. As with the index fund strategy, it is your orientation toward investing that should help guide your decision. Before taking on the challenge of active management, consider the following:

Issues to Consider	*Candidate for Active Management Strategy*
Time for Investments	"My schedule affords ample time for researching, evaluating and selecting investments."
Interest Level in Investing	"Investing is fun, interesting, challenging."
Stress Level	"Being totally at the mercy of the market (in index funds) is stressful."
Goals for Investment Performance	"I want to try to beat my benchmark"; AND/OR "I want benchmark returns with less fluctuation in values."
Attitude Toward Fees	"Risk and returns are far more important than fees."

CHART 15-1

Of course, there is nothing wrong with building a portfolio of mutual funds that includes both index funds and actively managed funds. Many investors and professionals alike choose to index their large cap stock position with an S&P 500 Index Fund, but choose to actively manage their allocations to all other equity asset classes, reasoning that there is more opportunity in mid/small, micro cap or international funds for individual judgment on stock selection to pay off.

Random Walk

In the previous chapter, it was pointed out that domestic large cap stocks have been the best performing asset class since the early 1980s. Because of this, the primary index of large cap stocks — the S&P 500 Index — has outperformed the majority of general equity mutual funds, as would be expected. Unfortunately, many industry observers have confused the performance of the large cap *asset class* with the performance of *passive* or *index investing*. Thus, passive management has been given undeserved credit for being able to outperform the average actively managed general U.S. stock fund. As was shown in Chapter 14, only domestic large cap funds had difficulty outperforming the S&P 500. Other domestic equity fund managers found it easier to outperform index funds for their asset classes.

Yet, the success of the S&P 500 Index for so many years has given renewed credence to the original theory that led to the development of index funds — the "efficient market theory" popularized by Burton Malkiel in his now famous A Random Walk Down Wall Street in 1973.

This theory suggests that neither a person nor a system of stock selection can consistently beat random selection of stocks over time. The foundation for this theory is that all public knowledge is instantaneously known by market participants and immediately reflected in equity prices, i.e. no one can know more than the all-knowing market. To its logical conclusion, random walk means that *every* fully invested portfolio of large cap stocks, for example, would eventually gravitate to the large cap market average, less fees and costs.

Common Sense Prevails

Until very recently, random walk was becoming entrenched as accepted wisdom, yet it defies common sense. It's as if Warren Buffett, Michael Price, Ben Graham, Ralph Wanger, Shelby Davis, Peter Lynch and all the other long-term "winners" never lived! Individual investment managers have indeed outperformed the market averages over very long time periods!

Recent exhaustive research has proved that superior *methods* of stock selection have consistently outperformed their target asset class.

A landmark study conducted by professors Eugene Fama and Kenneth French of the University of Chicago scrutinized the performance of 2,000 stocks from 1941 to 1990. Whereas efficient market theory suggests that no criterion of stock selection (other than market capitalization and volatility) would accurately predict *future* performance, the Fama/French study published in the Journal of Finance (June 1992) found that selection criteria such as the current market price of a stock as a multiple of its book value did in fact predict *future* performance.

Just as impressive is James O'Shaughnessy's study of every stock in Standard & Poor's (S&P) database from 1954 through 1994 as published in What Works on Wall Street (McGraw Hill, 1996). In his study, O'Shaughnessy pitted 40 combinations of selection criteria, i.e. *methods* of stock selection, against the S&P 500 Index and against a universe of all stocks for that 40-year period.

What Works on Wall Street, as its preface notes, "is the first all-inclusive, definitive guide to the long-term efficacy of Wall Street's favorite strategies." Using vast computer power and a method devoid of outside influences, O'Shaughnessy tested these 40 well-known strategies for returns, risk (standard deviations and Sharpe ratios) and consistency of performance. The result: "Forty years of data prove that the market follows a purposeful stride, not a random walk. The stock market consistently rewards some strategies and consistently punishes others."

☞ Active management employing disciplined strategies can add value to the relevant combination of indexes and, as importantly, can do so with *less risk* than that of a comparable index. Better still, certain methods of adding value to index performance are predictable!

Superior Mutual Fund Managers

Now that the air has been let out of the efficient market theory, it should be pointed out that there is some validity to the theory with regard to actively managed mutual funds. Among all mutual funds, there is an observable gravitation toward the mean (average). Perhaps the theory could be restated as follows:

> Most mutual funds and other managed portfolios will trend toward the average performance of the asset classes they are employing. Winners in one period may lose in the next—or just win with less margin over average. From the other side, losers in one time period may win in the next— or just lose with less margin. Over many time periods, perhaps 80% of mutual funds will cluster around the average; *less than* 10% will be persistent winners and *more than* 10% will be consistent losers.

This really should come as no great surprise. Money management is as fiercely competitive as professional sports. There are few— very few—who possess the remarkable talent, the work ethic and discipline to stand out like Michael Jordan, Martina Navratilova, Carl Lewis or Jack Nicklaus have in their respective professions over long careers.

Managing a Portfolio of Mutual Funds

The conclusion of these studies and of those cited in Chapter 14 is that a small proportion of actively managed mutual funds will consistently add value to the average or index returns of the asset class within which they invest. The key word is *consistently*. Anyone can look at one-year, three-year and five-year performance charts and point out those mutual funds that beat their relevant index. But without consistency it has questionable meaning with regard to predicting *future* superior performance.

As a long-term investor in actively managed mutual funds, you want a selection criteria that identifies one or two mutual fund managers that are more likely than not to outperform the asset class they are filling within your Wealth and Retirement Portfolio...over the long haul.

Put simply, can *you* identify such consistent, long-term, superior mutual fund managers? And, once identified, can you stay with them? The second question will be dealt with in Chapter 17. The first question is the subject of the balance of this chapter. Before addressing the question directly, there is one other characteristic of equity mutual funds with which you need to be aware.

Your Stock Fund Has Style

Benjamin Graham is known today as the father of value investing. This is a *style* of investing characterized by the goal of buying out-of-favor individual stocks for less than a third-party buyer would pay for the whole company or for less than the cash-out value of the company if it were liquidated.

Graham's credentials are impeccable. He wrote the bible of investment evaluation technique for professionals in 1934, Security Analysis. He also wrote what is still among the best investment books for individuals, The Intelligent Investor (1973). His personal and professional investment track record is among the very best of this century and perhaps the best of the Deflation Era.

T. Rowe Price is thought by many students of 20th century investing to be the father of growth investing. This is the *style* of investing noted by its attachment to the stocks of companies well-positioned for long-term growth of revenues and earnings.

Price wrote some of the most insightful pieces ever written on investing and broad economic trends, including a series of articles written for Barron's in 1939 entitled "Picking Growth Stocks." More than anyone else, he influenced investors to look beyond the balance sheet and toward the future and the positioning of each company for sustainable growth. His personal investment record and that of the mutual funds he founded are a testament to his successful methods.

Growth Vs. Value

The two schools of investing have spawned the so-called growth-versus-value debate. There are many dimensions to this debate that have ramifications for your mutual fund evaluation, selection and performance measurement.

☞ As this book takes a long-term focus, it should be stated quite clearly that this debate has no winner...or loser. When applied consistently, investing techniques based on both philosophies have produced superior results. In other words, superior mutual fund managers have emerged from both the growth and value camps.

Also, superior fund managers may have elements of both investment philosophies within their stock selection criteria. Warren Buffett confessed that he was caught up in the growth vs. value debate early in his career, but after a point, learned that "they are joined at the hip." Few superior value managers totally ignore the earnings prospects of a company and few superior growth managers will pay any price for perceived future growth. Mutual fund managers who acknowledge that their investment philosophy incorporates elements of both camps are referred to as "growth-at-a-price" managers, and Morningstar categorizes them under the style box heading "blend."

So why pay any attention to this particular debate? Because one style or the other—or even a subset style—may be dominating short-term performance statistics. Therefore, diversifying your equity mutual funds among the distinctive style categories serves to smooth out short-term portfolio performance without sacrificing long-term returns.

How do you know what style a particular domestic stock fund falls into? Each individual mutual fund's prospectus and marketing materials, as well as analytical industry observers like Morningstar and Value Line, available at many public libraries, will prove helpful in determining a fund's style. Possibly the best source of style comparisons by asset class is the No-Load Fund Analyst (Orinda, California). This firm pioneered much of the research in this area of mutual fund analysis. As their name suggests, however, they analyze no-load mutual funds only.

Style Yardsticks

A second reason for segregating your domestic stock funds by style is so that you apply the appropriate yardstick for measuring each fund's individual performance. A mid/small cap growth fund should be measured against other mid/small cap growth funds. This compares *apples to apples*.

On the other hand, comparing any large cap value fund to a large cap growth fund will quickly lead to bouts of euphoria or feelings of depression. You will find that one style will "zig" while another "zags" — for prolonged periods of time. It's a constant *apples to oranges* dilemma.

This misleads investors into selling good funds at the wrong time and for the wrong reasons or, conversely, buying poor or average funds merely because their style (or asset class) is temporarily in vogue.

The No-Load Fund Analyst referred to above provides the best style yardsticks by asset class. Morningstar's newly reorganized format (1996) has come a long way in this regard and covers a significantly larger group of mutual funds — load and no-load. (However, keep in mind that Morningstar's large, medium and small asset class definitions do not match up exactly with those of CRSP/Ibbotson — the convention used in this book.)

Identifying Consistently Superior Mutual Fund Managers

Focus on the Manager

This book focuses on evaluating mutual fund managers — not mutual funds themselves. In most cases, the performance that a mutual fund delivers is a direct result of the judgment of the fund manager. The mutual fund organization may provide terrific technical support, insightful research and talented analysts, yet in the end, it is up to the portfolio manager to make the decisions that are the primary determinant of the fund's results during his or her tenure. This has two notable ramifications:

- Mutual fund performance records are valid only back to the inception of the current (lead) portfolio manager and

- A manager's track record may be pieced together from prior mutual fund or private money management experience if the manager was the primary manager with the same investment mandate as held currently.

As a consequence, a mutual fund with a great long-term track record but with a new, unproven portfolio manager is of no interest, while a brand new mutual fund with a proven superior manager may be quite appealing.

Historical Risk/Reward

Historical Risk/Reward charts are especially designed for long-term analysis and therefore are of great value in evaluating the risks and rewards of asset classes and portfolio designs. Unfortunately, few mutual fund managers have been at the helm for the requisite 20-year period or longer. Of those that do qualify, there are some outstanding performers.

Chart 15-2 is a Historical Risk/Reward chart of a superior large cap growth-at-a-price fund, Davis New York Venture, continuously managed since 1969 by Shelby Davis. (Davis has also managed no-load Selected American Shares since 1993.)

Chart 15-3 compares the performance of Shelby Davis's New York Venture Fund against that of the S&P 500, his targeted asset class, for the 1972-1996 period of study.

Chart 15-4 is a Historical Risk/Reward chart of a superior mid/small cap growth fund, Acorn, continuously managed since 1970 by Ralph Wanger.

Chart 15-5 compares the performance of Ralph Wanger's Acorn Fund against that of mid/small caps, his targeted asset class, for the 1972-1996 period of study.

Historical Risk/Reward

Davis NY Venture A: Shelby Davis
Growth of $100,000
(12/31/71 – 12/31/96)

Year	Jan	Feb	Mar	Apr	May	Jun	Jul	Aug	Sep	Oct	Nov	Dec	Annual Returns
1972	$100,000	↓	↓	↑	↓	22% 12 mo.		↑	↓	↑	↑	$122,200	22.2
1973													-24.1
1974					<44%> 21 mo.				$68,900	↑	↓	↑	-20.1
1975	↑	↓	↓	↑	↓	↑	↓	↓	↑	↑	↓	↓	23.2
1976	↑	↓	↓	↓	↓	↑	↓	↓	↑	↓	↑	↑	20.6
1977	↓	↓	↑	↑	↓	↑	↓	↓	↑	↓	↑	↓	4.5
1978	↓	↑	↑	↑	↓	+211% 65 mo.		↑	↓	↓	↑	↓	19.5
1979	↑	↓	↑	↓	↓	↑	↓	↑	↓	↓	↑	↓	38.9
1980	↑	$214,300	<15%>1 mo.	↑	↑	↓	↑		+61% 14 mo.		↑	↓	43.9
1981	↓	↑	↑	↓	$293,200	<18%> 14 mo.							1.2
1982							$240,500	↑	↓	↑	↓	↓	25.4
1983	↑	↓	↑	↑	↓	↑	↓	↑	↑	↓	↑	↓	23.0
1984	↑	↓	↑	↓	↓	↑	↓	↑	↓	↑	↓	↑	4.8
1985	↑	↓	↓	↑	↑	+290% 61 mo.		↑	↓	↑	↑	↓	37.5
1986	↑	↑	↓	↓	↑	↓	↓	↑	↓	↑	↓	↓	22.0
1987	↑	↓	↓	↓	↑	↑	↓	$937,800	<26%> 3 mo.		$694,000	↑	-1.5
1988	↓	↓	↓	↑	↑	↑	↓	↓	↑	↓	↓	↑	21.4
1989	↑	↓	↑	↑	↓	+81% 32 mo.		↓	↑	↓	↑	↑	34.8
1990	↓	↑	↓	↓	↑	↓	$1,256,100	<15%> 3 mo.		$1,067,700	↑	↓	-2.9
1991	↑	↑	↓	↓	↑	↓	↑	↓	↓	↓	↓	↑	40.6
1992	↓	↑	↓	↑	↑	↓	↑	↓	↑	↓	↑	↑	12.0
1993	↑	↑	↑	↓	↑	↑	↓	↑	↓	↓	↓	↑	16.1
1994	↑	↓	↓	↑	↑	+253% 74 mo.		↑	↓	↑	↓	↑	-1.9
1995	↑	↑	↓	↑	↓	↓	↑	↓	↑	↓	↑	↓	40.6
1996	↑	↓	↓	↓	↑	↓	↓	↑	↑	↓	↑	$3,768,800	26.5

Total Return: Includes dividends reinvested   **Standard Deviation: 18.0**

Source: Davis Selected Advisors

↑ ↓ *Up or Down Month* ⬤ *Cyclical Declines* ⬤ *Recovery (to pre-decline level)* ⬤ *Net New Advancement*

	REWARD*			**RISK**	
	Total Return (1972-1996)	15.6%		Worst Decline	44 % 21 mo.
	Riskless Return (T-bills)	<7.0%>		Average Decline	19 % 5 mo.
	AVERAGE ANNUAL REWARD OF			Average Recovery	14 mo.
	DAVIS NY VENTURE A: **SHELBY DAVIS**	**8.6%**		**COMPOSITE RISK**	**103 points**

EFFICIENCY RATING = 84

Annualized   *(Reward ÷ Composite Risk x 1,000)*

CHART 15-2

Face Off: Shelby Davis vs. S&P 500

		S&P 500	Shelby Davis Davis NY Venture Fund
Advances & Declines			
Jan 1972→Dec 1972	End of Advance	19%	22%
Jan 1973→Sep 1974	(Worst-Case Decline)	-46%	-44%
Oct 1974→Feb 1980	Advance	132%	211%
Mar 1980	(Cyclical Decline)	-10%	-15%
Apr 1980→Nov 1980	Advance	43%	61%
Dec 1980→Jul 1982	(Cyclical Decline)	-17%	-18%
Aug 1982→Aug 1987	Advance	282%	290%
Sep 1987→Nov 1987	(Cyclical Decline)	-30%	-26%
Dec 1987→May 1990	Advance	71%	81%
Jun 1990→Oct 1990	(Cyclical Decline)	-15%	-15%
Nov 1990→Dec 1996	Advance	190%	253%
Jan 1972→Dec 1996:	**Total Gain**	**1820%**	**3650%**
	Annualized Gain	**12.5%**	**15.6%**
Full Market Cycles			
Jan 1973→Feb 1980	High to High	30%	74%
Oct 1974→Mar 1980	Low to Low	109%	164%
Mar 1980→Nov 1980	High to High	29%	37%
Apr 1980→Jul 1982	Low to Low	19%	32%
Dec 1980→Aug 1987	High to High	217%	220%
Aug 1982→Nov 1987	Low to Low	167%	189%
Sep 1987→May 1990	High to High	20%	34%
Dec 1987→Oct 1990	Low to Low	45%	54%
Jun 1990→Dec 1996	High to High Point	147%	200%
Reward (annualized return above T-bills)		**5.5%**	**8.6%**
Composite Risk		**101 points**	**103 points**
Efficiency Rating		**54**	**84**

CHART 15-3

Historical Risk/Reward

Acorn: Ralph Wanger
Growth of $100,000
(12/31/71 – 12/31/96)

Year	Jan	Feb	Mar	Apr	May	Jun	Jul	Aug	Sep	Oct	Nov	Dec	Annual Returns
1972	$100,000	↑	↓	↑	↓	+11% 11 mo.		↑	↑	↑	$110,850		8.9
1973					<45%> 22 mo.								-24.0
1974									$61,000	↑	↓	↓	-27.7
1975	↑	↓	↓	↑	↑	↑	↓	↓	↑	↓	↓	↓	30.2
1976	↑	↓	↓	↓	↑	↑	↓	↑	↑	↓	↑	↑	66.0
1977	↓	↓	↑	↓	+265% 47 mo.		↓	↓	↑	↓	↑	↓	18.1
1978	↓	↑	↑	↑	↓	↓	↓	↑	$222,500	<20%> 2 mo.	↑		16.9
1979	↑	↓	↑	↓	↑	↑	↓	↑	↓	↑	↑	↓	50.2
1980	↑	↓	↓	↑ +134% 31 mo. ↓		↑	↓	↑	↓	↑	↓		30.9
1981	↓	↑	↑	↓	$416,600	<21%> 14 mo.							-7.3
1982						$329,100		↑	↓	↑	↓	↓	17.6
1983	↑	↓	↓	↑	↑	↓	↓	↑	↑	↓	↑	↓	25.2
1984	↓	↓	↑	↓	↓	↑	↓	↑	↓	→	↓	↑	4.4
1985	↑	↓	↓	↑	↑	+242% 62 mo.		↓	↓	↑	↑	↓	31.4
1986	↑	↑	↓	↓	↑	↓	↓	↑	↓	↑	↓	↓	17.0
1987	↑	↓	↓	↓	↑	↑	↓	↑	$1,125,600	<26%> 2 mo.	↑		4.5
1988	↑	↑	↓	↑	↓	↑	↓	↓	↑	↓	↓	↑	24.8
1989	↑	↓	↓	↑	↓	+70% 31 mo.		↓	↓	↑	↓	↑	24.9
1990	↓	↑	↑	↓	↑	$1,415,000	<26%> 4 mo.		$1,047,800	↑	↓		-17.6
1991	↑	↑	↓	↓	↑	↑	↑	↓	↓	↑	↓	↑	47.4
1992	↑	↑	↓	↓	↑	↓	↑	↓	↑	↑	↑	↑	24.2
1993	↑	↓	↑	↓	↑	+257% 74 mo. ↑		↓	↑	↓	↑		32.4
1994	↓	↓	↓	↑	↓	↓	↑	↑	↓	↑	↓	↑	-7.5
1995	↓	↑	↓	↓	↑	↑	↑	↓	↑	↓	↑	↓	20.8
1996	↓	↑	↓	↑	↓	↓	↓	↑	↓	↓	↑	$3,735,800	22.6

Total Return: Includes dividends reinvested   **Standard Deviation: 21.9**

Source: Morningstar Principa ™ Plus for Mutual Funds

↑ ↓ *Up or Down Month*   ⬤ *Cyclical Declines*   ⬤ *Recovery (to pre-decline level)*   ◯ *Net New Advancement*

REWARD*		RISK	
Total Return (1972-1996)	15.6%	Worst Decline	45 % 22 mo.
Riskless Return (T-bills)	<7.0%>	Average Decline	23 % 6 mo.
AVERAGE ANNUAL REWARD OF		Average Recovery	9 mo.
ACORN: RALPH WANGER	**8.6%**	**COMPOSITE RISK**	**105 points**

EFFICIENCY RATING = 82
Annualized   (Reward ÷ Composite Risk x 1,000)

CHART 15-4

Face Off: Ralph Wanger vs. Mid/Small Cap Stocks - (1972-1996)

		Domestic Mid/ Small Cap Stocks (Asset Class)	Ralph Wanger Acorn Fund
Advances & Declines			
Jan 1972→Nov 1972	(End of Advance)	9%	11%
Dec 1972→Sep 1974	(Worst-Case Decline)	-50%	-45%
Oct 1974→Aug 1978	Advance	225%	265%
Sep 1978→Oct 1978	(Cyclical Decline)	-17%	-20%
Nov 1978→May 1981	Advance	115%	134%
Jun 1981→Jul 1982	(Cyclical Decline)	-19%	-21%
Aug 1982→Aug 1987	Advance	256%	242%
Sep 1987→Nov 1987	(Cyclical Decline)	-31%	-26%
Dec 1987→May 1990	Advance	65%	70%
Jun 1990→Oct 1990	(Cyclical Decline)	-24%	-24%
Nov 1990→Dec 1996	Advance	242%	257%
Jan 1972→Dec 1996:	**Total Gain**	**2610%**	**3636%**
	Annualized Gain	**14.1%**	**15.6%**
Full Market Cycles			
Jan 1972→Aug 1978	High to High	63%	101%
Oct 1974→Oct 1978	Low to Low	170%	192%
Sep 1978→May 1981	High to High	78%	87%
Nov 1978→Jul 1982	Low to Low	74%	85%
Jun 1981→Aug 1987	High to High	188%	170%
Aug 1982→Nov 1987	Low to Low	146%	153%
Sep 1987→May 1990	High to High	14%	26%
Dec 1987→Oct 1990	Low to Low	25%	29%
Jun 1990→Dec 1996	High to High Point		
Reward (annualized return above T-bills)		**7.1%**	**8.4%**
Composite Risk		**110 points**	**105 points**
Efficiency Rating		**65**	**80**

CHART 15-5

Note: The Standard Deviations for Mid/Small Cap stocks and Acorn for this period of study are 20.6 and 21.9, respectively. By this measure, Acorn is more risky than its target asset class. Yet, Acorn's Composite Risk Score is *less* than that of Mid/Small Cap stocks. This is a good example of how a Composite Risk Score may offer a better view of an investor's actual long-term risks.

Winning the War

Neither Shelby Davis nor Ralph Wanger won every skirmish, but they did win most battles and in the end they won the war. Each manager trailed his target asset class occasionally during a particular advance or decline, but Davis *never* trailed during a full market cycle and Wanger fell short only once. This is the picture of consistency.

For the entire 25-year period, their outstanding performances are clearly shown in both their rewards and efficiency ratings relative to those of their respective target asset classes (Chart 15-6). Their efficiency ratings, in particular, are truly remarkable. They demonstrate clearly that superior risk-adjusted performance is not only possible but also sustainable.

Two Superior Mutual Fund Managers vs. Asset Class
(1972-1996)

	Shelby Davis	vs.	S&P 500	Ralph Wanger	vs.	Mid/Small Cap
Return (Annualized)	15.6%		12.5%	15.4%		14.1%
Riskless Return (T-bills)	-7.0%		-7.0%	-7.0%		-7.0%
Reward	8.6%		5.5%	8.4%		7.1%
Composite Risk	103		101	105		110
Efficiency Rating	84		54	80		65

CHART 15-6

Target Asset Class

Some proponents of asset allocation will not invest in Ralph Wanger's Acorn Fund because in recent years he has invested between 15% and 20% of the fund's assets internationally. These asset allocation purists want to strip away from their fund managers the right to exercise investment judgment outside of the confines of their primary asset class, i.e. to only invest within one asset class.

This book takes a different view. For such purists, the index fund strategy outlined in Chapter 14 should be ideal. With index funds, they can control the asset class representations within their portfolio precisely. With index funds, companies are routinely bought and sold as they enter and leave the applicable universe of the specific index.

What separates actively managed funds from index funds is the exercise of judgment. Of course, much of this judgment is aimed at discerning which securities within a target asset class best fit a manager's own specifications of exceptional stocks. However, there are good reasons to allow a fund manager to exercise judgment in a wider field of vision.

For example, suppose a mid/small cap domestic stock manager has owned a specific company for some time, understands its growth prospects, knows its management well and is very satisfied with the current value of its stock and the prospects for a higher price. If this company's market cap grows to large cap status, should she automatically sell the stock like an index fund would (and pay a large capital gains tax), or should she continue to own this stock for as long as she continues to judge the stock as a particularly good stock for her portfolio?

Another example. Many exceptional managers like Ralph Wanger and Michael Price of the Mutual Series Funds do buy international stocks for their primarily U.S. stock funds. As Price puts it, "If I can buy a company in Europe for a 40-50% discount over the price I would pay for a similar stock of a U.S. company, it makes sense for me to buy it."

Superior managers like Wanger, Price and Davis know their target asset classes very well. If their judgment leads them to a purchase outside of that asset class, you can be sure that they believe it will add value to their portfolio. Therefore, this book takes the position that a fund manager's performance may be judged against that of his or her target asset class even if some percentage of the fund's portfolio falls into other asset classes. This is one area in which a mutual fund manager exercises judgment to whatever extent allowed within his or her fund's prospectus. The cumulative effect of that judgment is displayed for all to see in the manager's performance history. But the big question remains, *"What technique of fund manager evaluation can be used to identify those few, consistent, long-term winners?"*

Full Market Cycle

As was stated earlier, very few mutual fund managers offer a 20+-year track record to evaluate as do Shelby Davis and Ralph Wanger. Therefore, an alternate evaluation technique to Historical Risk/Reward is required.

Recall the discussion of asset classes and model portfolios during the Great Depression (Chapter 11). It was stated then that the only fair evaluation of a short or intermediate time period would be that of a full market cycle. The same logic applies to mutual fund managers. Obviously, the more market cycles over which a fund manager can be evaluated relative to his or her target asset class the better.

One particularly relevant argument for evaluating a fund manager's performance over a market cycle is that various styles of fund management tend to earn their rewards at different times. Therefore, beginning mid-cycle will unfairly penalize managers employing one style while benefiting managers with different styles. Another reason to look at full cycles is that some managers do their best during the advancing half of the cycle and others are at their best during the declining part of the cycle.

☞ The bottom line is simply this: fund managers cannot be considered "superior" until they have *proved* their ability to outperform their target asset class over at least one full market cycle. The more full cycles of continuous outperformance by a manager, the more confidence you can develop in their ability to keep delivering superior long-term performance. The idea is to isolate the cream of the crop

Superior Mutual Fund Manager Candidates

Charts 15-7 through 15-12 compare the full market cycle performance of superior mutual fund manager candidates with that of their target asset class. The comparisons begin with the earliest peak or trough for which performance information on the manager is available.

Face Off: Michael Price vs. Mid/Small Cap Stocks   *VALUE STYLE*
(June 1981 - December 1996)

		Domestic Mid/ Small Cap Stocks (Asset Class)	Michael Price Mutual Qualified Fund
Advances & Declines			
Jun 1981→Jul 1982	(Cyclical Decline)	-19%	15%
Aug 1982→Aug 1987	Advance	256%	242%
Sep 1987→Nov 1987	(Cyclical Decline)	-31%	-20%
Dec 1987→May 1990	Advance	65%	55%
Jun 1990→Oct 1990	(Cyclical Decline)	-24%	-14%
Nov 1990→Dec 1996	Advance	242%	214%
Jun 1981→Dec 1996:	**Total Gain**	753%	1216%
	Annualized Gain	14.7%	18.0%
Full Market Cycles			
Jun 1981→Aug 1987	High to High	188%	293%
Aug 1982→Nov 1987	Low to Low	146%	174%
Sep 1987→May 1990	High to High	14%	24%
Dec 1987→Oct 1990	Low to Low	25%	33%
Jun 1990→Dec 1996	High to High Point	260%	270%

Sources: Morningstar, Inc., Advanced Analytics for Principia™ and Center for Research in Security Prices (CRSP)

CHART 15-7

Mutual Qualified is a value-style mutual fund that has been continuously managed by Michael Price since inception. The performance of the fund is compared here to the fund's target asset class, mid/small cap stocks, beginning with the first market peak after the fund's inception. As you can see, Michael Price has greatly outdistanced the total return of his target asset class while *underperforming* every single major advance. Price's superiority clearly is a function of significant outperformance during cyclical declines. This downside focus did not keep Price from winning all five full market cycles. This is an example of how to evaluate the performance histories that are presented herein.

Chapter 15

Face Off: Bill Sams vs. S&P 500   *VALUE STYLE*
(December 1980 - December 1996)

		S&P 500	Bill Sams FPA Paramount
Advances & Declines			
Dec 1980→Jul 1982	(Cyclical Decline)	-17%	1%
Aug 1982→Aug 1987	Advance	282%	255%
Sep 1987→Nov 1987	(Cyclical Decline)	-30%	-20%
Dec 1987→May 1990	Advance	71%	61%
Jun 1990→Oct 1990	(Cyclical Decline)	-15%	6%
Nov 1990→Dec 1996	Advance	190%	179%
Dec 1980→Dec 1996:	**Total Gain**	**836%**	**1266%**
	Annualized Gain	**14.9%**	**17.6%**
Full Market Cycles			
Dec 1980→Aug 1987	High to High	217%	259%
Aug 1982→Nov 1987	Low to Low	167%	184%
Sep 1987→May 1990	High to High	20%	29%
Dec 1987→Oct 1990	Low to Low	45%	71%
Jun 1990→Dec 1996	High to High Point	147%	196%

Sources: Morningstar, Inc., Advanced Analytics for Principia™ and Standard & Poor's

CHART 15-8

FPA Paramount has been continuously managed by Bill Sams since December, 1980. Sams has been as effective a value-style manager in the large cap asset class as Michael Price has been in the mid/small cap asset class. In fact, his pattern of underperforming the advancing portion of market cycles and outperforming during cyclical declines is identical to that of Price. Yet, here again, Sams has outpaced his targeted asset class (the S&P 500) in every full market cycle during his tenure.

The next four superior mutual fund manager candidates are compared to their target asset class over the last three full market cycles. Mason Hawkins (value) and Ron Baron (growth) represent mid/small cap stocks while Bill Nasgovitz (value) and Larry Auriana (growth) represent micro caps. Two very successful aggressive growth managers, Gary Pilgrim and Foster Friess, are also shown.

Face Off: Mason. Hawkins vs. Mid/Small Cap Stocks   *VALUE STYLE*
(September 1987 - December 1996)

		Domestic Mid/ Small Cap Stocks (Asset Class)	Mason Hawkins Longleaf Partners Fund
Advances & Declines			
Sep 1987→Nov 1987	(Cyclical Decline)	-31%	-25%
Dec 1987→May 1990	Advance	65%	69%
Jun 1990→Oct 1990	(Cyclical Decline)	-24%	-23%
Nov 1990→Dec 1996	Advance	242%	289%
Sep 1987→Dec 1996:	**Total Gain**	**196%**	**280%**
	Annualized Gain	**12.3%**	**15.3%**
Full Market Cycles			
Sep 1987→May 1990	High to High	14%	27%
Dec 1987→Oct 1990	Low to Low	25%	30%
Jun 1990→Dec 1996	High to High Point	160%	200%

Face Off: Ron Baron vs. Mid/Small Cap Stocks   *GROWTH STYLE*
(September 1987 - December 1996)

		Domestic Mid/ Small Cap Stocks (Asset Class)	Ron Baron Baron Asset Fund
Advances & Declines			
Sep 1987→Nov 1987	(Cyclical Decline)	-31%	-20%
Dec 1987→May 1990	Advance	65%	76%
Jun 1990→Oct 1990	(Cyclical Decline)	-24%	-28%
Nov 1990→Dec 1996	Advance	242%	302%
Sep 1987→Dec 1996:	**Total Gain**	**196%**	**308%**
	Annualized Gain	**12.3%**	**16.2%**
Full Market Cycles			
Sep 1987→May 1990	High to High	14%	41%
Dec 1987→Oct 1990	Low to Low	25%	27%
Jun 1990→Dec 1996	High to High Point	160%	189%

Sources: Morningstar, Inc., Advanced Analytics for Principia™ and Center for Research in Security Prices (CRSP)

CHART 15-9

Face Off: Bill Nasgovitz vs. Micro Cap Stocks   *VALUE STYLE*
(September 1987 - December 1996)

		Domestic Micro Cap Stocks (Asset Class)	Bill Nasgovitz Heartland Value Fund
Advances & Declines			
Sep 1987→Nov 1987	(Cyclical Decline)	-33%	-32%
Dec 1987→Sep 1989	Advance	54%	58%
Oct 1989→Oct 1990	(Cyclical Decline)	-32%	-28%
Nov 1990→Dec 1996	Advance	275%	323%
Sep 1987→Dec 1996:	**Total Gain**	**163%**	**227%**
	Annualized Gain	**10.9%**	**13.5%**
Full Market Cycles			
Sep 1987→Sep 1989	High to High	3%	9%
Dec 1987→Oct 1990	Low to Low	5%	14%
Oct 1989→Dec 1996	High to High Point	155%	205%

Face Off: L. Auriana & H. Utsch vs. Micro Cap Stocks   *GROWTH STYLE*
(September 1987 - December 1996)

		Domestic Micro Cap Stocks (Asset Class)	Auriana and Utsch Kaufmann Fund
Advances & Declines			
Sep 1987→Nov 1987	(Cyclical Decline)	-33%	-39%
Dec 1987→Sep 1989	Advance	54%	174%
Oct 1989→Oct 1990	(Cyclical Decline)	-32%	-30%
Nov 1990→Dec 1996	Advance	275%	401%
Sep 1987→Dec 1996:	**Total Gain**	**163%**	**486%**
	Annualized Gain	**10.9%**	**20.8%**
Full Market Cycles			
Sep 1987→Sep 1989	High to High	3%	67%
Dec 1987→Oct 1990	Low to Low	5%	92%
Oct 1989→Dec 1996	High to High Point	155%	251%

Sources: Morningstar, Inc., Advanced Analytics for Principia™ and © computed using data from Stocks, Bonds, Bills & Inflation 1996 Yearbook™ with data updated January 1997, Ibbotson Associates, Chicago

CHART 15-10

Face Off: G. Pilgrim vs. Mid/Small Cap Stocks   *AGGRESSIVE GROWTH*
(September 1987 - December 1996)

		Domestic Mid/ Small Cap Stocks (Asset Class)	Gary Pilgrim PBHG Growth
Advances & Declines			
Sep 1987→Nov 1987	(Cyclical Decline)	-31%	-33%
Dec 1987→May 1990	Advance	65%	86%
Jun 1990→Oct 1990	(Cyclical Decline)	-24%	-32%
Nov 1990→Dec 1996	Advance	242%	477%
Sep 1987→Dec 1996:	**Total Gain**	**196%**	**389%**
	Annualized Gain	**12.3%**	**18.5%**
Full Market Cycles			
Sep 1987→May 1990	High to High	14%	25%
Dec 1987→Oct 1990	Low to Low	25%	26%
Jun 1990→Dec 1996	High to High Point	160%	292%

Face Off: F. Friess vs. Mid/Small Cap Stocks   *AGGRESSIVE GROWTH*
(September 1987 - December 1996)

		Domestic Mid/ Small Cap Stocks (Asset Class)	Foster Friess Brandywine Fund
Advances & Declines			
Sep 1987→Nov 1987	(Cyclical Decline)	-31%	-41%
Dec 1987→May 1990	Advance	65%	114%
Jun 1990→Oct 1990	(Cyclical Decline)	-24%	-18%
Nov 1990→Dec 1996	Advance	242%	278%
Sep 1987→Dec 1996:	**Total Gain**	**196%**	**291%**
	Annualized Gain	**12.3%**	**15.7%**
Full Market Cycles			
Sep 1987→May 1990	High to High	14%	26%
Dec 1987→Oct 1990	Low to Low	25%	75%
Jun 1990→Dec 1996	High to High Point	160%	210%

Sources: Morningstar, Inc., Advanced Analytics for Principia™ and Center for Research in Security Prices (CRSP)

CHART 15-11

Note: Aggressive Growth is a subset of the Growth style employing a combination of earnings and price momentum strategies. Brandywine may now be categorized as large cap, yet its track record was built primarily with mid/small cap stocks.

Face Off: H. Castegren vs. Int'l Stocks (EAFE)
(September 1987 - December 1996)

		International Stocks (EAFE) (Asset Class)	Hakan Castegren Ivy International A
Advances & Declines			
Sep 1987→Oct 1987	(Cyclical Decline)	-15%	-25%
Nov 1987→Dec 1989	Advance	48%	73%
Jan 1990→Sep 1990	(Cyclical Decline)	-31%	-14%
Oct 1990→Dec 1996	Advance	87%	145%
Sep 1987→Dec 1996:	**Total Gain**	62%	173%
	Annualized Gain	5.3%	11.4%
Full Market Cycles			
Sep 1987→Dec 1989	High to High	26%	30%
Nov 1987→Sep 1990	Low to Low	2%	49%
Jan 1990→Dec 1996	High to High Point	29%	111%

Sources: Morningstar, Inc., Advanced Analytics for Principia™ and Morgan Stanley Capital International

CHART 15-12

International stock funds present a quandry. Few, if any, managers that were active during the 1980s outperformed the EAFE international stock index in U.S. dollars. On the other hand, the vast majority of active international fund managers have outperformed this index in the 1990s. The primary reason for both the 1980s underperformance and the 1990s outperformance lies with the dominance of one country—Japan—in the index and the tendency of international fund managers to underweight Japanese stocks in their portfolios. During the 1980s when the Japanese market was flying high, the underweighting of Japan could not be made up from the performance of stocks in lesser performing markets. During the 1990s, the exact opposite has occurred. The Japanese market has been a woeful underperformer, and therefore, the underweighting of this market has boosted fund performance relative to the EAFE index. Castegren is one of the few to outperform the index in the late 1980s.

Note: The general market advance that began in November of 1990 for most domestic stock asset classes is still in progress as this book is completed in January 1997. At over six years in duration, this particular advance qualifies as a complete advance for the purposes herein, as virtually every style of management has come into and out of vogue at least once during this long advance.

Managed Mutual Fund Portfolios - Pairing

Earlier in this chapter, it was pointed out that superior fund managers have emerged from both the *growth* and *value* camps. This is now clearly evident from the performance of the managers illustrated herein. It was also noted that the reason for recognizing the different styles was that each tended to outperform at different times. The performance histories of these funds show that growth managers tend to outperform during the advancing portion of the market cycle, while value managers typically outperform during major market declines. Therefore, pairing two superior managers in each equity asset class, one with a growth style and the other from the value camp, should smooth your overall performance and offer the opportunity of outperforming the results from the asset class in *both* the advancing and declining portions of the target asset class's market cycle.

The following charts, 15-13, 15-14 and 15-15, pair a growth manager and a value manager and illustrate their combined results against that of their target asset class. One pairing is represented for each of the three domestic asset classes: large cap (S&P 500), mid/small cap and micro cap. Each pairing demonstrates that outstanding results relative to those of the asset class are possible and with a smoother overall delivery than that provided by the index of the asset class. This is truly the best of all worlds.

Mutual Fund Pairing: Large Cap Stocks (S&P 500)

		S&P 500	Paired Performance	VALUE: Bill Sams	GROWTH: Shelby Davis
Advances & Declines					
Dec 1980→Jul 1982	(Cyclical Decline)	-17%	-9%	1%	-18%
Aug 1982→Aug 1987	Advance	282%	273%	255%	290%
Sep 1987→Nov 1987	(Cyclical Decline)	-30%	-23%	-20%	-26%
Dec 1987→May 1990	Advance	71%	71%	61%	81%
Jun 1990→Oct 1990	(Cyclical Decline)	-15%	-5%	6%	-15%
Nov 1990→Dec 1996	Advance	190%	216%	179%	253%
Dec 1980→Dec 1996:	**Total Gain**	**836%**	**1242%**	**1266%**	**1185%**
	Annualized Gain	**14.9%**	**17.5%**	**17.6%**	**17.2%**
Full Market Cycles					
Dec 1980→Aug 1987	High to High	217%	239%		
Aug 1982→Nov 1987	Low to Low	167%	187%		
Sep 1987→May 1990	High to High	20%	32%		
Dec 1987→Oct 1990	Low to Low	45%	62%		
Jun 1990→Dec 1996	High to High Point	147%	200%		

Sources: Morningstar, Inc., Advanced Analytics for Principia™; Standard & Poor's; Davis Selected Advisors

CHART 15-13

Selecting a superior value manager and a superior growth manager for each equity asset class comes closest to delivering on the goal of achieving both a reduced risk and a higher reward than that of the relevant asset class.

Mutual Fund Pairing: Mid/Small Cap Stocks

		Domestic Mid/Small Cap Stocks (Asset Class)	Paired Performance	VALUE: Mason Hawkins	GROWTH: Ron Baron
Advances & Declines					
Sep 1987→Nov 1987	(Cyclical Decline)	-31%	-22%	-25%	-20%
Dec 1987→May 1990	Advance	65%	71%	65%	76%
Jun 1990→Oct 1990	(Cyclical Decline)	-24%	-26%	-23%	-28%
Nov 1990→Dec 1996	Advance	242%	296%	289%	302%
Sep 1987→Dec 1996:	**Total Gain**	**196%**	**291%**	**280%**	**308%**
	Annualized Gain	**12.3%**	**15.7%**	**15.3%**	**16.2%**
Full Market Cycles					
Sep 1987→May 1990	High to High	14%	33%		
Dec 1987→Oct 1990	Low to Low	25%	27%		
Jun 1990→Dec 1996	High to High Point	160%	193%		

Sources: Morningstar, Inc., Advanced Analytics for Principia™ and Center for Research in Security Prices (CRSP)

CHART 15-14

Mutual Fund Pairing: Micro Cap Stocks

		Domestic Micro Cap Stocks* (Asset Class)	Paired Performance	VALUE: Bill Nasgovitz	GROWTH: L. Auriana H. Utsch
Advances & Declines					
Sep 1987→Nov 1987	(Cyclical Decline)	-33%	-36%	-32%	-39%
Dec 1987→Sept 1989	Advance	54%	116%	58%	174%
Oct 1989→Oct 1990	(Cyclical Decline)	-32%	-29%	-28%	-30%
Nov 1990→Dec 1996	Advance	275%	362%	323%	401%
Sep 1987→Dec 1996:	**Total Gain**	**163%**	**353%**	**227%**	**486%**
	Annualized Gain	**10.9%**	**17.6%**	**13.5%**	**20.8%**
Full Market Cycles					
Sep 1987→Sep 1989	High to High	3%	38%		
Dec 1987→Oct 1990	Low to Low	5%	53%		
Oct 1989→Dec 1996	High to High Point	155%	228%		

Sources: Morningstar, Inc., Advanced Analytics for Principia™ and © computed using data from Stocks, Bonds, Bills & Inflation 1996 Yearbook™ with data updated January 1997, Ibbotson Associates, Chicago

* DFA 9-10 Fund

CHART 15-15

Other Candidates

The following mutual fund managers also qualify as candidates for your Wealth and Retirement Portfolio. Each has proved his ability to outperform his or her target asset class over at least two full market cycles, while bettering the performance of the target asset class over his or her entire management tenure. (Be aware that many of the best known, best performing fund managers over one-, three- and five-year periods *fail* this test and that many other *potentially* superior mutual fund managers have not proved themselves over this long of a time period.)

Asset Class	Manager	Style	Mutual Fund(s) Available Through:
Domestic Large Cap	Spiros Segalas[1]	Aggressive Growth	Harbor Capital Appreciation
	James Margard[1]	Growth-at-a-Price	Rainier Core Equity
	William Ruane/ Richard Cunniff	Value	Sequoia[2]
	David Fowler/ J. Parker Hall	Growth	Vanguard U.S. Growth
Domestic Mid/ Small Cap	Wilmot Kidd	Growth-at-a-Price	Central Securities (closed-end)
	James Margard[1]	Growth-at-a-Price	Rainier Small/Mid Cap Equity
	William Dutton	Growth at-a-Price	Skyline Special Equities
	Kenneth Heebner	Aggressive Growth	CGM Capital Development[2]
	Robert Rodriquez	Growth-at-a-Price	FPA Capital[2]
	Stephen Johnes	Growth	Merrill Lynch Growth B
Domestic Micro Cap	Mason Hawkins[1]	Value	Longleaf Small Cap
	Jeanne Sinquefield[3]	N/A	DFA 9-10 Small Co.
International Stock	Jean-Marie Eveillard[1]	Value	SoGen Overseas
	Mark Holowesko	Value	Templeton Foreign
	Richard Foulkes	Growth	Vanguard International Growth

[1] *Track record partially developed outside of this mutual fund.*

[2] *Closed to new investors as of January 1997.*

[3] *Although used as the index for small companies in SBBI, this fund has substantially outperformed the complete micro cap asset class since its inception (see pages 31-34).*

Note: Our apologies to any mutual fund manager who qualified but did not come to our attention.

What Works on Wall Street

A new and different approach to actively managed mutual funds has recently become available. Instead of relying on the judgment and discipline of a human manager, these funds mechanically buy and sell stocks that fall within the guidelines of a proven long-term strategy.

In a sense, these new mutual funds are a variation of index funds. Instead of matching an entire asset class, they match a select group of stocks within an asset class that best meet the criteria of the strategy. Stocks are held only so long as they meet that criteria. The academic justification for such strategies began with the Fama/French study referred to on page 184.

The most well known strategy of this type is referred to as the "Dogs of the Dow" (Dogs). It was popularized by Michael O'Higgins in his 1992 book Beating the Dow. The essence of this strategy is to buy the 10 highest yielding stocks in the Dow Jones Industrial Average (Dow) and hold them exactly one year. At the end of the year, you merely repeat the process. O'Higgins demonstrated that this strategy, and several variations, have all outperformed the Dow since 1972—and with less risk.

Initially, this strategy was better suited to unit trusts than to mutual funds. A unit trust is not perpetual. The sponsor raises all of the money before employing the strategy, then closes the trust, executes the strategy and liquidates when the strategy is fulfilled (one year later in this case).

The results of the Dogs strategy were verified back to 1954 in James O'Shaughnessy's What Works on Wall Street. As discussed earlier (see page 184), his book illustrated the superior results of several "look ahead" strategies including this one. Each of O'Shaughnessy's strategies calls for the purchase of the 50 stocks within the domestic stock market (except Micro Caps) that best fit the criteria of that specific strategy. These stocks are held one full year, then sold and replaced by the 50 stocks that then best meet the strategy's criteria. There is no magic to the starting date for a strategy as long as the stocks are held only one full year.

In December 1996 O'Shaughnessy introduced four mutual funds, each based on one of the top-performing strategies illustrated in his book, including one variation of the Dogs strategy. What separates these funds from actively managed funds is the strict adherence to a defined long-term strategy without human judgment. The long-term element is fundamental. As O'Shaughnessy has stated, even the most superior of strategies can underperform for a period of years. Dedication to stay with any such strategy for a period of more than 10 years—the longer the better—has been necessary to ensure the superior results eventually were achieved.

Funds or unit trusts based on proven long-term strategies may one day become as popular as indexing. However, it should be apparent that such strategies are tax *insensitive* and belong in the tax-deferred or tax-sheltered slices of your Wealth and Retirement Portfolio.

Bond Funds

5-Year U.S. Treasury Bond Asset Class

Intermediate-term government bond funds come closest to capturing the risks and rewards of the 5-year U.S. Treasury bond asset class used throughout this book. Individual funds within this group may vary their criteria to differentiate their fund from the others within the group. Typical of such distinguishing characteristics are:

- Lengthening or shortening the target average maturity of the fund

- Broadening the scope of acceptable bonds to government agency securities or mortgage notes issued or guaranteed by quasi-government agencies such as FNMA or GNMA (mortgage backed securities)

- Developing an expansive charter which allows illiquid securities and/or options, futures or warrants to be purchased and

- Adopting exotic or leveraged strategies in the hope of boosting yields and returns.

This book takes the view that it is preferable with this asset class to focus on reliability. Plain vanilla intermediate government bond funds with a very low fee structure, such as the index funds discussed in Chapter 14, are preferable to higher risk and uncertain strategies for most investors. Reaching for perhaps a one-quarter to one-half percent total return advantage over the index (if you were to be very successful over time) may not be worth the risk or time involved.

In fact, if your portfolio is large enough to allow it, purchases of U.S. Treasury bonds either directly or through a broker may be preferable to a mutual fund in this asset class.

However, for those investors who have the time to research and evaluate bond funds that lie outside of this asset class, there are ample opportunities to add value to the return from intermediate-term Treasury bonds. Three bond fund managers that should be on the short-list of such research are Dan Fuss (Loomis Sayles Bond), Ernest Monrad (Northeast Investors) and Bill Gross (PIMCO bond funds). These three managers have provided consistently superior results relative to their target bond asset classes over several bond market cycles.

Two caveats: 1) no other bond asset class has yet provided reliable and efficient risk/reward data for 20 years or more; 2) successful bond managers seem to achieve their results by jumping from one bond asset class to another as they identify pockets of value. Both of these strategies are in conflict with the express objective of this book of building reliability and predictability into long-term portfolios.

Mutual Funds' Rapid Growth

It is no secret that the mutual fund industry is enjoying a period of rapid growth. While good for the mutual fund sponsoring companies, it is not necessarily good news to fund shareholders.

Top-performing mutual fund managers are inundated with huge inflows of new money to manage. In just the first few months of 1996, many funds *doubled* in size or more. One fund manager started 1996 with no money under management yet had over $1 billion to manage before mid-year.

This can be harmful to fund shareholders. The new dollars must be put to work regardless of market conditions or available stock opportunities. If not, the dollars will pile up in the fund. Huge slugs of cash can dilute performance.

Mutual funds specializing in micro caps or the smaller stocks within the mid/small cap universe will find it particularly hard to put the new money to work in their favorite stocks without pressuring prices upward (getting less long-term value). Therefore, many successful managers in a smaller market cap universe are forced into bigger and bigger market cap stocks where they may not be able to get the same results.

A mutual fund organization has its internal business side, too. Operations, computer capability, shareholder services, custody and administration can easily consume more and more of the manager's time in a fast-growing fund. This obviously takes away from his ability to perform for the fund. And this does not even take into consideration the need to find, interview and hire good analysts to support the expanding needs for research.

This is not a new phenomenon. It is just in a very intense phase in the 1990s. One caveat to reviewing the historical performance of any mutual fund manager you are considering is simply, "How much of her exceptional performance was delivered when her fund was in its first year or managing substantially fewer dollars than now?" Many a fund is quick out of the gate only to deliver very average performance afterward. Yet, their 3-year, 5-year and "since inception" returns look good for years *after the great performance is over*!

One solution is to close the fund. This is the route taken by some of the fund managers most concerned about their existing shareholders. While often beneficial for these shareholders, it closes some very good opportunities to you in your evaluation of superior managers.

Ever so often, a great manager, whose primary fund is closed, does open a new, different fund that is still well within his/her expertise and experience. These occasions provide some exceptional opportunities to those looking to fill out their Wealth and Retirement Portfolios.

Tax Strategies

All That Matters

Sir John Templeton, the founder of the highly regarded Templeton Group of funds, was fond of saying throughout his career that "the only return that counts is the after-tax, after-inflation return on your investments." There is more than an element of truth in his insight. Whatever you pay Uncle Sam from your investments will not add to your wealth nor will it supplement your retirement income.

Therefore, it makes good sense to be aware of tax mistakes to avoid as well as smart moves you may be able to take advantage of in your Wealth and Retirement Portfolio.

Year-End Distributions

In order to eliminate double taxation, each mutual fund must distribute the net capital gains it has realized throughout the year, either by the end of December or at the end of October. The date chosen is at the option of each fund.

If you purchase a mutual fund in a taxable account just prior to its making a large taxable distribution, you may wish you had waited to purchase it...or had purchased this mutual fund in a tax deferred account (IRA, IRA rollover, 401(k), etc.). This is an area where you must be proactive. Mutual funds will rarely alert you as to either the exact date or the amount of such distributions.

Tax Efficiency

If some or all of your Wealth and Retirement Portfolio is in a taxable account, pay attention to a fund's tax efficiency. The pinnacle of tax efficiency would be having your after-tax returns equal your pre-tax returns. No taxes due. A mutual fund that delivered such a stellar result would be 100% tax efficient.

Many mutual funds—including some of the higher performing ones—have 90%+ tax efficient ratings. As a comparison, at the end of 1996 Morningstar reports that the Vanguard 500 Index Trust had a tax efficiency of 88% versus an 81% rating for the average general equity mutual fund.

Three of the superior fund managers highlighted on the past few pages of this chapter have demonstrated exemplary after-tax returns. These three fund managers, their flagship fund and year-end 1996 tax efficiency ratings are: Gary Pilgrim's PBHG Growth (94%), Ron Baron's Baron Asset (97%), and Mason Hawkin's Longleaf Partners (90%). A discussion with each of these three fund managers makes clear that tax efficiency is not accidental; it is a primary focus of their individual mission statements.

Of course, a poor performing mutual fund would not jump into consideration just because it is highly tax efficient. (A "zero" total return with no tax due is 100% tax efficient!) In the same vein, a great fund should not be totally discounted just because it is somewhat below average in this area. (Hopefully, you could place such a fund in a tax-deferred *slice* within your portfolio.)

Tax efficiency ratings are included in Morningstar's individual mutual fund evaluations. Many periodicals pick up these ratings and include them in their own mutual fund rankings.

Another variation of this theme is the introduction of tax managed index funds. Vanguard Funds and Charles Schwab & Company, Inc. have both introduced index mutual funds specifically designed to be highly tax efficient. The underlying strategy of these funds is to not sell any security unless forced to do so. If a sale is necessary, first sell the higher cost shares and, when possible, sell losing security positions to offset the gains. This relatively new wrinkle in the mutual fund world may prove to be a winner for those not averse to index funds for their taxable accounts.

Taxable Yields

If you have a tax-deferred account within your Wealth and Retirement Portfolio, attempt to place as many of your higher yielding mutual funds into this account. Bond funds and equity mutual funds of the value style, i.e. those that produce high levels of dividend and interest income, would typically be higher yielding than other types of funds.

The reason for this focus on yields is two-fold. First, the total tax bite on interest and dividend income typically exceeds that of long-term capital gains. Second, mutual fund managers cannot reduce the tax bill on interest and dividend income through strategies such as realizing offsetting capital losses discussed above.

Selling Funds

When you have a need to sell some portion of any one of several mutual funds within your taxable portfolio, check the tax basis of each mutual fund relative to its current market value. In other words, what percentage of the sales price will be taxable to you? All else being equal, sell the fund with the lowest tax hit (highest tax basis).

Once you build up significant tax-deferred gains within a particular mutual fund, think twice before selling it. This is particularly true if you are merely switching to a different but similar fund within your taxable portfolio. You will have a lot fewer dollars—after taxes—to invest in the new fund.

Getting Started

One final hurdle remains if you will be acting as your own investment manager. This is the question of how to commit new dollars to equity mutual funds. The stock market often seems high or vulnerable to a correction—or worse. The reality, of course, is that no one knows how high is too high or, for that matter, if a new low is low enough.

If this is a concern, there are two viable strategies:

- Begin with a defensive strategy, i.e. choose only actively managed funds from the value investing style. Even within these styles, some superior managers have proved more defensive than others, so do your homework.

- The other strategy is to phase in your new dollar commitment over a period of time (perhaps 6-18 months). This virtually guarantees you will not invest the bulk of the new investment dollars at a major top in the market cycle.

Dollar Cost Averaging

A commonly recommended stock market strategy is referred to as dollar cost averaging. This strategy can be boiled down to simply this: buy shares in stock mutual funds at regular intervals with a set dollar amount.

It is a very good strategy for those who are adding to their Wealth and Retirement Portfolio from wages—either through company-sponsored 401(k) plans or through direct purchases.

One of the advantages attributed to a dollar-cost-average program is that you buy more shares when the market is down and fewer when the market is up with your fixed commitment of dollars, thereby producing a lower average cost than the market average over time.

Although this is true, the real strength of this strategy is the force of its discipline. Once set up, it takes on a life of its own. You will find it very hard to talk yourself out of continuing the program. This is the hallmark of a truly great strategy.

Maintain Controls

It was noted in Chapter 1 that most investors do not know how their portfolio is performing. Many investors know they don't know, many others think they know but really don't.

The only way you can control your portfolio properly and know if you are on track toward your objectives is to nail down the performance of your portfolio—and your benchmark portfolio performance—at least once a year.

The easiest and perhaps best way to do this is to join the computer age in this area of your life if you haven't already done so. This is one of those areas where software is delivering on its promise of quality, flexibility, low cost and ease of use. Software such as Intuit's "Quicken" or Meca Software's "Managing Your Money" can track all of your investments quickly and easily. "Wealthbuilder" by Reality Technologies is also good. With these programs you can subscribe to on-line services which will provide automatic pricing and performance updates for your mutual funds. You can easily set up two portfolios and update them both when checking on your portfolio (actual and benchmark).

These software packages will not only do the math for you, they will properly differentiate between new contributions or withdrawals and those items that contribute to your total return (interest, dividends, capital gains, unrealized appreciation, etc.). They may also help you with tax planning and tax preparation.

Making it easy to see your investments *as a portfolio* and to track overall performance is much more than half the battle. You can't properly plan, you can't adjust, if you don't know the performance and status of your investments.

Rebalancing Your Portfolio

Chapter 10 illustrated the *magic* of annually rebalancing a portfolio so that its portfolio design is maintained over time. Actually, a portfolio can be rebalanced on any regular interval, such as quarterly or semi-annually, without losing the benefits previously discussed. However, do not let more than a year go by without adjusting your mutual fund positions, i.e. selling off a little of those that have done so well that they now represent more than that called for by your portfolio design and acquiring more of those funds that have underperformed to bring them back up to their prescribed percentage in your portfolio. This is a necessary element of achieving the results contemplated by your portfolio design.

Conclusion

Superior mutual fund managers are available to your Wealth and Retirement Portfolio. These managers have proved themselves where it counts — over several full market cycles. Choosing superior fund managers to fill out your portfolio design offers the highest probability of providing long-term performance which outdistances that of your benchmark (index) portfolio. There are many other benefits possible with an active management strategy. Among them are the personal enjoyment of active involvement in your financial future, the satisfaction of success and the ability to personalize the risks and rewards of your Wealth and Retirement Portfolio.

16

Health Spa of Finance –
A "One Decision"
Strategy that Works

Selecting a professional money manager may be the best way for many investors to implement the ideas outlined in this book. While remaining responsible for evaluating and selecting a portfolio design that suits your needs and objectives, hiring a professional manager can assure the discipline and time required to execute your plan. Evaluating the professional's skills, your rapport, and the related services you can expect to receive are all critical to a successful long-term relationship. Other important factors include the advisor's compensation, forms of client communication and performance reviews which compare your account's risks and returns with those of your benchmark (portfolio design).

"The emergence of this new profession of disinterested
investment [advisors], who have no allegiance or
alliances and whose only job is to judge a security on
its merits, is one of the most constructive and healthy
developments of the last half century."
— Bernard Baruch (1957)

Do you know someone who has gone to a health spa?

People who just can't seem to eat right or exercise with consistency in their normal life seem to fall right in step with the spa's healthy lifestyle.

Why do these programs work? They succeed because it takes only one decision—the decision to do it. Once you have made that decision, paid the price, arranged the ticket, you don't have to make any more decisions. No temptations. No hesitations. You avoid the noise of the 1,000 and more distractions and excuses that come your way in your everyday "normal" life. You surrender both your normal self and normal surroundings to be totally enmeshed in an atmosphere that is completely supportive of your higher goal. Everything is lined up for success—the facility (all good stuff, no bad stuff), the staff (positive, goal-oriented, encouraging) and your fellow campers ("we're all in this together") make it almost impossible to fail.

Best of all, you do it gladly. You know it works, it's what you want and this is the way to make sure it gets done, even if it costs more than doing it on your own.

One Decision

In the same sense, choosing a money manager can be your one decision that makes everything in this book work for you. The management firm can be your Health Spa of Finance.

Candidates for a Money Manager

In Chapters 14 and 15 we looked at the types of investors who would be good candidates for investing with index funds and those that would be a better fit with actively managed mutual funds. The differences revolved around their attitude and expectations from investing. Let's look at who might be a good candidate for hiring a personal money manager.

Issue	Candidate for Money Manager
Time	"I wish to spend as little time on my investments as possible." (same as Index Investor)
Interest Level	"Investments are boring" or "too difficult to judge." (same as Index Investor)
Stress	"Being totally at the mercy of the market is stressful." (same as Active Fund Investor)
Market Returns	"I want to try to beat my benchmark." OR "I want benchmark returns but with less risk." (same as Active Fund Investor)
Fees	"Returns and fluctuations are far more important than fees." (same as Active Fund Investor)
Guidance	"I want personal consulting and guidance to make sure my objectives, portfolio design and related financial issues are on track." (unique to money manager)
Service	"I would like a complete package of account services that include consolidated performance reports, accounting, tax preparation, rebalancing and special services such as income distributions and tracking." (unique to money managers)
Discipline	"I'm not sure that I will have the discipline on my own to stay with my portfolio design or my mutual fund strategy during substantial changes in market conditions." (unique to money managers)

CHART 16-1

If you decide to hire an investment professional to manage some or all of your Wealth and Retirement Portfolio, understand that, at a minimum, you are still responsible for evaluating and selecting the appropriate investment policy (broad portfolio design) that is right for you. The manager then selects the mutual funds (or individual securities) that best executes your portfolio design.

Certainly your investment manager may be a big help to you in assembling your financial information in whatever manner helps you both understand where you are today. Your investment advisor can also help clarify your future needs and objectives.

☞ However, in the end, the investment policy that is the most appropriate trade-off between long-term returns and degree of market setbacks is *your* call. You must accept responsibility in advance for the major parameters your advisor will observe. There is no escaping from the fact that this is your money, that the long-term returns will greatly affect your retirement or wealth and that only you know what degree of temporary loss (it will seem like a permanent loss when it occurs—even if it is only a setback to be recovered later) you can tolerate without emotional trauma.

Selecting a Professional Investment Manager

For those who hire a personal money manager, the most important determinant of long-term investment success will be in choosing the right manager to begin with. Start with the basics, screen out any candidates who are not:

- **Professionally Competent.** Is this money manager a full-time professional with an established counseling practice? There is no reason for your account to be a guinea pig or after-thought. A true professional should be registered with the Securities and Exchange Commission (SEC) by filing a form "ADV." Ask for a copy, review it thoroughly. It will detail all the nuts and bolts of the advisor's practice as well as his principal investment philosophy and experience.

  A good money manager is a craftsman. He or she is building a performance record that has his or her unique risk and reward characteristics. Take a long, hard look at this track record for accounts with similar objectives to your own.

- **Fee-Only.** The advisor charges an annual fee for managing your account and does not receive per-transaction commissions. Fee-only managers are professionals whose interest is identical to your own—to maximize the value of your account relative to your risk parameters. As transaction costs are a detriment to account growth, the money manager's interest will be to keep transaction costs to a minimum. The advisor's method(s) of compensation should be clearly set forth in the firm's ADV filing (see above).

    Note: The fee-only rule need only apply to compensation related to investment selection and supervision. Other services that financial planners provide such as estate planning may be reasonably compensated in other ways.

- **Fee Conscious.** There is a trade-off to hiring your own money manager. The typical fee charged by a money manager is approximately one percent of the money under his direct management per year. Some investment advisors will charge as little as one-half of one percent per year and others as much as two percent per year or more. Buyer beware...cost and quality do not necessarily go hand in hand.

Initial Appointment

For those who pass this first screening and whose philosophies ring appropriate chords with you, set up an initial appointment. The purpose of this investigatory meeting should include:

- **Quarterback.** Will this money manager help you evaluate your entire retirement portfolio—including the parts not to be directly managed—in order to help formulate and adhere to the overall portfolio design?

- **Portfolio Design.** Will the advisor help you establish your portfolio design? Will the advisor agree to stay within the boundaries of your agreed portfolio design? (Maintaining your portfolio's superstructure is fundamental to achieving the expected long-term returns with the anticipated degree of periodic setbacks in market values.) Will the advisor provide a suitable benchmark for performance comparisons?

- **Enjoyable Relationship.** This should be entered into as a long-term relationship. Make sure it feels right from the beginning. Is there a spirit of trust, cooperation and mutual respect?

If the results of this initial appointment are satisfactory for you, then ask the advisor for a least two referrals of long-term clients of the firm that share similar characteristics and objectives to your own. Call them. Ask them to speak candidly of their relationship with the advisor. Ask them to address the advisor's strengths and weaknesses. This may provide good insights and help you decide on—or prepare for—a second meeting.

Counseling and Communication

In our health spa analogy at the beginning of this chapter, it was pointed out that one of the reasons it works is the completely supportive atmosphere, including staff and fellow campers. Good money management firms will put a lot of effort into providing you with high-quality support for your Wealth and Retirement Portfolio objectives.

This is one area where there are significant differences between money management firms.

Your management firm should prepare simple, consolidated reports to reflect your portfolio design. These will illustrate your asset allocation, your individual mutual fund holdings, your current-period performance and your historical performance. Your fee will be clearly shown and netted against your gross return to reflect your bottom-line return. Your net returns are then compared to your portfolio design's benchmark returns (see Chapter 14). This provides you with a measuring tool for both returns and setbacks.

This is important. Meetings with your advisor should include complete discussions of just how your account is doing relative to its objectives. With appropriate benchmarks, you are not guessing, you are not at the mercy of your manager's presentation…*you know!*

Some advisors prepare detailed quarterly reports to keep their clients informed of their current market insights and the reasoning behind any changes that have either just occurred or are anticipated within your portfolio. The quality of these reports varies widely.

Some money managers add interim client reports and special individual correspondence to highlight specific activity within the firm or within your individual portfolio.

Some professionals organize quarterly or annual meetings in which all clients are invited to participate. This is a great way to hear your money manager's broader views as well as interact with other clients of the firm and hear their questions and comments. This can be very positive reinforcement. (For those who cannot attend, a cassette tape may be offered.)

Annual Reviews

Of course, many money managers offer personalized annual reviews to update your retirement plan and to get valuable feedback from you. Have you had a change of circumstances that could directly or indirectly influence your Wealth and Retirement Portfolio? The true professional wants to know about it.

Without preparation, annual reviews may end up as little more than social contact or involve interesting but relatively unimportant remarks about investment markets or current events. The following outline may prove beneficial for productive annual reviews:

- Set an agenda. What will be discussed by each party.

- Be prepared. Bring all of your relevant documentation and have your advisor do the same (or send it to you in advance of the meeting).

- Review the portfolio design of your Total Wealth and Retirement Portfolio (both managed and un-managed assets). Does it still fit your circumstances?

- Discuss any changes thoroughly; understand the changes in income needs, retirement date, new capital (how it will be phased into the portfolio), long-term returns and fluctuations to expect in market values.

- Discuss performance of your account and your comparable benchmark portfolio in terms of both returns and setbacks.

- Question specific moves within your portfolio so you can take a deep look into the thinking process of your manager.

- Request written follow-up.

Remember, your primary role in these reviews is to be candid in discussing areas of dissatisfaction and to insist on adherence to the agreed upon portfolio design.

It is very important that you take advantage of all the counseling and communication that your money manager offers. It is both informing and supportive.

Making Life Easier - Other Services

A high-quality money management firm will provide other services that may not add to the long-term rate of return of your retirement portfolio but will surely add to your overall satisfaction by taking over all the minutiae and aggravations of servicing a portfolio.

Tax Reporting and Accounting. Your money manager should make life much easier at tax time. Many professionals provide full and complete accounting for your account(s).

Tax reports will be prepared that reconcile exactly with your 1099s. Preliminary reports can easily be put together in the fall of the year to help with any year-end planning you may wish to do.

Accounting reports can be prepared that comply with almost any needs either you or your accountant require. An underrated part of the money manager's all-around service is troubleshooting when problems occur—and they will occur.

Retirement Income and Other Payouts. Your money management firm will oversee the payment (from the Custodian) of your monthly retirement income—by check or wire. In addition, any non-recurring needs for money from your Wealth and Retirement Portfolio (new roof, new car, etc.) are easily handled with a phone call. All such transactions are a part of your permanent accounting record and show up on your statements in easy-to-read form.

Rebalancing. The financial markets are not symmetrical (correlated). Your Wealth and Retirement Portfolio needs periodic rebalancing to make sure it does in fact continue to meet your portfolio design. This is obviously a continuous and dynamic part of your manager's service.

Conclusion

A qualified money manager is an excellent strategy for those who want a third-party to enforce the discipline of their portfolio design. Given the myriad temptations to alter a well-thought-out, long-term portfolio design *at just the wrong time*, using a professional's services may be a better choice than either utilizing index funds or developing your own portfolio of managed funds. In addition, your investment advisor can customize your strategy to focus on increasing the returns and/or decreasing the risks within your portfolio.

17

The Not-So-Secret Key Ingredient

Several studies reveal that investors do not achieve the same returns as the mutual funds within which they invest. They have made *significantly* less! The culprit is usually either market timing or performance chasing (dumping a fund currently out of favor in order to buy a hot fund). Clearly, the advice of sage investors as well as the results of serious studies show that selecting an investment strategy and staying the course is the most important ingredient in attaining investment success and the one in least supply.

"Our stay-put behavior reflects our view that the stock market serves as a relocation center at which money is moved from the active to the patient."
— Warren Buffett

Have you ever sat on a river bank, one with a fast-moving current and scattered rapids? Perhaps you threw pieces of bark or branches into the water. If your "ship" made it to the main current—off it went—caught in the major force of the river. It bobbed and weaved wildly, but its course was undeniable. You had no doubt where it was heading.

If your ship did not make the main current, it may have been caught in swirling eddies, dead-end side streams or the calm water near the edge. Not being part of the major force of the river, your ship might end up anywhere, while the major rush of the river passed it by.

We want our *investment* ships in the main current. The ride may be spirited, but we know where we're going, and we know we'll get there.

The "If Only" Fallacy

In early 1995, a Los Angeles firm, Fundminder, Inc., commissioned Morningstar to find out how well individuals have done when they buy and sell mutual funds.

The study was commissioned because individual investors hold no-load mutual funds for only 21 months on average. This suggests that fund owners do not achieve the same long-term results as the funds themselves. The study sought to either validate or dispel the reputation of individual investors as poor market timers.

The study evaluated 199 growth mutual funds for which Morningstar had performance data from 1989 through 1994. The average total return for the 199 funds over this six-year period was **12.01%**. This was the annualized return any investor would have achieved by simply buying and holding these funds for the full six years.

So, how well did all of the owners of those same 199 do for their various periods of ownership? Not good. The average annualized return was just **2.02%**! *They turned 12% returns into 2% returns!*

This study reveals the single biggest misconception that investors hold—the "if only" fallacy. Most investors look at the past returns of a mutual fund with extraordinary returns and think to themselves, "if only I had invested in this fund five years ago, then I could have made these marvelous returns." As this study shows, even those who did invest in the super mutual fund five years ago did *not* get the return! At some point, either market timing or performance chasing drove them out!

Further proof of this finding was provided by Peter Lynch, the highly regarded manager of the Fidelity Magellan Fund during its glory years, who told an audience of investment advisors in 1992: "Over half of my investors in Fidelity Magellan during my tenure at the helm lost money due to poorly timed buy and sell decisions." This despite Magellan being the number one performing mutual fund over those 10 years! Think about that. **Discipline is far more important than any other aspect of your investment strategy.**

How to Turn 2% Into 12%

Can you figure out how to turn 2% returns into 12% returns? Stay put! The single most important rule of investing is simply this: *Choose your investment game plan prudently and wisely and then stay with it.*

 Research continually shows that, among individuals and professionals alike, those with a consistent approach win, and those who keep changing strategies lose.

Twist on Load Vs. No-Load Mutual Funds

For mutual fund investors, another interesting proof of maintaining a strict discipline comes from combining the results of two different studies on mutual funds and their investors.[20]

The first study was conducted by finance professor Mark Carhart of the University of Southern California. He constructed a comprehensive mutual fund database that included virtually every diversified equity mutual fund that has existed since 1962—including those that no longer exist.

The study concluded that the average no-load mutual fund outperformed the average load mutual fund by 0.6% per year. And that does not take into consideration the commissions load fund investors must pay. All other fund expenses were included so that the net results would be comparing apples to apples.

The second study was conducted by Dalbar Financial Services, a Boston-based consulting firm. Dalbar studied the actual returns of *investors*, as opposed to the returns of the funds themselves (much like the Morningstar study previously sited). Dalbar found that the average load fund investor (before loads) made 1.2% per year more than the average no-load fund investor! How can that be?

Like the Fundminder/Morningstar study cited earlier, the culprit is market timing. The average load fund investor earned more than the average no-load fund investor simply because he/she stayed put longer...even though the load funds themselves did not perform as well. Investors who have paid a sales charge are less likely to attempt market timing.

Market Timing in All Its Guises

Market timing comes in many different disguises, but the results are nearly always the same. Whether based on technical indicators, fundamental values, market sentiment (moods), cycles or even jumping from one strategy to another...they just rob you of your valuables: *time* and *compounding*.

Peter Lynch put it in different terms: "Far more money has been lost by investors in preparing for corrections, or anticipating corrections, than has been lost in the corrections themselves."

The allure of market timing is not hard to grasp. Once again, look at the Historical Risk/Reward Chart S-1 of the Total U.S. Stock Market in the special two-color supplement found in Chapter 8. Looking back at the past quarter century, wouldn't it have been wonderful to have enjoyed the advances while neatly side-stepping the five worst declines illustrated.

What may not be so obvious is just how difficult a challenge market timing truly is. Most market timers state clearly that their "system" will neither get you out at the top of a market cycle nor get you back in at the bottom. In other words, they will be early or late. Take another look at Chart S-1. Three of the five worst declines in the past quarter century came and went in one to five months. How could such declines be successfully timed?

For example, many investors would jump at the chance to participate in a market timing system that guaranteed they would be out of the market three months before the top and be back in the market three months after the bottom. They may "leave the party" early and miss the initial bounce back, but they would be out of the market during every single month of its worst declines. With the perfect hindsight of historical performance, how would such a system have performed?

On the one hand, this system would have been very profitable for the worst-case market decline of 1973-'74. In that case, the happy participant would have re-entered the market 36% below his selling price (side-stepping a net four-fifths of the 45% decline in the market).

On the other hand, this system would have been a dismal failure the rest of the time. For the four cyclical declines in the past 25 years, the re-entry to the market are at levels 11% higher, 10% higher, 7% lower, and 5% higher than where the investor exited the market.

This is with perfect hindsight. In reality, most market timing systems incur whipsaws, exiting the market before perceived major declines and then scurrying back into the market at higher levels when the phantom decline doesn't materialize. Is it any wonder that market timing over long time periods has not financially delivered on its emotional appeal?

Experience Builds Patience

Let's listen in again on another part of Louis Rukeyser's insightful interview on April 28, 1995, with Phil Carret, the voice of 77 years of investment management experience.

RUKEYSER:	"What is the most important thing that you have learned about investing over the past three-quarters of a century?"
CARRET:	"Patience."
RUKEYSER:	"What do you think of this stock market today?"
CARRET:	"I think it is dangerous at current levels. There's a lot of froth on the bloom. I think we're in for maybe something like 1987 when the market went down 500 points in one day...But in the long run...the market will recover, and people who buy the right stocks and sit on them are going to do very well."
RUKEYSER:	"What do you do, given your experience, when you think there may be too much froth, when you think there may be a major correction, even a crash? Do you sell all your stocks?"
CARRET:	*"No, I really don't do anything."*

Don't Just Sit There — Do Nothing!

It appears that the great philosopher Blaise Pascal could have been discussing investment philosophy in 1670 when he said, "I have discovered that all human evil comes from this, man's being unable to sit still in a room."[21]

Your portfolio design will control your risks—let it! Any market timing you attempt to enhance returns and/or reduce setbacks has a very high probability of doing exactly the opposite—lower your long-term returns and increase the risk that you will fall well short of your retirement income objective.

 Your portfolio design is much more powerful and predictable than any system of market timing! Let it work for you.

> *"We have striven throughout to guard the student against over emphasis upon the superficial and the temporary...this over emphasis is at once the delusion and the nemesis of the world of finance."*
> — Benjamin Graham and David Dodd,
>   Security Analysis, 1934

Action Summary

Here is a simple summary of the important points in this book. Understanding and acting upon them will help assure your investment success.

Motivate yourself to invest better. Understand that the rate of return you achieve on your investments may be the single most important determinant of the retirement income available to you.

Organize your retirement portfolio—all of it—on one page. Begin thinking of it as an entity in itself, not a collection of separate investments. Purchase financial software that makes this much easier.

Educate yourself as to the long-term returns that asset classes and combinations of asset classes are likely to provide. Also, appreciate the interim fluctuations in market values that are a part of each class. Be armed and prepared *not to act*!

Select a portfolio design that is appropriate for your Wealth and Retirement Portfolio—the right combination of long-term return and fluctuation in market values that is satisfying and livable for you.

Choose your strategy for investing within the portfolio design you select. Index funds? Actively managed funds? Your own personal money manager? One of these is the best choice for you. Size yourself up based on your attitude and expectations from investing.

Research and uncover those few superior mutual fund managers experienced in the styles appropriate to your objective (actively managed fund strategy)—OR—select a professional money manager to do this for you.

Stay put with your portfolio design and investment strategy. To get the benefits of a well-thought-out investing program, you still need the patience and discipline to stay the course—either on your own or with help from an advisor.

Rebalance your portfolio design annually.

Build Wealth and. . . .Have a Great Retirement!

Appendix

Note: Charts in the Appendix are the letter A (for Appendix) followed by the chapter number in which the chart is introduced or to which it is referred. A hyphen follows these two digits which is followed by the individual chart number.

This page left intentionally blank.

How Much Retirement Income Will Your Current
Tax-Sheltered Account Provide?

(Inflation-Adjusted, Retirement Income as a Percentage of Your Current Tax-Sheltered Retirement Account)

Years to Retirement	Annual Rates of Return							
	5%	6%	7%	8%	9%	10%	11%	12%
0	4.3%	4.9%	5.5%	6.2%	7.0%	7.8%	8.6%	9.4%
10	5.2%	6.6%	8.1%	10.1%	12.4%	14.9%	18.0%	21.8%
15	5.7%	7.6%	9.8%	12.8%	16.4%	20.7%	26.2%	33.1%
20	6.3%	8.7%	11.9%	16.2%	21.8%	28.8%	38.0%	50.4%
25	6.9%	10.1%	14.4%	20.6%	28.9%	40.0%	55.3%	76.6%
30	7.6%	11.7%	17.4%	26.1%	38.4%	55.6%	80.4%	116.4%
35	8.4%	13.5%	21.1%	33.1%	50.9%	77.2%	116.8%	176.9%
40	9.2%	15.5%	25.5%	41.9%	67.6%	107.2%	169.8%	269.0%

CHART A1-1

Note: In order to estimate future income from a portfolio, it is necessary to make certain assumptions:
- Inflation is assumed to be 3.0% per year (both before and after retirement).
- Retirement income will be adjusted annually by the increase in inflation.
- Retirement income will be paid out for 30 years before the investment principal is depleted.

Example: Assume you currently have $300,000 in a tax-deferred account, such as a Rollover IRA, 401(k), profit sharing plan or deferred annuity. Further assume you are 15 years away from beginning to take retirement distributions from this account (shaded on chart). Based on the assumptions noted, your maximum level of retirement income will be determined by the rate of return from your investments both before and after retirement. Assume your investment return averages 7% per year (shaded on chart). At this rate of return, your maximum retirement income will be $29,400 ($300,000 x 9.8%) per year *in today's dollars* for 30 years. A year-by-year illustration of this example is shown on Chart A1-2.

This chart is designed to illustrate the impact on your retirement income of merely changing the rate of return on your current investment portfolio. Changing your rate of return has a dramatic impact on your available retirement income. In the example above, a 5% annual rate of return reduces retirement income to only $17,100 per year in current dollars, whereas increasing the rate of return to 9% results in an annual retirement income of $49,200 per year in present value dollars.

Tax Sheltered Net Worth

Lump Sum:	$300,000
Years to Retirement:	15
Inflation Rate:	3%
Pre-Retirement Total Return:	7%
Post-Retirement Total Return	7%

Years Before and After Retirement	Accumulated Wealth	Retirement Income	
1	$321,000	N/A	
2	343,470	N/A	
3	367,513	N/A	
4	393,239	N/A	
5	420,766	N/A	
6	450,219	N/A	
7	481,734	N/A	
8	515,456	N/A	
9	551,538	N/A	
10	590,145	N/A	
11	631,456	N/A	*$46,027 equates to*
12	675,657	N/A	*$29,400 in present*
13	722,954	N/A	*dollars at 3% inflation.*
14	773,560	N/A	*Each annual retirement*
15	$827,709	$46,027	*income distribution*
1	838,241	47,408	*increases by 3%;*
2	848,089	48,830	*however, the buying*
3	857,160	50,295	*power of each year's*
4	865,358	51,804	*income remains $29,400*
5	872,575	53,358	*in present dollars.*
6	878,697	54,958	
7	883,598	56,607	
8	887,145	58,305	
9	889,190	60,055	
10	889,577	61,856	
11	888,136	63,712	
12	884,682	65,623	
13	879,018	67,592	
14	870,929	69,620	
15	860,186	71,708	
16	846,540	73,860	
17	829,722	76,075	
18	809,445	78,358	***30 Years of***
19	785,398	80,708	***Retirement***
20	757,246	83,130	***Distributions***
21	724,630	85,623	
22	687,162	88,192	
23	644,425	90,838	
24	595,972	93,563	
25	541,320	96,370	
26	479,951	99,261	
27	411,309	102,239	
28	334,794	105,306	
29	249,765	108,465	
30	155,529	111,719	
	$ 51,345	**Final Distribution - Principal Depleted**	

CHART A1-2

10% SALARY DEFERRAL

What Percentage of Your "Final Salary" Will Your 401(k) Replace?

(Your Retirement Income as a Percentage of Your Final Compensation)

Years to Retirement	Annual Rates of Return							
	5%	6%	7%	8%	9%	10%	11%	12%
10	4.9%	5.9%	7.0%	8.4%	9.9%	11.6%	13.5%	15.6%
15	7.5%	9.3%	11.4%	13.9%	16.9%	20.2%	24.3%	29.0%
20	9.8%	12.3%	15.4%	19.2%	23.9%	29.3%	36.0%	44.0%
25	13.3%	17.3%	22.4%	28.8%	37.0%	47.2%	60.3%	76.5%
30	16.2%	21.7%	28.9%	38.4%	50.9%	67.8%	88.6%	116.5%
35	19.5%	26.8%	36.8%	50.4%	69.1%	94.0%	128.8%	175.7%
40	22.7%	32.1%	45.4%	64.1%	90.9%	129.7%	184.4%	261.3%

CHART A1-3

Assumptions:
- Annual rate of return is for both "years to retirement" *and* 30 years after retirement.
- Annual Inflation: 3.0% (both before and after retirement)
- Annual Salary Increases: 1.0% (over inflation)

Example: You anticipate you will retire in 20 years (shaded on chart). You and your employer together will set aside 10% of your growing annual salary each year. (Your salary is assumed to grow 1.0% per year above inflation.) If your investments average a 9% rate of return (shaded on chart) both before and after retirement, your investments from the 20 years of salary deferral will replace 23.9% (shaded on chart) of your *final* salary. Your retirement income will fully adjust for changes in the Consumer Price Index (CPI), that is the income paid out to you during your retirement will rise each year by the inflation rate. The income will last 30 years at which time all of the investment principal would be consumed. (See opposite page for a full illustration of this example.)

This chart is designed to illustrate the impact on your retirement income of merely changing the rate of return on your 401(k) investments.

Retirement Income as a % of Final Compensation

Compensation:	$25,000	Inflation Wage Adjustment:	3%
Contribution Level:	10%	Portfolio Rate of Return (Pre-Retirement):	9%
Merit Wage Adjustment:	1%	Portfolio Rate of Return (Post-Retirement):	9%

Years Before and After Retirement	Compensation	Plan Contribution	Plan Accumulation/ Retirement Fund	Retirement Income	
1	$26,000	$2,600	$ 2,834	0	
2	27,040	2,704	6,036	0	
3	28,122	2,812	9,645	0	
4	29,246	2,925	13,701	0	
5	30,416	3,042	18,249	0	
6	31,633	3,163	23,340	0	
7	32,898	3,290	29,026	0	
8	34,214	3,421	35,368	0	
9	35,583	3,558	42,430	0	
10	37,006	3,701	50,282	0	
11	38,486	3,849	59,002	0	
12	40,026	4,003	68,675	0	
13	41,627	4,163	79,393	0	
14	43,292	4,329	91,258	0	
15	45,024	4,502	104,378	0	
16	46,825	4,682	118,876	0	*Each annual*
17	48,698	4,870	134,883	0	*retirement income*
18	48,698	4,870	134,883	0	*distribution increases*
19	50,645	5,065	152,543	0	*by 3%; however, the*
20	$52,671	$5,267	$172,013	$12,081	*buying power of each*
1			175,050	12,444	*year's income*
2			177,988	12,817	*remains at 23.9% of*
3			180,805	13,202	*final compensation.*
4		*Increasing/(Decreasing)*	183,480	13,598	
5		*Value of*	185,987	14,006	
6		*Retirement Fund*	188,300	14,426	
7			190,389	14,859	
8			192,219	15,304	
9			193,756	15,764	
10			194,957	16,236	
11			195,780	16,724	
12			196,175	17,225	
13			196,089	17,742	
14			195,462	18,274	
15			194,231	18,822	
16			192,325	19,387	
17			189,666	19,969	*30 Years of*
18			186,168	20,568	*Retirement*
19			181,738	21,185	*Distributions*
20			176,274	21,820	
21			169,664	22,475	
22			161,784	23,149	
23			152,501	23,844	
24			141,667	24,559	
25			129,122	25,296	
26			114,688	26,055	
27			98,173	26,836	
28			79,368	27,641	
29			58,040	28,471	
30			33,939	29,325	

$ 6,789   *Final Distribution - Principal Depleted*

CHART A1-4

How Much Retirement Income Will Your Current After-Tax Account Provide?

(Inflation-Adjusted, Retirement Income as a Percentage of Your Current After-Tax Retirement Account)

Years to Retirement	*Annual Rates of Return*							
	5%	6%	7%	8%	9%	10%	11%	12%
0	3.5%	3.8%	4.2%	4.6%	5.1%	5.5%	6.1%	6.6%
10	3.6%	4.3%	5.1%	6.0%	7.0%	8.1%	9.5%	11.0%
15	3.7%	4.6%	5.6%	6.8%	8.2%	9.8%	11.9%	14.2%
20	3.8%	4.8%	6.1%	7.7%	9.6%	11.9%	14.8%	18.3%
25	3.9%	5.1%	6.7%	8.7%	11.2%	14.4%	18.5%	23.6%
30	4.0%	5.4%	7.4%	9.9%	13.1%	17.4%	23.2%	30.5%
35	4.1%	5.7%	8.1%	11.2%	15.4%	21.1%	29.0%	39.4%
40	4.2%	6.1%	8.8%	12.6%	18.0%	25.5%	36.2%	50.9%

CHART A1-5

Note: In order to estimate future income from a portfolio, it is necessary to make certain assumptions:
- Inflation is assumed to be 3.0% per year (both before and after retirement).
- Retirement income will be adjusted annually by the increase in inflation.
- Retirement income will be paid out for 30 years before the investment principal is depleted.

Example: You assume you will retire in 25 years (shaded on chart). You currently have a Wealth and Retirement Portfolio of $300,000. If your portfolio averages a 10% rate of return (shaded on chart) both before and after retirement, your after-tax retirement income (distributions from your portfolio) will have the same purchasing power as 14.4% (shaded on chart) of today's $300,000 throughout your retirement (30 years). In other words, your retirement income from your current nest egg is the equivalent of $43,200 per year (14.4% x $300,000) in today's dollars after taxes. (See opposite page for a full illustration of this example.)

This chart is designed to illustrate the impact on your retirement income of merely changing the rate of return on your current investment portfolio.

Non-Tax Sheltered Net Worth

Lump Sum:	$300,000
Years to Retirement:	25
Inflation Rate:	3%
Tax Rate:	30%
% Taxable (Accumulation):	100%
Pre- and Post-Retirement Total Return:	10%
Pre- and Post-Retirement After-Tax Return:	7%

Years Before and After Retirement	Accumulated Wealth	Retirement Income	
1	$ 321,000	N/A	
2	343,470	N/A	
3	367,513	N/A	
4	393,239	N/A	
5	420,766	N/A	
6	450,219	N/A	
7	481,734	N/A	
8	515,456	N/A	
9	551,538	N/A	
10	590,145	N/A	
11	631,456	N/A	
12	675,657	N/A	
13	722,954	N/A	
14	773,560	N/A	
15	827,709	N/A	
16	885,649	N/A	
17	947,645	N/A	
18	1,013,980	N/A	
19	1,084,958	N/A	
20	1,160,905	N/A	*$90,542 equates to $43,200 in present dollars. Each annual retirement income distribution increases by 3%; however, the buying power of each year's income remains $43,200 in present dollars.*
21	1,242,169	N/A	
22	1,329,121	N/A	
23	1,422,159	N/A	
24	1,521,710	N/A	
25	$1,628,230	$ 90,542	
1	1,648,948	93,258	
2	1,668,318	96,056	
3	1,686,163	98,937	
4	1,702,289	101,906	
5	1,716,487	104,963	
6	1,728,529	108,112	
7	1,738,171	111,355	
8	1,745,148	114,696	
9	1,749,172	118,136	
10	1,749,933	121,681	
11	1,747,098	125,331	
12	1,740,304	129,091	
13	1,729,161	132,964	
14	1,713,250	136,953	***30 Years of Retirement Distributions***
15	1,692,116	141,061	
16	1,665,272	145,293	
17	1,632,189	149,652	
18	1,592,301	154,141	
19	1,544,996	158,766	
20	1,489,618	163,528	
21	1,425,456	168,434	
22	1,351,751	173,487	
23	1,267,682	178,692	
24	1,172,367	184,053	
25	1,064,858	189,574	
26	944,137	195,262	
27	809,107	201,119	
28	658,591	207,153	
29	491,325	213,368	
30	305,949	219,769	
	$ 101,004	*Final Distribution - Principal Depleted*	

CHART A1-6

Measures of Risk

Standard deviation is a common measure of volatility of yearly returns. The standard deviation is defined as $\sigma = \{[(r_1 - r_A)^2 + (r_2 - r_A)^2 + \ldots (r_n - r_A)^2]/n\}^{1/2}$, where $r_1, r_2 \ldots r_n$ are the individual yearly returns and r_A is the average, or *mean* of the yearly returns (σ^2 is called the *variance*): if yearly returns follow a normal distribution, popularly known as the *bell-shaped curve*, then about two thirds of the time the asset will have a return equal to the mean plus or minus one standard deviation. That is, the return on the asset will be within one standard deviation of its average, or mean, about two thirds of the time. About 95 percent of the time, the return on the asset will be within two standard deviations of its mean.

Composite Risk is an investor's tool, not an academic measurement, for portraying the long-term risks of an asset class or portfolio. It takes into consideration all three primary characteristics of risk as applied to the major cyclical declines the asset class or portfolio has actually incurred over a long period of study. These three risk characteristics are:

- Degree of decline - the reduction in market value as a percentage of the prior high valuation

- Duration of the decline - the number of months over which the decline unfolds

- Duration of recovery - the number of months to re-attain the prior high in market value measured from the low point of the decline

The number of major declines to be evaluated is determined by dividing by 5 the total number of years being studied. (Fractions add one additional decline to the study.) For example, in the 1960-1996 period of study (37 years), the eight most severe declines in market value are included ($37 \div 5 = 7\text{-}2/5$ — rounded up to 8).

The rationale for dividing by five is simply that the total U.S. stock market has incurred one major decline *on average* about every five years. These declines do not operate on a predictable cycle, and therefore some five-year periods have no major declines and some five-year periods have more than one major decline. See the Historical Risk/Reward Chart A5-1 to visually see this illustrated for the total U.S. stock market.

Declines, recoveries and advances are measured from calendar month-ends to subsequent calendar month-ends. (This lines up with the timing of brokerage and custodial valuations, i.e. month-end statements.) The end of a decline is established when a recovery restores the entire market value temporarily lost in the decline. All calculations are made on a total return basis without consideration of taxes or costs.

The most significant decline in the period of study is dubbed the *worst-case* decline. Both the percentage and duration of the worst-case decline enter into the Composite Risk compilation. On Chart A5-1, the worst decline for the total U.S. stock market in the 1960-1996 period is the decline that began in January 1973 and ended 21 months later in September 1974. The domestic market fell a full 45% during the 21-month duration of this decline. In the bottom right-hand corner of Chart A5-1, the worst decline shows as "45%" and "21 months."

All the remaining major declines (the next seven most severe declines in this period of study) are averaged together to determine the average cyclical decline to which an investor was exposed. On Chart A5-1, the average cyclical decline (without including the worst-case decline already illustrated) of the domestic stock market in the 1960-1996 period was 20% over a period of 9 months.

Finally, the recovery periods for all of the cyclical declines (including the worst-case) are averaged together. On Chart A5-1, you can see that the domestic stock market took 10 months on average to fully recover from the eight cyclical declines of the 1960-1996 period. The basic premise is that each additional percentage of a major decline adds to risk as does each additional month that the decline unfolds and each additional month that it takes to fully recover.

A large part of the attractiveness of this particular investor's tool is its consistency. Composite Risk scores among the domestic asset classes evaluated were amazingly consistent in their relationship to each other in each of several long-term periods studied including the full 1926-1996 modern financial era.

Total Domestic Stock Market
Growth of $100,000
(12/31/59 – 12/31/96)

Year	Jan	Feb	Mar	Apr	May	Jun	Jul	Aug	Sep	Oct	Nov	Dec	Annual Returns
1960	$100,000	↓	↓	↓	↑	+26% 26 mo.		↑	↓	↓	↑	↑	0.8
1961	↑	↑	↑	↑	↑	↓	↑	↑	↓	↑	↑	→	27.4
1962	↓	$126,200	<22%> 4 mo.			$98,800	↑	↑	↓	↑	↑	↑	-10.2
1963	↑	↓	↑	↑	↑	↓	↓	↑	↓	↑	↓	↑	20.9
1964	↑	↑	↑	↑	↑	↑	+90% 43 mo.		↑	↑	↑	↑	16.1
1965	↑	↑	↓	↑	↓	↓	↑	↑	↑	↑	↑	↑	14.4
1966	$187,500		<15%> 8 mo.					$158,600	↑	↑	↑	↑	-8.7
1967	↑	↑	↑	↑	+56% 32 mo.		↑	↓	↓	↓	↓	↓	28.7
1968	↓	↓	↑	↑	↑	↑	↓	↑	↑	↑	↑	↓	14.2
1969	↓	↓	↑	↑	$246,900	<31%> 13 mo.							-10.9
1970						$171,400	↑	↑	↑	↓	↑	↑	0.0
1971	↑	↑	↑	↑	↓	+76% 30 mo.		↑	↓	↓	↓	↑	16.2
1972	↑	↑	↑	↑	↑	↓	↓	↑	↓	↑	↑	$301,100	16.9
1973					<45%> 21 mo.								-18.1
1974								$164,900	↑	↓	↓		-27.2
1975	↑	↑	↑	↑	↑	↑	↓	↓	↓	↑	↑	↓	38.7
1976	↑	↑	↑	↓	↓	↑	↓	↓	↑	↓	↑	↓	26.7
1977	↓	↓	↓	↑	↓	↑	↓	↓	↑	↓	↑	↑	-4.2
1978	↓	↓	↑	↑	↑	+228% 78 mo.		↑	↓	↓	↑	↑	7.5
1979	↑	↓	↑	↑	↓	↑	↑	↑	↑	↓	↑	↑	23.0
1980	↑	↑	↓	↑	↑	↑	↑	↑	↑	↑	↑	↓	32.7
1981	↓	↑	$541,300	<16%> 16 mo.									-3.7
1982							$456,400	↑	↑	↑	↑	↑	20.8
1983	↑	+68% 11 mo.		↑	↑	$766,900	<10%> 11 mo.				↑	↑	22.0
1984			$689,800	↓	↓	↑	↑	↑	↓	↑	↓	↑	4.3
1985	↑	↑	↓	↓	↑	↓	↑	↓	↓	↑	↑	↑	32.2
1986	↑	↑	↑	↓	↑	+136% 39 mo.		↑	↓	↑	↑	↓	16.1
1987	↑	↑	↑	↓	↑	↑	↑	$1,627,400	<30%> 3 mo.		$1,143,400	↑	1.8
1988	↑	↑	↓	↑	↑	↑	↑		↓			↑	18.0
1989	↑	↓	↑	↑	↑	+68% 30 mo.		↓	↓	↑	↑	↑	28.9
1990	↓	↑	↑	↓	$1,914,800	<17%> 5 mo.			$1,592,600		↑	↑	-5.9
1991	↑	↑	↑	↑	↑	↑	↑	↑	↓	↑	↓	↑	34.7
1992	↓	↑	↓	↑	↑	↓	↑	↓	↑	↑	↑	↑	9.8
1993	↑	↑	↑	↓	↑	↑	↓	↑	↑	↑	↓	↑	11.1
1994	↑	↓	↓	↓	↑	+200% 74 mo.		↑	↓	↑	↓	↑	-0.1
1995	↓	↑	↑	↑	↑	↑	↑	↑	↑	↓	↑	↑	36.8
1996	↑	↑	↑	↑	↑	↓	↓	↑	↑	↑	↑	$4,782,200	21.3%

Total Return: Includes reinvested dividends and capital gains   **Standard Deviation: 16.1**

Source: Center for Research in Security Prices (CRSP) University of Chicago

↑ ↓ *Up or Down Month*   ▬ *Cyclical Declines*   ▬ *Recovery (to pre-decline level)*   ◯ *Net New Advancement*

REWARD*		RISK	
Total Return (1960-1996)	11.0%	Worst Decline	45 % / 21 mo.
Riskless Return (T-bills)	<6.1%>	Average Decline	20 % / 9 mo.
		Average Recovery	10 mo.
AVERAGE ANNUAL REWARD OF TOTAL DOMESTIC STOCK MARKET	4.9%	COMPOSITE RISK	105 points

EFFICIENCY RATING = 47

*Annualized   (Reward ÷ Composite Risk x 1,000)

CHART A5-1

Historical Risk/Reward

Large Cap Stocks
Growth of $100,000
(12/31/59 – 12/31/96)

Year	Jan	Feb	Mar	Apr	May	Jun	Jul	Aug	Sep	Oct	Nov	Dec	Annual Returns
1960	$100,000	↑	↓	↓	↑	+25% 26 mo.		↑	↑	→	↓	↑	0.9
1961	↑	↑	↑	↑	↑	↑	↑	↑	↓	↑	↑	↑	27.0
1962	↑	$125,400	<21%> 4 mo.			$98,800	↑	↑	↓	↑	↑	↑	-9.0
1963	↑	↓	↑	↑	↑	↓	↓	↑	↓	↑	↓	↑	22.2
1964	↑	↑	↑	↑	↑	↓	↑	+15% 43 mo.	↑	↑	↑	↑	15.7
1965	↑	↑	↓	↓	-↑	↓	↑	↑	↑	↑	↑	↑	10.7
1966	$182,900	<15%> 8 mo.							$155,100	↑	↑	→	-9.4
1967	↑	↑	↑	↑	↑	↑	↑	↓	↑	↓	↑	↑	21.8
1968	↓	↓	↑	↑	↑	+48% 26 mo.	↑	↑	↑	$229,400			9.3
1969	<29%> 19 mo.												-7.4
1970					$163,000	↑	↑	↑	↑	↓	↑	↑	2.3
1971	↑	↑	↑	↑	↓	↑	↓	+77% 30 mo.		↓	↑	↑	14.7
1972	↑	↑	↑	↑	↑	↓	↑	↑	↓	↓	↑	$288,000	20.5
1973	<44%> 21 mo.												-14.5
1974									$162,000	↑	↓	↓	-27.6
1975	↑	↑	↑	↑	↑	↑	↓	↓	↓	↑	↑	↑	34.1
1976	↑	↓	↑	↓	↓	↑	↓	↑	↑	↓	↓	↑	22.5
1977	↓	↓	↓	↑	↓	↑	↓	↓	↓	↓	↑	↑	-7.8
1978	↓	↓	↑	↑	↑	↓	+124% 65 mo.	↑	↓	↓	↑	↑	5.6
1979	↑	↓	↑	↑	↑	↑	↑	↑	↑	↓	↑	↑	18.2
1980	↑	$362,300	<10%>1 mo.	↑	↑	+37% 12 mo.	↑	↑	↑	↑	↑	↑	32.9
1981	↓	↑	$445,700	<16%> 16 mo.						↑	↑	↑	-6.4
1982							$375,400	↑	↑	↑	↑	↑	19.0
1983	↑	↑	↑	↑	↓	↑	↑	↑	↑	↓	↑	↓	19.8
1984	↓	↓	↑	↑	↓	↑	↑	↑	↑	↑	↓	↑	8.0
1985	↑	↑	↑	↓	↑	+269% 61 mo.	↓	↓	↓	↑	↑	↑	32.8
1986	↑	↑	↑	↓	↑	↑	↓	↑	↓	↑	↑	↓	17.9
1987	↑	↑	↑	↑	↑	↑	↑	$1,385,100	<29%> 3 mo.	$984,000	↑		4.0
1988	↑	↑	↓	↑	↓	↑	↓	↓	↑	↑	↓	↑	16.0
1989	↑	↓	↑	+70% 30 mo.	↓	↑	↑	↑	↑	↓	↑	↑	32.3
1990	↓	↑	↑	↓	$1,673,500	<14%> 5 mo.			$1,444,600	↑	↑		-2.6
1991	↑	↑	↑	↑	↑	↓	↑	↑	↓	↑	↓	↑	31.2
1992	↓	↑	↓	↑	↑	↓	↑	↓	↑	↑	↑	↑	6.9
1993	↑	↑	↑	↓	↑	+185% 74 mo.	↑	↑	↓	↑	↓	↑	8.5
1994	↑	↓	↓	↑	↑	↓	↑	↑	↓	↑	↓	↑	1.0
1995	↑	↑	↑	↑	↑	↑	↑	↓	↑	↓	↑	↑	38.6
1996	↑	↑	↑	↑	↑	↑	↓	↑	↑	↑	↑	$4,122,300	22.9%

Total Return: Includes reinvested dividends and capital gains   **Standard Deviation: 15.4**

Source: Center for Research in Security Prices (CRSP) University of Chicago

↑ ↓ Up or Down Month   ■ Cyclical Declines   ▨ Recovery (to pre-decline level)   ⬭ Net New Advancement

REWARD*		RISK	
Total Return (1960-1996)	10.6%	Worst Decline	44 %
			21 mo.
Riskless Return (T-bills)	<6.1%>	Average Decline	19 %
			8 mo.
AVERAGE ANNUAL REWARD OF		Average Recovery	10 mo.
LARGE CAP STOCKS	**4.5%**	**COMPOSITE RISK**	**102 points**

EFFICIENCY RATING = 44

Annualized   (Reward ÷ Composite Risk x 1,000)

CHART A5-2

Historical Risk/Reward

Mid/Small Cap Stocks
Growth of $100,000
(12/31/59 – 12/31/96)

Year	Jan	Feb	Mar	Apr	May	Jun	Jul	Aug	Sep	Oct	Nov	Dec	Annual Returns
1960	$100,000	↓	↓	↓	↑	↑	+30% 26 mo.		↓	↓	↑	↑	0.8
1961	↑	↑	↑	↑	↑	↓	↓	↑	↓	↑	↑	↓	29.2
1962	↓	$129,800	<24%> 4 mo.			$98,700	↑	↑	↓	↓	↑	↓	-14.0
1963	↑	↓	↑	↑	↑	↓	↑	↑	↓	↑	↓	↑	16.7
1964	↑	↑	↑	↓	↑	+112% 46 mo.		↓	↑	↑	↑	↓	17.9
1965	↑	↑	↑	↑	↓	↑	↑	↑	↑	↑	↑	↑	28.0
1966	↑	↑	↓	$208,800	<18%> 5 mo.			$171,200	↑	↑	↑		-6.2
1967	↑	↑	↑	↑	↓	↑	↑	↓	↓	↓	↑	↓	46.5
1968	↓	↓	↓	↑	↑	+103% 26 mo.		↑	↑	↑	$347,500		25.1
1969	<43%> 19 mo.												-17.4
1970						$198,100	↑	↑	↑	↑	↑	↑	-4.7
1971	↑	↑	↑	↑	↑	↓	↑	↑	↓	↓	↓	↑	20.5
1972	↑	↑	↑	→	↓	+77% 29 mo.		↑	↓	↓	$350,700		7.8
1973	<50%> 22 mo.												-28.5
1974								$176,600	↑	↑	↓	↓	-25.4
1975	↑	↑	↑	↑	↑	↑	↓	↓	↓	↑	↑	↓	57.7
1976	↑	↑	↑	↓	↓	↑	↓	↓	↑	↓	↑	↑	42.2
1977	↓	↓	↑	↑	↓	+225% 47 mo.		↓	↑	↑	↑	↑	7.5
1978	↓	↑	↑	↑	↑	↓	↑	$573,500	<17%> 2 mo.		↑	↑	12.5
1979	↑	↑	↑	↑	↓	↑	↑	↑	↓	↑	↑	↑	37.1
1980	↑	↓	↓	+115% 31 mo.	↑	↑	↑	↑	↑	↑	↑	↓	31.9
1981	↓	↑	↑	↑	$1,022,500	<19%> 14 mo.							3.5
1982							$836,700	↑	↑	↑	↑	↑	26.0
1983	↑	↑	↑	↑	↑	↑	↓	↑	↓	↑	↓		28.7
1984	↓	↓	↓	↓	↓	↑	↓	↑	↓	↓	↑		-1.2
1985	↑	↑	↓	↓	+256% 61 mo.		↑	↓	↓	↑	↑		31.8
1986	↓	↑	↑	↑	↑	↑	↑	↑	↓	↑	↑	↑	13.3
1987	↑	↑	↑	↓	↑	↑	↑	$2,982,400	<31%> 3 mo.	$2,047,100	↑		-1.5
1988	↑	↑	↑	↑	↓	↑	↓	↓	↑	↑	↑		22.6
1989	↑	↑	↑	↑	↑	↓	↑	+65% 30 mo.		↓	↑	↑	23.1
1990	↓	↑	↑	↓	$3,367,400	<24%> 5 mo.			$2,551,100	↑	↑		-12.9
1991	↑	↑	↑	↑	↑	↓	↑	↑	↓	↑	↓	↑	44.3
1992	↑	↑	↓	↓	↑	↓	↑	↓	↑	↑	↑	↑	16.7
1993	↑	↓	↑	↓	↑	+242% 74 mo.		↑	↑	↑	↓	↑	16.9
1994	↑	↓	↓	↑	↑	↑	↑	↑	↓	↑	↓	↑	-2.2
1995	↑	↑	↑	↑	↑	↑	↑	↑	↑	↓	↑	↑	32.3
1996	↑	↑	↑	↑	↑	↓	↓	↑	↑	↓	↑	$8,724,400	17.5%

Total Return: Includes reinvested dividends and capital gains   **Standard Deviation: 20.6**

Source: Center for Research in Security Prices (CRSP) University of Chicago

↑ ↓ *Up or Down Month*   ⬛ *Cyclical Declines*   ⬛ *Recovery (to pre-decline level)*   ⬭ *Net New Advancement*

REWARD[*]		**RISK**	
Total Return (1960-1996)	12.8%	Worst Decline	50 % 22 mo.
Riskless Return (T-bills)	<6.1%>	Average Decline	25 % 7 mo.
AVERAGE ANNUAL REWARD OF		Average Recovery	11 mo.
MID/SMALL CAP	6.7%	**COMPOSITE RISK**	**115 points**

EFFICIENCY RATING = 58
Annualized   (Reward ÷ Composite Risk x 1,000)

CHART A5-3

Micro Cap Stocks
Growth of $100,000
(12/31/59 – 12/31/96)

Year	Jan	Feb	Mar	Apr	May	Jun	Jul	Aug	Sep	Oct	Nov	Dec	Annual Returns
1960	$100,000	↓	↓	↓	↑	+33% 27 mo.		↑	↓	↓	↑	↓	-3.3
1961	↑	↑	↑	↑	↑	↓	↑	↑	↓	↑	↑	↑	32.1
1962	↑	↑	$132,700			<24%> 7 mo.				$100,900	↑	↓	-11.9
1963	↑	↑	↑	↑	↑	↓	↑	↑	↓	↑	↓	↓	23.6
1964	↑	↑	↑	↑	↑	↑	+172% 42 mo.		↑	↑	↑	↓	23.5
1965	↑	↑	↑	↑	↓	↑	↑	↑	↑	↓	↓	↑	41.8
1966	↑	↑	↓	$273,900		<22%> 6 mo.				$214,400	↑	↑	-7.0
1967	↑	↑	↑	↑	↓	↑	↑	↓	↑	↓	↑	↑	83.6
1968	↑	↓	↓	↑	+124% 26 mo.		↓	↑	↑	↑	↑	$565,100	36.0
1969													-25.1
1970													-17.4
1971					<58%> 72 mo.								16.5
1972													4.4
1973													-30.9
1974												$235,300	-19.9
1975	↓	↓	↑	↑	↑	↑	↓	↓	↓	↓	↑	↑	52.8
1976	↑	↑	↓	↓	↓	↑	↑	↑	↑	↓	↑	↑	57.4
1977	↑	↓	↓	↑	+352% 44 mo.		↑	↓	↑	↓	↑	↑	25.4
1978	↓	↑	↑	↑	↑	↓	↑	$1,063,600	<25%> 2 mo.		↑	↑	23.5
1979	↑	↓	↑	↑	↑	+70% 15 mo.		↑	↓	↓	↑	↑	43.5
1980	$1,362,000	<20%> 2 mo.		↑	↑	↑	↑	↑	↑	↑	↑	↓	39.9
1981	↑	↑	↑	↑	↑	+242% 39 mo.		↑	↓	↑	↑	↓	13.9
1982	↓	↓	↓	↑	↓	↓	↓	↑	↑	↑	↑	↓	28.0
1983	↑	↑	↑	↑	↑	$3,719,200	<15%> 13 mo.						39.7
1984						$3,156,900	↑	↑	↓	↓	↑	-6.7
1985	↑	↑	↓	↓	↑	↑	↑	↓	↓	↑	↑	↑	24.7
1986	↑	↑	↑	+80% 37 mo.		↓	↑	↑	↓	↓	↓	6.9
1987	↑	↑	↑	↓	↓	↑	↑	$5,688,400	<33%> 3 mo.	$3,836,700	↑	-9.3
1988	↑	↑	↑	↑	↓	↑	↓	↓	↑	↓	↓	↑	22.9
1989	↑	↑	↑	↑	+54% 22 mo.		↑	$5,924,800			↓	↓	10.2
1990	<32%> 13 mo.								$4,023,500	↑	↑	-21.6
1991	↑	↑	↑	↑	↑	↓	↑	↑	↑	↑	↓	↑	44.6
1992	↑	↑	↓	↓	↓	↓	↑	↓	↑	↑	↑	↑	23.3
1993	↑	↓	↑	↓	↑	↓	↑	↑	↑	↑	↓	↑	21.0
1994	↑	↓	↓	↑	↓	+275% 74 mo.		↑	↑	↑	↓	↑	3.1
1995	↑	↑	↑	↑	↑	↑	↑	↑	↑	↓	↑	↑	34.5
1996	↑	↑	↑	↑	↑	↓	↓	↑	↑	↓	↑	$15,084,900	17.6%

Total Return: Includes reinvested dividends and capital gains

Standard Deviation: 25.2

Source: © Computed using data from Stocks, Bonds, Bills & Inflation 1996 Yearbook™ *with data updated January 1997, Ibbotson Associates, Chicago*

↑ ↓ *Up or Down Month* ⬤ *Cyclical Declines* ⬤ *Recovery (to pre-decline level)* ◯ *Net New Advancement*

REWARD*		**RISK**	
Total Return (1960-1996)	14.5%	Worst Decline	58 %
			72 mo.
Riskless Return (T-bills)	<6.1%>	Average Decline	24 %
			7 mo.
AVERAGE ANNUAL REWARD OF		Average Recovery	10 mo.
MICRO CAP STOCKS	**8.4%**	**COMPOSITE RISK**	**171 points**

EFFICIENCY RATING = 49
(Reward ÷ Composite Risk x 1,000)

*Annualized

CHART A5-4

5-Year Government Bonds

Growth of $100,000
(12/31/59 – 12/31/96)

Year	Jan	Feb	Mar	Apr	May	Jun	Jul	Aug	Sep	Oct	Nov	Dec	Annual Returns
1960	$100,000↑	↑	↑	↓	↑	↑	↑	↓	↑	↑	↓	↑	11.8
1961	↓	↑	↑	↑	↓	↓	↑	↑	↑	↑	↓	↑	1.8
1962	↓	↑	↑	↑	↑	↓	↑	↑	↑	↑	↑	↑	5.6
1963	↑	↑	↑	↑	↑		→	↑	↑	↑	↑	→	1.6
1964	↑	↑	↑	↑	↑	+45% 106 mo.		↑	↑	↑	↓	↑	4.0
1965	↑	↑	↑	↑	↑	↑	↑	↓		→	↑	↑	1.0
1966	→	↓	↑	↓	↑	↓	↓	↓	↑	↑	↑	↑	4.7
1967	↑	↓	↑	↓	↑	↓	↑	↓	↑	↓	↑	↑	1.0
1968	↑	↑	↓	↓	↑	↑	↑	↑	↑	$144,600 [bar]			4.5
1969	[<3%> 11 mo. bar]								$139,700	↑	↓	↓	-0.7
1970	↑	↑	↑	↓	↑	+25% 18 mo.		↑	↑	↑	↑	↑	16.9
1971	↑	↑	$174,300 <5%> 3 mo.		$165,600	↓	↑	↑	↑	↑	↑	↑	8.7
1972	↑	↑	↑	↑	↑	↑	↑	↑	↑	+19% 32 mo.		↑	5.2
1973	↓	↓	↑	↑	↓	↓	↓	↑	↑	↑	↑	↑	4.6
1974	↑	$197,700 <4%> 2 mo.		↑	↓	↑	↓	↑	↑	↑	↑		5.7
1975	↑	↑	↓	↓	↑	↑	↓	↓	↑	↑	↓	↑	7.8
1976	↑	↑	↑	↑	↓	+47% 62 mo.		↑	↑	↑	↑	↑	12.9
1977	↓	↑	↑	↑	↑	↑	↑	↑	↑	↓	↑	↑	1.4
1978	↑	↑	↑	↑	→	↓	↑	↑	↑	↓	↑	↑	3.5
1979	↑	↑	↑	↑	↑	$280,400			<9%>8 mo.				4.1
1980	$255,400	+19% 3 mo.		$304,300			<9%> 14 mo.						3.9
1981						$278,500	↑	↑	↑	↑	↑	↓	9.5
1982	↑	↑	↑	↑	↑	↑	↑	↑	↑	↑	↑	↑	29.1
1983	↑	↑	↓	↑	↓	+59% 30 mo.		↑	↑	↑	↑	↑	7.4
1984	$444,000	< 4%> 4 mo.			$428,500	↑	↑	↑	↑	↑	↑	↑	14.0
1985	↑	↓	↑	↑	↑	↑	↓	+64% 33 mo.		↑	↑	↑	20.3
1986	↑	↑	↑	↑	↓	↑	↑	↑	↓	↑	↑	↑	15.1
1987	↑	$700,600	<3%>7 mo.						$676,600	↑	↑	↑	2.9
1988	↑	↑	↓	↑	↑	↑	↓	↓	↑	↑	↓	↓	6.1
1989	↑	↓	↑	↑	↑	↑	↑	↓	↓	↑	↑	↑	13.3
1990	↓	↑	↓	↓	↑	↑	↑	↑	↑	↑	↑	↑	9.7
1991	↑	↑	↑	↓	↑	+93% 76 mo.		↑	↑	↑	↑	↑	15.5
1992	↓	↑	↓	↑	↑	↑	↑	↑	↑	↓	↓	↑	7.2
1993	↑	↑	↑	↑	↓	↑	↑	↑	↑	↑	↓	↑	11.2
1994	$1,305,000				<7%>10 mo.						$1,215,000	↑	-5.1
1995	↑	↑	↑	↑	↑	↓	↑	↑	↑	↑	↑	↑	16.8
1996	↓	↓	↓	↓	↓	+20% 25 mo.		↓	↑	↑	↑	$1,456,700	2.1

Total Return: Includes reinvested interest   **Standard Deviation: 7.0**

Source: © Computed using data from Stocks, Bonds, Bills & Inflation 1996 Yearbook™ with data updated January 1997, Ibbotson Associates, Chicago

↑↓ *Up or Down Month*   ■ *Cyclical Declines*   ▨ *Recovery (to pre-decline level)*   ⬭ *Net New Advancement*

REWARD*		RISK	
Total Return (1960-1996)	7.5%	Worst Decline	9 % / 15 mo.
Riskless Return (T-bills)	<6.1%>	Average Decline	5 % / 6 mo.
AVERAGE ANNUAL REWARD OF		Average Recovery	4 mo.
5-YEAR GOVERNMENT BONDS	**1.4%**	**COMPOSITE RISK**	**39 points**

EFFICIENCY RATING = 36

Annualized   (Reward ÷ Composite Risk x 1,000)

CHART A5-5

Long-Term Corporate Bonds

Growth of $100,000
(12/31/59 – 12/31/96)

Year	Jan	Feb	Mar	Apr	May	Jun	Jul	Aug	Sep	Oct	Nov	Dec	Annual Returns
1960	$100,000	↑	↑	↓	↓	↑	↑	↑	↓	↑	↓	↑	9.1
1961	↑	↑	↓	↓	↑	↓	↑	↓	↑	↑	↑	↓	4.8
1962	↑	↑	↑	↑	→	↓	↓	↑	↑	↑	↑	↑	7.9
1963	↑	↑	↑	↓	↑	+38% 104 mo.		↑	↑	↑	↑	↓	2.2
1964	↑	↑	↑	↓	↑		↑	↑	↑	↑	→	↑	4.8
1965	↑	↑	↑	↑	↓	→	↑	↓	↓	↓	↓	↓	-0.5
1966	↑	↓	↓	↑	↓	↑	↓	↓	↑	↑	↑	↑	0.2
1967	↑	↓	↑	↓	↓	↓	↑	↓	↑	↓	↓	↑	-5.0
1968	↑	↑	↓	↑	↑	↑	↑	$137,500	<14%> 16 mo.				2.6
1969												$118,100	-8.1
1970	↑	↑	↓	↓	↓	↑	↑	↑	↑	↓	↑	↑	18.4
1971	↑	↓	↑	↓	↓	↓	↑	↑	↓	↑	↑	↑	11.0
1972	↓	↑	↑	↑	↑	+42% 50 mo.		↑	↑	↑	↑	→	8.0
1973	↓	↑	↑	↑	↓	↓	↓	↑	↑	↓	↑	↓	1.1
1974	↓	$167,600				<12%> 6 mo.		$146,800	↑	↑	↑	↓	-3.1
1975	↑	↑	↓	↓	↑	↓	↓	↓	↓	↑	↓	↑	14.6
1976	↑	↑	↑	↓	↓	↑	↑	↑	↑	↑	↑	↑	18.6
1977	↓	↓	↑	↑	+63% 58 mo.		↓	↑	↓	↓	↑	↓	1.7
1978	↓	↑	↑	↓	↓	↑	↑	↑	↓	↓	↑	↓	-0.1
1979	↑	↓	↑	↓	↑	$239,600							-4.2
1980					<22%> 27 mo.								-2.8
1981									$186,000	↑	↑	↑	-1.2
1982	↓	↓	↑	↑	↑	+75% 19 mo.		↑	↑	↑	↑	↑	42.6
1983	↓	↑	↑	$324,900		<10%> 13 mo.							6.3
1984				$292,900	↑	↑	↑	↑	↑	↑	↑	↑	16.9
1985	↑	↓	↑	↑	↑	↑	↓	↑	↑	↑	↑	↑	30.1
1986	↑	↑	↑	↑	↓	+101% 33 mo.		↑	↓	↑	↑	↑	19.8
1987	↑	$588,900		<11%> 7 mo.					$526,100	↑	↑	↓	-0.3
1988	↓	↑	↑	↓	↑	↑	↑	↑	↑	↑	↓	↑	10.7
1989	↑	↓	↑	↑	+40% 27 mo.			↓	↑	↑	↑	$735,500	16.2
1990	<4% 4 mo.			$706,000	↑		↑	↓	↑	↑	↑	↑	6.8
1991	↑	↑	↑	↑	↑	↓	+69% 45 mo.		↑	↑	↑	↑	19.9
1992	↓	↑	↓	↑	↑	↑	↑	↑	↑	↓	↑	↑	9.4
1993	↑	↑	↑	↑	↑	↑	↑	↑	↑	↑	↓	↑	13.2
1994	$1,189,300				<9%> 9 mo.					$1,079,700	↑	↑	-5.8
1995	↑	↑	↑	↑	↑	+29% 14 mo.		↑	↑	↑	↑	$1,397,500	27.2
1996	<7% 4 mo.		$1,308,500	↑	↑	↑	↑	↑	+8% 8 mo.		↑	$1,417,100	1.4%

Total Return: Includes reinvested interest　　　　　　　　　　　　　　　　　　　**Standard Deviation: 7.9**

Source: © Computed using data from Stocks, Bonds, Bills & Inflation 1996 Yearbook™ *with data updated January 1997, Ibbotson Associates, Chicago*

↑ ↓ *Up or Down Month*　　■ *Cyclical Declines*　　▨ *Recovery (to pre-decline level)*　　▢ *Net New Advancement*

REWARD[*]		**RISK**	
Total Return (1960-1996)	7.4%	Worst Decline	22 % / 27 mo.
Riskless Return (T-bills)	<6.1%>	Average Decline	10 % / 8 mo.
AVERAGE ANNUAL REWARD OF		Average Recovery	6 mo.
LONG-TERM CORPORATE BONDS	**1.3%**	**COMPOSITE RISK**	**73 points**

EFFICIENCY RATING = 18

Annualized　　　　　　　　　　　　(Reward ÷ Composite Risk x 1,000)

CHART A5-6

Domestic Model Portfolio Guidelines

Certain guidelines were adopted in order to prevent any model from being too lopsided toward any one particular asset class. These guidelines are:

- No asset class can represent more than 50% of a model portfolio (to ensure appropriate diversification).

- Every asset class must be represented in each model (except in the All-Equity Model Portfolio).

- No domestic stock asset class can represent more than twice its normal weighting in the U.S. stock market.

Virtually every combination of domestic stock asset classes, 5-year Treasury bonds and 30-day T-bills that met the guidelines above was tested. The returns assumed a reinvestment of all dividends, interest and capital gains. The goal was to find the most favorable combination of the five asset classes that satisfied the objectives set out for each model portfolio.

If more than one portfolio design met the rate-of-return objective and produced an identical level of risk, the portfolio with the most even distribution of asset classes was selected as the domestic model.

All of the results of this study may be duplicated using the databases identified in Chart 8-1.

Domestic Model Portfolio: Moderate
(September 1929 through February 1937)
Illustrates annual gains/declines by asset class and annual rebalancing back to 47% Stocks, 47% Bonds, 6% Cash.

Year			47% Stocks	47% Bonds	6% Cash	Nominal Value of Total Portfolio	Value of U.S. $ Relative to 9/1/29	Real Value of Total Portfolio
1929	1-Sep		470,000	470,000	60,000	1,000,000	$1.00	$1,000,000
	Gain/<Loss>		<156,000>	18,000	1,000	<137,000>		
	31-Dec		314,000	488,000	61,000	863,000	$1.01	$ 872,000
1930	1-Jan	(Rebalanced)	405,000	405,000	52,000	863,000		
	Gain/<Loss>		<122,000>	28,000	1,000	< 94,000>		
	31-Dec		283,000	433,000	53,000	769,000	$1.07	$ 823,000
1931	1-Jan	(Rebalanced)	361,000	361,000	46,000	769,000		
	Gain/<Loss>		<163,000>	< 8,000>	1,000	<171,000>		
	31-Dec		198,000	353,000	47,000	598,000	$1.19	$ 712,000
1932	1-Jan	(Rebalanced)	281,000	281,000	36,000	598,000		
	Gain/<Loss>		< 20,000>	25,000	0	5,000		
	31-Dec		261,000	306,000	36,000	603,000	$1.33	$ 802,000
1933	1-Jan	(Rebalanced)	284,000	284,000	36,000	603,000		
	Gain/<Loss>		233,000	5,000	0	239,000		
	31-Dec		517,000	289,000	36,000	842,000	$1.32	$1,111,000
1934	1-Jan	(Rebalanced)	396,000	396,000	51,000	842,000		
	Gain/<Loss>		24,000	35,000	0	59,000		
	31-Dec		420,000	431,000	51,000	901,000	$1.30	$1,171,000
1935	1-Jan	(Rebalanced)	424,000	424,000	54,000	901,000		
	Gain/<Loss>		192,000	29,000	0	223,000		
	31-Dec		616,000	453,000	54,000	1,124,000	$1.26	$1,416,000
1936	1-Jan	(Rebalanced)	528,000	528,000	67,000	1,124,000		
	Gain/<Loss>		199,000	17,000	1,000	215,000		
	31-Dec		727,000	545,000	68,000	1,339,000	$1.24	$1,660,000
1937	1-Jan	(Rebalanced)	629,000	629,000	80,000	1,339,000		
	Gain/<Loss>		48,000	< 1,000>	0	47,000		
	28-Feb		677,000	628,000	80,000	1,386,000	$1.23	$1,705,000

Average Annual Return Over 90 Months: 4.4% (nominal)   **7.4%** (real)

CHART A11-1

Moderate Domestic Model
Maximum Perpetual "Real" Retirement Income
Full Adjustment for Inflation (CPI*) Increases

Initial Portfolio: $500,000   Initial Income: $19,500 (3.90% of Original Portfolio)

	The Numbers You See				The Numbers You Feel	
Year	The Portfolio Grows in Nominal $ Even After Paying Out Retiree Distributions	Retiree's Annual Distributions– Increasing Annually with the Full Change in Inflation	CPI: Annual Inflation Rate %	CPI: Cumulative Inflation %	This Portfolio Remains Fairly Stable in Real $ (Adjusted for Inflation)	Retiree's Annual Distributions in Real $ (Adjusted for Inflation)
1960	$ 509,967	$ 19,500	1.5%	1.5%	$ 502,431	$19,500
1961	562,999	19,637	0.7	2.2	550,823	19,500
1962	529,041	19,872	1.2	3.4	511,462	19,500
1963	563,889	20,190	1.6	5.1	536,567	19,500
1964	601,711	20,432	1.2	6.4	565,767	19,500
1965	644,378	20,821	1.9	8.4	594,588	19,500
1966	614,140	21,528	3.4	12.1	548,053	19,500
1967	703,480	22,174	3.0	15.4	609,494	19,500
1968	759,042	23,217	4.7	20.8	628,111	19,500
1969	687,265	24,633	6.1	28.2	536,019	19,500
1970	715,145	25,988	5.5	35.3	528,686	19,500
1971	777,341	26,871	3.4	39.9	555,769	19,500
1972	818,411	27,785	3.4	44.6	565,892	19,500
1973	725,864	30,230	8.8	57.3	461,305	19,500
1974	627,390	33,918	12.2	76.5	355,368	19,500
1975	755,586	36,292	7.0	88.9	399,982	19,500
1976	885,433	38,034	4.8	98.0	447,251	19,500
1977	857,795	40,620	6.8	111.4	405,703	19,500
1978	871,899	44,276	9.0	130.5	378,324	19,500
1979	959,098	50,165	13.3	161.1	367,308	19,500
1980	1,073,495	56,385	12.4	193.5	365,764	19,500
1981	1,068,402	61,404	8.9	219.6	334,278	19,500
1982	1,276,941	63,799	3.9	232.1	384,529	19,500
1983	1,418,857	66,223	3.8	244.7	411,623	19,500
1984	1,467,122	68,872	4.0	258.5	409,255	19,500
1985	1,760,697	71,489	3.8	272.1	473,167	19,500
1986	1,948,821	72,275	1.1	276.2	518,025	19,500
1987	1,920,013	75,455	4.4	292.8	488,858	19,500
1988	2,081,740	78,775	4.4	310.0	507,697	19,500
1989	2,400,591	82,399	4.6	328.9	559,712	19,500
1990	$2,338,749	$ 87,425	6.1%	355.1%	$ 513,942	$ 19,500

Retirement Income (Inflation-Adjusted) is Perpetual
Principal Value Fluctuates Around Original Real Value

*Consumer Price Index

CHART A13-1

Moderate Domestic Model
Maximum Perpetual "Real" Retirement Income
Two-Thirds Adjustment for Inflation (CPI*) Increases

Initial Portfolio: $500,000   Initial Income: $26,500 (5.30% of Original Portfolio)

	The Numbers You See				The Numbers You Feel	
Year	The Portfolio Grows in Nominal $ Even After Paying Out Retiree Distributions	Retiree's Annual Distributions– Increasing Annually with the ⅔ Change in Inflation	⅔ x CPI: Two-Thirds of Annual Inflation Rate %	⅔ x CPI: Two-Thirds of Cumulative Inflation %	This Portfolio Remains Fairly Stable in Real $ (Adjusted for ⅔ Inflation)	Retiree's Annual Distributions in Real $ (Adjusted for ⅔ Inflation)
1960	$ 502,967	$ 26,500	1.0%	1.0%	$ 497,985	$ 26,500
1961	548,014	26,624	0.5	1.5	540,064	26,500
1962	507,466	26,837	0.8	2.3	496,133	26,500
1963	533,137	27,123	1.1	3.4	515,727	26,500
1964	560,874	27,340	0.8	4.2	538,250	26,500
1965	592,366	27,687	1.3	5.5	561,358	26,500
1966	556,045	28,315	2.3	7.9	515,253	26,500
1967	628,129	28,881	2.0	10.1	570,630	26,500
1968	668,683	29,787	3.1	13.5	589,007	26,500
1969	596,152	30,999	4.1	18.1	504,589	26,500
1970	610,743	32,136	3.7	22.5	498,646	26,500
1971	653,942	32,865	2.3	25.3	522,076	26,500
1972	678,257	33,610	2.3	28.1	529,481	26,500
1973	591,029	35,583	5.9	35.6	435,806	26,500
1974	499,986	38,478	8.1	46.7	340,931	26,500
1975	590,797	40,275	4.7	53.5	384,883	26,500
1976	680,501	41,564	3.2	58.4	429,569	26,500
1977	647,030	43,449	4.5	65.6	390,718	26,500
1978	645,007	46,058	6.0	75.5	367,440	26,500
1979	696,482	50,143	8.9	91.1	364,434	26,500
1980	766,211	54,291	8.3	106.9	370,294	26,500
1981	748,890	57,513	5.9	119.2	341,642	26,500
1982	880,774	59,010	2.6	124.9	391,620	26,500
1983	963,833	60,505	2.5	130.6	417,957	26,500
1984	981,285	62,119	2.7	136.8	414,467	26,500
1985	1,161,764	63,694	2.5	142.8	478,566	26,500
1986	1,269,423	64,161	0.7	144.5	519,105	26,500
1987	1,233,763	66,044	2.9	151.7	490,139	26,500
1988	1,320,323	67,983	2.9	159.1	509,571	26,500
1989	1,504,744	70,068	3.1	167.1	563,460	26,500
1990	$ 1,447,861	$ 72,919	4.1%	177.9%	$ 520,963	$ 26,500

Retirement Income (Inflation-Adjusted) is Perpetual
Principal Value Fluctuates Around Original Real Value

*Consumer Price Index

CHART A13-2

Moderate Domestic Model
Worst Case Study* (Retire in 1968)
Maximum Perpetual "Real" Retirement Income
Full Adjustment for Inflation (CPI**) Increases)

Initial Portfolio: $500,000   Initial Income: $17,000 (3.40% of Original Portfolio)

	The Numbers You See				The Numbers You Feel	
Year	The Portfolio Grows in Nominal $ Even After Paying Out Retiree Distributions	Retiree's Annual Distributions– Increasing Annually with the Full Change in Inflation	CPI: Annual Inflation Rate %	CPI: Cumulative Inflation %	This Portfolio Remains Fairly Stable in Real $ (Adjusted for Inflation)	Retiree's Annual Distributions in Real $ (Adjusted for Inflation)
1968	$ 538,193	$ 17,000	4.7%	4.7%	$ 514,033	$ 17,000
1969	485,881	18,037	6.1	11.1	437,389	17,000
1970	504,041	19,029	5.5	17.2	430,082	17,000
1971	546,215	19,676	3.4	21.2	450,743	17,000
1972	573,297	20,345	3.4	25.3	457,534	17,000
1973	506,467	22,135	8.8	36.3	371,507	17,000
1974	435,420	24,836	12.2	53.0	284,663	17,000
1975	521,755	26,574	7.0	63.7	318,791	17,000
1976	608,523	27,850	4.8	71.5	354,777	17,000
1977	586,304	29,744	6.8	83.2	320,058	17,000
1978	592,262	32,421	9.0	99.7	296,616	17,000
1979	647,112	36,733	13.3	126.2	286,042	17,000
1980	719,112	41,288	12.4	154.3	282,800	17,000
1981	709,758	44,962	8.9	176.9	256,310	17,000
1982	841,766	46,716	3.9	187.7	292,571	17,000
1983	928,202	48,491	3.8	198.6	310,803	17,000
1984	952,031	50,430	4.0	210.6	306,521	17,000
1985	1,134,117	52,347	3.8	222.4	351,779	17,000
1986	1,246,438	52,923	1.1	225.9	382,412	17,000
1987	1,218,425	55,251	4.4	240.3	358,063	17,000
1988	1,310,653	57,682	4.4	255.3	368,933	17,000
1989	1,500,107	60,336	4.6	271.6	403,692	17,000
1990	1,449,069	64,016	6.1	294.3	367,538	17,000
1991	1,745,160	66,001	3.1	306.5	429,328	17,000
1992	1,839,355	67,915	2.9	318.3	439,749	17,000
1993	1,984,616	69,748	2.7	329.6	462,003	17,000
1994	1,864,643	71,632	2.7	341.2	422,662	17,000
1995	2,247,639	73,566	2.7	353.1	496,083	17,000
1996	$ 2,411,433	$ 75,993	3.3%	368.0%	$ 515,232	$ 17,000

*1968 was the worst possible year to retire in the Inflation Era (1960-1996). This was the kick-off year for the Super Bowl, the huge 14-year bout of inflation, and (not coincidentally) the worst stock market conditions since the Great Depression (1968-1974).

**Consumer Price Index

CHART A13-3

Moderate Domestic Model
Worst Case Study* (Retire in 1968)
Maximum Perpetual "Real" Retirement Income
Two-Thirds Adjustment for Inflation (CPI**) Increases

Initial Portfolio: $500,000   Initial Income: $24,500 (4.90% of Original Portfolio)

	The Numbers You See				The Numbers You Feel	
Year	The Portfolio Grows in Nominal $ Even After Paying Out Retiree Distributions	Retiree's Annual Distributions– Increasing Annually with the ⅔ Change in Inflation	⅔ x CPI: Two-Thirds of Annual Inflation Rate %	⅔ x CPI: Two-Thirds of Cumulative Inflation %	This Portfolio Remains Fairly Stable in Real $ (Adjusted for ⅔ Inflation)	Retiree's Annual Distributions in Real $ (Adjusted for ⅔ Inflation)
1968	$ 530,724	$ 24,500	3.1%	3.1%	$ 514,592	$ 24,500
1969	471,465	25,497	4.1	7.3	439,262	24,500
1970	481,157	26,432	3.7	11.3	432,429	24,500
1971	513,203	27,032	2.3	13.8	451,001	24,500
1972	530,150	27,645	2.3	16.4	455,563	24,500
1973	459,597	29,267	5.9	23.2	373,040	24,500
1974	386,081	31,649	8.1	33.2	289,788	24,500
1975	453,138	33,127	4.7	39.4	324,949	24,500
1976	518,561	34,187	3.2	43.9	360,328	24,500
1977	489,306	35,738	4.5	50.4	325,248	24,500
1978	483,537	37,883	6.0	59.5	303,211	24,500
1979	517,179	41,244	8.9	73.6	297,882	24,500
1980	563,216	44,655	8.3	88.0	299,617	24,500
1981	543,972	47,306	5.9	99.1	273,164	24,500
1982	632,573	48,536	2.6	104.3	309,603	24,500
1983	684,355	49,766	2.5	109.5	326,667	24,500
1984	688,157	51,094	2.7	115.1	319,945	24,500
1985	805,359	52,389	2.5	120.5	365,180	24,500
1986	870,040	52,774	0.7	122.2	391,636	24,500
1987	834,840	54,322	2.9	128.7	365,077	24,500
1988	881,743	55,917	2.9	135.4	374,594	24,500
1989	992,258	57,632	3.1	142.6	408,996	24,500
1990	940,975	59,977	4.1	152.5	372,694	24,500
1991	1,114,983	61,217	2.1	157.7	432,667	24,500
1992	1,156,237	62,402	1.9	162.7	440,161	24,500
1993	1,227,938	63,525	1.8	167.4	459,187	24,500
1994	1,133,414	64,669	1.8	172.2	416,342	24,500
1995	1,345,136	65,834	1.8	177.1	485,374	24,500
1996	$ 1,421,386	$ 67,283	2.2%	183.2%	$ 501,842	$ 24,500

*1968 was the worst possible year to retire in the Inflation Era (1960-1996). This was the kick-off year for the Super Bowl, the huge 14-year bout of inflation, and (not coincidentally) the worst stock market conditions since the Great Depression (1968-1974).

** Consumer Price Index

CHART A13-4

Moderate Domestic Model
Maximum 30-Year "Real" Retirement Income
Full Adjustment for Inflation (CPI*) Increases

Initial Portfolio: $500,000   Initial Income: $27,000 (5.40% of Original Portfolio)

	The Numbers You See				The Numbers You Feel	
Year	The Portfolio is Depleted After 30 Years of Paying Increasing Retiree Distributions	Retiree's Annual Distributions– Increasing Annually with the Full Change in Inflation	CPI: Annual Inflation Rate %	CPI: Cumulative Inflation %	The Real Value of this Portfolio is Fairly Stable at First– then Declines Steadily	Retiree's Annual Distributions in Real $ (Adjusted for Inflation)
1960	$ 502,467	$ 27,000	1.5%	1.5%	$ 495,041	$ 27,000
1961	546,878	27,189	0.7	2.2	535,051	27,000
1962	505,680	27,515	1.2	3.4	488,877	27,000
1963	530,332	27,956	1.6	5.1	504,636	27,000
1964	556,829	28,291	1.2	6.4	523,566	27,000
1965	586,753	28,829	1.9	8.4	541,415	27,000
1966	549,013	29,809	3.4	12.1	489,934	27,000
1967	617,999	30,703	3.0	15.4	535,433	27,000
1968	655,059	32,146	4.7	20.8	542,065	27,000
1969	580,266	34,107	6.1	28.2	452,567	27,000
1970	589,765	35,983	5.5	35.3	435,996	27,000
1971	626,010	37,206	3.4	39.9	447,573	27,000
1972	642,989	38,471	3.4	44.6	444,596	27,000
1973	552,172	41,857	8.8	57.3	350,920	27,000
1974	456,101	46,963	12.2	76.5	258,346	27,000
1975	525,430	50,251	7.0	88.9	278,145	27,000
1976	589,511	52,663	4.8	98.0	297,774	27,000
1977	541,911	56,244	6.8	111.4	256,302	27,000
1978	517,487	61,306	9.0	130.5	224,542	27,000
1979	529,556	69,459	13.3	161.1	202,805	27,000
1980	545,779	78,072	12.4	193.5	185,959	27,000
1981	489,388	85,021	8.9	219.6	153,118	27,000
1982	525,797	88,336	3.9	232.1	158,335	27,000
1983	519,808	91,693	3.8	244.7	150,801	27,000
1984	467,361	95,361	4.0	258.5	130,371	27,000
1985	484,669	98,985	3.8	272.1	130,249	27,000
1986	456,276	100,073	1.1	276.2	121,285	27,000
1987	362,721	104,477	4.4	292.8	92,353	27,000
1988	299,082	109,074	4.4	310.0	72,940	27,000
1989	242,638	114,091	4.6	328.9	56,573	27,000
1990	$ 124,174	$ 121,051	6.1%	355.1%	$ 27,287	$ 27,000

Principal is Depleted
Retirement Income (Inflation-Adjusted) Lasts 30 Years

*Consumer Price Index

CHART A13-5

Moderate Domestic Model

Maximum 30-Year "Real" Retirement Income
Two-Thirds Adjustment for Inflation (CPI*) Increases

Initial Portfolio: $500,000   Initial Income: $32,000 (6.40% of Original Portfolio)

	The Numbers You See				The Numbers You Feel	
Year	The Portfolio is Depleted After 30 Years of Paying Increasing Retiree Distributions	Retiree's Annual Distributions– Increasing Annually with the ⅔ Change in Inflation	⅔ x CPI: Two-Thirds of Annual Inflation Rate %	⅔ x CPI: Two-Thirds of Cumulative Inflation %	The Real Value of this Portfolio is Fairly Stable at First– then Declines Steadily	Retiree's Annual Distributions in Real $ (Adjusted for ⅔ Inflation)
1960	$ 497,467	$ 32,000	1.0%	1.0%	$ 492,539	$ 32,000
1961	536,205	32,149	0.5	1.5	528,426	32,000
1962	490,383	32,407	0.8	2.3	479,431	32,000
1963	508,646	32,753	1.1	3.4	492,036	32,000
1964	528,179	33,015	0.8	4.2	506,874	32,000
1965	550,475	33,433	1.3	5.5	521,660	32,000
1966	508,844	34,191	2.3	7.9	471,514	32,000
1967	566,363	34,875	2.0	10.1	514,518	32,000
1968	593,817	35,969	3.1	13.5	523,062	32,000
1969	519,503	37,432	4.1	18.1	439,712	32,000
1970	521,416	38,805	3.7	22.5	425,714	32,000
1971	546,670	39,685	2.3	25.3	436,435	32,000
1972	554,507	40,585	2.3	28.1	432,875	32,000
1973	469,317	42,968	5.9	35.6	346,059	32,000
1974	381,113	46,464	8.1	46.7	259,873	32,000
1975	432,399	48,634	4.7	53.5	281,692	32,000
1976	478,282	50,191	3.2	58.4	301,917	32,000
1977	432,827	52,467	4.5	65.6	261,369	32,000
1978	406,668	55,617	6.0	75.5	231,666	32,000
1979	410,187	60,550	8.9	91.1	214,630	32,000
1980	417,668	65,558	8.3	106.9	201,850	32,000
1981	370,127	69,450	5.9	119.2	168,851	32,000
1982	393,216	71,257	2.6	124.9	174,836	32,000
1983	384,247	73,063	2.5	130.6	166,625	32,000
1984	340,957	75,012	2.7	136.8	144,011	32,000
1985	348,884	76,913	2.5	142.8	143,716	32,000
1986	323,005	77,478	0.7	144.5	132,086	32,000
1987	250,985	79,752	2.9	151.7	99,709	32,000
1988	200,331	82,092	2.9	159.1	77,317	32,000
1989	154,333	84,611	3.1	167.1	57,791	32,000
1990	$ 67,925	$ 88,053	4.1%	177.9%	$ 24,440	$ 32,000

Principal is Depleted
Retirement Income (Inflation-Adjusted) Lasts 30 Years

* *Consumer Price Index*

CHART A13-6

Moderate Domestic Model
Worst Case Study* (Retire in 1968)
Maximum 30-Year "Real" Retirement Income
Full Adjustment for Inflation (CPI**) Increases)

Initial Portfolio: $500,000   Initial Income: $22,500 (4.50% of Original Portfolio)

	The Numbers You See				The Numbers You Feel	
Year	The Portfolio is Depleted After 30 Years of Paying Increasing Retiree Distributions	Retiree's Annual Distributions– Increasing Annually with the Full Change in Inflation	CPI: Annual Inflation Rate %	CPI: Cumulative Inflation %	The Real Value of this Portfolio is Fairly Stable at First– then Declines Steadily	Retiree's Annual Distributions in Real $ (Adjusted for Inflation)
1968	$ 532,434	$ 22,500	4.7%	4.7%	$ 508,533	$ 22,500
1969	474,370	23,873	6.1	11.1	427,027	22,500
1970	485,182	25,185	5.5	17.2	413,991	22,500
1971	518,343	26,042	3.4	21.2	427,742	22,500
1972	536,064	26,927	3.4	25.3	427,820	22,500
1973	464,572	29,297	8.8	36.3	340,775	22,500
1974	388,838	32,871	12.2	53.0	254,209	22,500
1975	453,958	35,172	7.0	63.7	277,367	22,500
1976	516,229	36,860	4.8	71.5	300,968	22,500
1977	482,581	39,367	6.8	83.2	263,437	22,500
1978	470,498	42,910	9.0	99.7	235,634	22,500
1979	493,721	48,617	13.3	126.2	218,239	22,500
1980	524,423	54,645	12.4	154.3	206,236	22,500
1981	489,626	59,509	8.9	176.9	176,816	22,500
1982	549,697	61,829	3.9	187.7	191,057	22,500
1983	572,101	64,179	3.8	198.6	191,565	22,500
1984	549,449	66,746	4.0	210.6	176,904	22,500
1985	613,630	69,283	3.8	222.4	190,335	22,500
1986	631,046	70,045	1.1	225.9	193,607	22,500
1987	569,587	73,127	4.4	240.3	167,387	22,500
1988	561,002	76,344	4.4	255.3	157,915	22,500
1989	585,525	79,856	4.6	271.6	157,570	22,500
1990	503,055	84,727	6.1	294.3	127,594	22,500
1991	538,376	87,354	3.1	306.5	132,446	22,500
1992	495,259	89,887	2.9	318.3	118,405	22,500
1993	457,382	92,314	2.7	329.6	106,475	22,500
1994	347,754	94,806	2.7	341.2	78,826	22,500
1995	331,605	97,366	2.7	353.1	73,189	22,500
1996	$ 262,203***	$ 105,307	3.3%	368.0%	$ 56,023	$ 22,500

*1968 was the worst possible year to retire in the Inflation Era (1960-1996). This was the kick-off year for the Super Bowl, the huge 14-year bout of inflation, and (not coincidentally) the worst stock market conditions since the Great Depression (1968-1974).

**Consumer Price Index

***Minimum of two years' income remaining.

CHART A13-7

Moderate Domestic Model
Worst Case Study* (Retire in 1968)
Maximum 30-Year "Real" Retirement Income
Two-Thirds Adjustment for Inflation (CPI**) Increases

Initial Portfolio: $500,000   Initial Income: $28,500 (5.70% of Original Portfolio)

	The Numbers You See				The Numbers You Feel	
Year	The Portfolio is Depleted After 30 Years of Paying Increasing Retiree Distributions	Retiree's Annual Distributions– Increasing Annually with the ⅔ Change in Inflation	⅔ x CPI: Two-Thirds of Annual Inflation Rate %	⅔ x CPI: Two-Thirds of Cumulative Inflation %	The Real Value of this Portfolio is Fairly Stable at First– then Declines Steadily	Retiree's Annual Distributions in Real $ (Adjusted for ⅔ Inflation)
1968	$ 526,598	$ 28,500	3.1%	3.1%	$ 510,592	$ 28,500
1969	463,302	29,660	4.1	7.3	431,657	28,500
1970	467,904	30,748	3.7	11.3	420,518	28,500
1971	493,748	31,445	2.3	13.8	433,904	28,500
1972	504,317	32,158	2.3	16.4	433,364	28,500
1973	430,803	34,046	5.9	23.2	349,669	28,500
1974	354,518	36,816	8.1	33.2	266,098	28,500
1975	407,722	38,535	4.7	39.4	292,381	28,500
1976	457,298	39,769	3.2	43.9	317,758	28,500
1977	421,127	41,572	4.5	50.4	279,928	28,500
1978	404,339	44,068	6.0	59.5	253,548	28,500
1979	418,559	47,977	8.9	73.6	241,079	28,500
1980	439,516	51,945	8.3	88.0	233,812	28,500
1981	405,817	55,029	5.9	99.1	203,787	28,500
1982	451,030	56,461	2.6	104.3	220,749	28,500
1983	464,841	57,892	2.5	109.5	221,885	28,500
1984	441,918	59,436	2.7	115.1	205,461	28,500
1985	489,026	60,943	2.5	120.5	221,743	28,500
1986	498,037	61,390	0.7	122.2	224,184	28,500
1987	444,786	63,191	2.9	128.7	194,505	28,500
1988	433,415	65,046	2.9	135.4	184,129	28,500
1989	447,811	67,042	3.1	142.6	184,582	28,500
1990	380,627	69,769	4.1	152.5	150,756	28,500
1991	403,108	71,212	2.1	157.7	156,425	28,500
1992	366,425	72,590	1.9	162.7	139,492	28,500
1993	333,698	73,897	1.8	167.4	124,786	28,500
1994	248,549	75,228	1.8	172.2	91,301	28,500
1995	230,885	76,582	1.8	177.1	83,312	28,500
1996	$ 175,162***	$ 78,268	2.2%	183.2%	$ 61,844	$ 28,500

*1968 was the worst possible year to retire in the Inflation Era (1960-1996). This was the kick-off year for the Super Bowl, the huge 14-year bout of inflation, and (not coincidentally) the worst stock market conditions since the Great Depression (1968-1974).

**Consumer Price Index

***Minimum of two years' income remaining.

CHART A13-8

Endnotes

[1] Investor's Business Daily, 5/29/96, p.1.

[2] Gary P. Brinson, L. Randolph Hood, and Gilbert L. Beebower, "Determinants of Portfolio Performance," Financial Analysts Journal, July-August, 1986.

[3] Andrew Tobias, The Only Investment Guide You'll Ever Need, rev. 1996.

[4] Lowell Bryan and Diana Farrell, The McKinsey Quarterly Report, No. 2, 1996.

[5] Investor's Business Daily, 9/26/96.

[6] Standard & Poor's Statistical Service, "Description of Method Used in Computation."

[7] Jeremy J. Siegel, Stocks for the Long Run, 1994.

[8] Jeremy J. Siegel, Stocks for the Long Run, 1994.

[9] David Roche, economist in London at International Strategy, Ltd., The Wall Street Journal, 11/22/95.

[10] Associated Press release in Houston Chronicle, 5/27/96.

[11] Peter Lynch, Beating the Street, 1993.

[12] Robert G. Hagstrom, Jr., The Warren Buffett Way, 1994.

[13] Ray Dalio, Bridgewater Associates, The Wall Street Journal, 4/9/96.

[14] Charles Carignan, Letter to the Editor, Barron's, 6/3/96.

[15] Gary P. Brinson, L. Randolph Hood, and Gilbert L. Beebower, "Determinants of Portfolio Performance," Financial Analysts Journal, July-August, 1986.

[16] Gary P. Brinson, L. Randolph Hood, and Gilbert L. Beebower, "Determinants of Portfolio Performance," Financial Analysts Journal, July-August, 1986.

[17] John Kenneth Galbraith, The Great Crash 1929, 1954.

[18] Worth magazine, 3/97, p. 125.

[19] Kenneth Volpert, Vanguard Funds, Investor's Business Daily, 1/24/97.

[20] Mark Hulbert, column in Forbes, 7/1/96.

[21] From Longleaf Partners Fund's Shareholder Letter dated 7/8/96.

Bibliography

Bernstein, Peter L. <u>Against the Gods, The Remarkable Story of Risk</u>. New York: John Wiley & Sons, 1996.

Bogle, John C. <u>Bogle on Mutual Funds: New Perspectives for the Intelligent Investor</u>. New York: Irwin Professional Publishing, 1994.

Bryan, Lowell and Farrell, Diana. <u>Market Unbound: Unleashing Global Capitalism</u>. New York: John Wiley & Sons, 1996.

Ellis, Charles D. <u>Investment Policy: How to Win the Loser's Game</u>. Homewood, Illinois: Business One Irwin, 1985.

Ellis, Charles D. and Vertin, James R. <u>Classics II: Another Investor's Anthology</u>. Homewood, Illinois: Dow Jones-Irwin, 1989

Ellis, Charles D. and Vertin, James R. <u>Classics: An Investor's Anthology</u>. Homewood, Illinois: Dow Jones-Irwin, 1989

Fisher, Kenneth L. <u>The Wall Street Waltz</u>. Chicago: Contemporary Books, Inc., 1987.

Galbraith, John Kenneth. <u>The Great Crash 1929</u>. Boston, Massachusetts: Houghton Miffin Co., 1954.

Gibson, Roger C. <u>Asset Allocation</u>. Homewood, Illinois: Business One Irwin, 1990.

Graham, Benjamin. <u>The Intelligent Investor</u>. New York: Harper & Row, 1973.

Hagstrom, Robert G., Jr. <u>The Warren Buffett Way</u>. New York: John Wiley & Sons, 1994.

Hoff, Benjamin. <u>The Tao of Pooh</u>. New York: Penguin Books, 1982.

Ibbotson Associates. <u>Stocks, Bonds, Bills & Inflation 1996 Yearbook</u>. Chicago, Illinois: Ibbotson Associates, 1996.

Ibbotson, Roger G. and Brinson, Gary P. <u>Global Investing</u>. New York: McGraw-Hill, Inc., 1993.

Lederman, Jess and Klein, Robert A. (Editors). <u>Global Asset Allocation</u>. New York: John Wiley & Sons, 1994.

Leuthold, Steven C. <u>The Myths of Inflation and Investing</u>. Chicago: Crain Books, 1980.

Lynch, Peter. <u>Beating the Street</u>. New York: Simon & Schuster, 1993.

Malkiel, Burton G. <u>A Random Walk Down Wall Street</u>. New York: W. W. Norton, 1973, rev. 1991.

O'Higgins, Michael. <u>Beating the Dow</u>. New York: Harper-Perennial, 1992.

O'Shaughnessy, James P. <u>What Works On Wall Street</u>. New York: McGraw-Hill, Inc., 1997.

Rosenberg, Claude N., Jr. <u>Investing with the Best</u>. New York and Toronto: John Wiley & Sons, 1986.

Siegel, Jeremy J. <u>Stocks for the Long Run</u>. Burr Ridge, Illinois: Irwin Professional Publishing, 1994.

<u>The Vanguard Retirement Investing Guide</u>. Chicago: Irwin Professional Publishing, 1995.

Tobias, Andrew. <u>The Only Investment Guide You'll Ever Need</u>. San Diego: Harcourt Brace & Co., 1978, rev. 1996.

Train, John. <u>The Money Masters</u>. New York: Harper & Row, 1985.

Train, John. <u>The New Money Masters</u>. New York: Harper & Row, 1989.

Index

Order Form

✳ Fax orders: 713-622-7307

☎ Telephone orders: 1-800-772-0072 (Toll Free) Have your AMEX, VISA or MasterCard ready.

💻 On-line orders: John Merrill
104662.2150@compuserve.com

✉ Postal orders: Tanglewood Publishing
770 South Post Oak Lane, Suite 410
Houston, TX 77056, USA
Tel: 713-840-8880

Please send the following books:

Title	*Qty.*	
_____	_____	@ $29.95 each = $_____
_____	_____	@ $29.95 each = $_____
_____	_____	@ $29.95 each = $_____

Please send to: (your address)

Name: _____

Company Name: _____

Address: _____

City: _____ State: _____ Zip: _____-_____

Telephone: (____) _____

Sales Tax:

Please add 8.25% for books shipped to Texas addresses.

Shipping:

Book Rate: $2.50 for the first book and $1.00 for each additional book. (Surface shipping may take three to four weeks.)

Air Mail: $3.50 per book

Payment:

❑ Check

❑ Credit Card: ❑ Visa ❑ MasterCard ❑ AMEX

Name on card: _____ Card no. _____

Signature: _____

Expiration date: _____ / _____

Call *toll free* and order now

Order Form

✳   Fax orders: 713-622-7307

☎   Telephone orders: 1-800-772-0072 (Toll Free) Have your AMEX, VISA or MasterCard ready.

💻   On-line orders: John Merrill
                                     104662.2150@compuserve.com

✉   Postal orders: Tanglewood Publishing
                             770 South Post Oak Lane, Suite 410
                             Houston, TX 77056, USA
                             Tel: 713-840-8880

Please send the following books:

Title	_Qty._	
_____	_____	@ $29.95 each = $_____
_____	_____	@ $29.95 each = $_____
_____	_____	@ $29.95 each = $_____

Please send to: (your address)

Name: _____

Company Name: _____

Address: _____

City: _____ State: _____ Zip: _____-_____

Telephone: (____) _____

Sales Tax:

Please add 8.25% for books shipped to Texas addresses.

Shipping:

Book Rate: $2.50 for the first book and $1.00 for each additional book. (Surface shipping may take three to four weeks.)

Air Mail: $3.50 per book

Payment:

❑ Check

❑ Credit Card: ❑ Visa ❑ MasterCard ❑ AMEX

Name on card: _____Card no. _____

Signature: _____

Expiration date: ____ / ____

Call _toll free_ and order now